COVID-19 Pandemic, Public Policy, and Institutions in India

This book looks at the institutional and governance issues faced by India during the first and second wave of the COVID-19 pandemic and its adverse impact on the vulnerable sectors and groups.

The book is split into four parts, with preceding chapters informing later ones. Part One outlines the approach of the study, in particular their examination of policy responses and the effect of the pandemic. Part Two delves into the governance challenges in containing the pandemic while giving the theoretical rationale for institutional responses. Part Three looks at how the pandemic affected economically vulnerable households, workers, and small industries. The effect of pandemic on the informal sector is also detailed. Lastly, Part Four examines the impacts and responses of Indian public infrastructure and services to the pandemic, in particular the impact of the COVID-19 pandemic on health care and schooling. It also explores the challenges caused by infrastructure inadequacies in Indian cities. The book closes by looking at how businesses in the private sector have responded to the COVID-19 pandemic, with a focus on Corporate Social Responsibility.

The book will be a useful reference to researchers, policymakers, and practitioners who are interested in institutions and development, especially in the context of India.

Indranil De is Associate Professor in Social Sciences at the Institute of Rural Management Anand (IRMA), Gujarat, India.

Soumyadip Chattopadhyay is Associate Professor at the Department of Economics and Politics, Visva-Bharati University, India.

Hippu Salk Kristle Nathan is Associate Professor in Social Sciences at the Institute of Rural Management Anand (IRMA), Gujarat, India.

Kingshuk Sarkar is Joint Commissioner, Department of Labour, Government of West Bengal, India.

Routledge Research in Public Administration and Public Policy

For more information about this series, please visit: www.routledge.com/ Routledge-Research-in-Public-Administration-and-Public-Policy/book-series/ RRPAPP

COVID-19 Pandemic, Public Policy, and Institutions in India

Issues of Labour, Income, and Human Development

Edited by
Indranil De, Soumyadip Chattopadhyay, Hippu Salk Kristle Nathan, and Kingshuk Sarkar

Routledge
Taylor & Francis Group

LONDON AND NEW YORK

First published 2022
by Routledge
4 Park Square, Milton Park, Abingdon, Oxon OX14 4RN

and by Routledge
605 Third Avenue, New York, NY 10158

Routledge is an imprint of the Taylor & Francis Group, an informa business

British Library Cataloguing-in-Publication Data
A catalogue record for this book is available from the British Library

Library of Congress Cataloging-in-Publication Data
A catalog record has been requested for this book

ISBN: 978-1-032-12947-1 (hbk)
ISBN: 978-1-032-12949-5 (pbk)
ISBN: 978-1-003-22697-0 (ebk)

DOI: 10.4324/9781003226970

Typeset in Galliard
by codeMantra

Contents

Figures

Tables

Contributors

Soumyadip Chattopadhyay teaches at the Department of Economics and Politics, Visva-Bharati University, India. He holds a PhD from University of Calcutta. He was associated with Graduate School of Geography Clark University as a C V Raman Fellow and Department of Urban Studies and Planning University of Sheffield as a Commonwealth Academic Fellow. His research works have been published in the *Progress in Development Studies, Development in Practice, Environment and Urbanization ASIA, Journal of Infrastructure Development, South Asian Survey, Economic and Political Weekly, Journal of Rural Development, Journal of Development Policy and Practice* and *Review of Market Integration*, as well as in other Journals and edited volumes.

Surajit Das is Assistant Professor at Centre for Economic Studies and Planning (CESP), Jawaharlal Nehru University (JNU), New Delhi.

Indranil De is Associate Professor in Social Sciences at the Institute of Rural Management Anand (IRMA), Gujarat, India. He holds PhD from Jawaharlal Nehru University, New Delhi. He has recently published a book "Social Norms, Gender and Collective Behaviour: Development Paradigms in India" with Palgrave Macmillan. He has published several research articles in reputed journals including Housing studies, Development Policy Review, Water Policy, Journal of Water, Sanitation and Hygiene for Development, International Journal of Social Economics and Economic and Political Weekly. He is Editor of International Journal of Rural Management.

Amrita Ghatak is an applied microeconomist working at the intersections of inclusive development, labour, health, environment, and women. She is currently an Assistant Professor at the Gujarat Institute of Development Research in Ahmedabad, India.

Rooba Hasan is Research Associate at SVEP, Entrepreneurship Development Institute of India, Ahmedabad, India.

Mubashshir Iqbal was Junior Research Fellow at the Institute of Rural Management Anand (IRMA), Gujarat, India.

Md Sahidul Islam is Research Scholar pursuing a fellowship programme in management (Rural Management) at the Institute of Rural Management Anand (IRMA), Gujarat, India.

Hippu Salk Kristle Nathan is Associate Professors in Social Sciences at the Institute of Rural Management Anand, Gujarat, India. He has a masters from Indian Institute of Technology, Delhi, and Ph.D. from Indira Gandhi Institute of Development Research, Mumbai. His areas of interest lie in energy, economic measurement, sustainable use of resources, human development, and disarmament. His most significant research contributions are conceptualization and development of frameworks for both structuring and selection of sustainable development indicators. In his co-authored works he proposed an alternative approach to measure human development index and conceived a novel method to assess energy poverty.

Saswati Paik is an Associate Professor at Azim Premji University, Bengaluru. She holds a Ph.D. from JNU, New Delhi. A Geographer by training, she has a keen interest in research on schooling processes in challenging locations, educational leadership, educational governance, policy implementation, intervention design, monitoring, and evaluation. She was earlier associated with the Institute for Social & Economic Change (ISEC) Bengaluru, for the midterm evaluation of the 11th Five Year Plan. Her fervour for research is visible through her several publications that include chapters in books, journals, magazines, and popular social media.

Partha Pratim Sahu is Associate Professor at the Centre for Entrepreneurship Development and Financial Inclusion (CEDFI, National Institute of Rural Development and Panchayati Raj (NIRDPR), Hyderabad, India. He was a visiting fellow at Korea Institute for International Economic Policy (KIEP), South Korea. His research interests include issues related to enterprise and entrepreneurship development, skill development, labour and employment. He is also a member of the Editorial Advisory Board of Journal of Rural Development (JRD) of NIRDPR.

Driven by the need for better schooling in India, **Roshan M Samuel** pursued a Master's course in Education at Azim Premji University, Bengaluru. Prior to this he was working in the corporate sector developing Artificial Intelligence and Machine Learning modules at Samsung Research Institute, Bengaluru. A Master's degree holder in English Literature from the University of Westminster, London, Roshan found his calling to influence and inspire students to evolve with education. He is currently the Academic and Technical Director at Royal Public School, Bhandara, Maharashtra.

Kingshuk Sarkar primarily worked for Govt. of West Bengal as a Labour Administrator. He is presently visiting faculty at the Goa Institute of Management, Goa. He has PhD in Economics from Jawaharlal Nehru University, New Delhi. His areas of interests are labour economics, industrial relation, labour administration, informal sector labour etc. He has worked as Fellow at the V V Giri National Labour Institute, Noida. He had also worked as Assistant Professor in the National Institute of Rural Development, Hyderabad. He has in his credit number of publications in reputed journals. Attended and conducted numerous conferences, workshops, seminars in India and outside. He has carried out important research assignments in India and abroad and has represented India on global forums on few occasions

Shyam Singh is Associate Professor in Social Sciences at the Institute of Rural Management Anand (IRMA), Gujarat, India. Bangalore. He was the Scholar-in-Residence at the University of Antwerp, Belgium, in 2018. His research interests include community development and governance, monitoring and evaluation, CSR, and social networks. He teaches Rural Society and Polity, Monitoring and Evaluation, and Social Network Analysis at IRMA.

Sudhir Kumar Sinha is Professor of Practice at the Institute of Rural Management Anand (IRMA), Gujarat, India.

Abbreviations

AMRUT	Atal Mission for Rejuvenation and Urban Transformation
CSR	Corporate Social Responsibility
DRDO	Defence Research and Development Organisation
DST	Department of Science and Technology
FCI	Food Corporation of India
FSSAI	Food Safety and Standard Authority of India
GDI	Gender Development Index
GST	Goods and Services Tax
HDI	Human development index
ICMR	Indian Council of Medical Research
IMR	Infant mortality rate
JNNURM	Jawaharlal Nehru National Urban Renewal Mission
MCivilA	Ministry of Civil Aviation
MGNREGS	Mahatma Gandhi Employment Guarantee Scheme
MHA	Ministry of Home Affairs
MoCI	Ministry of Commerce and Industry
MoEFC	Ministry of Environment, Forest and Climate Change
MoF	Ministry of Finance
MoHFW	Ministry of Health and Family Welfare
MoR	Ministry of Railway
MoRD	Ministry of Rural Development
MoST	Ministry of Science and Technology
MoT	Ministry of Tourism
OOPE	Out-of-pocket expenditure
PDS	Public Distribution System
PMGKP	Pradhan Mantri Garib Kalyan Package
PMGKY	Pradhan Mantri Garib Kalyan Yojana
PMKAY	Pradhan Mantri Krishi Sinchayee Yojana
RAY	Rajiv Awas Yojana
RTE	Right to Education

SAFE	SIDBI Assistance to Facilitate Emergency Response Against Coronavirus
SBM-U	Swachh Bharat Mission – Urban
SoPs	Standard Operating Procedures
SCM	Smart Cities Mission

Part I

COVID-19 Pandemic and Challenges

1 Introduction

The COVID-19 Pandemic, Challenges and Policy

*Indranil De, Hippu Salk Kristle Nathan,
Soumyadip Chattopadhyay, and Kingshuk Sarkar*

1.1 Overview

We begin with three assertions. First, the COVID-19 pandemic has thrown challenge to the ability of mankind to manage shock. It has made it imperative to not only innovate clinical means to contain the disease but also manage human behaviour. Second, institutions which develop and govern rules and regulations can play a pivotal role in managing human behaviour. Third, public policy can provide support to cope up with the losses due to pandemic. It can not only provide resources but also policy paradigms under which the institutions would operate.

COVID-19 infection was first reported in India on 30th January 2020 and since then, there have been more than 32 million new cases and 0.4 million deaths being reported (Covid19India, 2021). The country has been affected by different waves of the pandemic. These waves are periods when number of new infections and deaths rose high (Figure 1.1). The first wave of pandemic can be identified between May to December 2020. After a brief lull the cases and deaths again started raging from April 2021. This was the beginning of second wave which lasted till the end of June 2021. The second wave spanned over a shorter period but the incidence of new infection and deaths per day was approximately four times as compared to the first wave. In other words, the second wave was much more devastating than the first wave. Management of the pandemic to contain the spread of disease and extending support to the vulnerable proved challenging during both the waves. During the first wave, there was lack of knowledge and preparedness. The lull between the two waves was assumed to be the end of the pandemic by many. Hence, the second wave was more shocking. It was devastating and damaging, placing the community and administration in unprecedented stress.

To manage the pandemic, it is also important to know how the pandemic has impacted the human life. Due to the norms of social distancing, the pandemic has taken away the freedom of movement, which has impacted economic progress and human capital formation. The impact on households is varied depending on the vulnerability of occupation and livelihood of the members of the household. It would also depend on the savings and other endowments

DOI: 10.4324/9781003226970-2

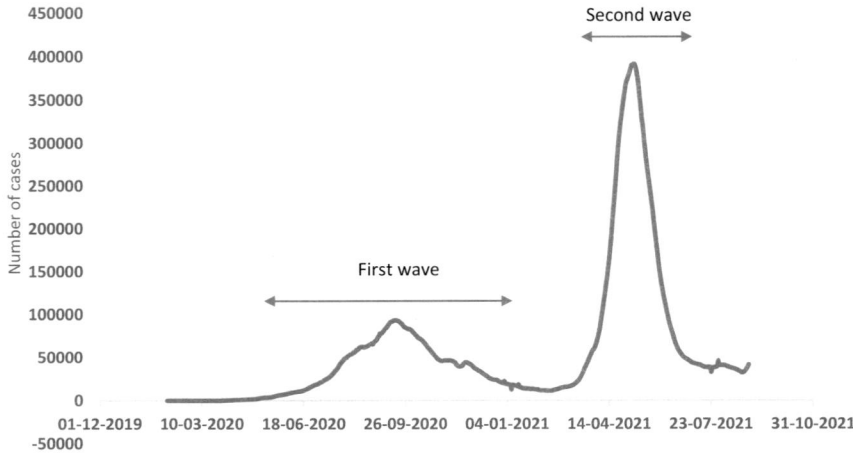

Figure 1.1 Number of daily new cases of COVID-19 in India.
Data Source: OWID (2021).

of the households to fall back on. The impact has been not only economic. It has affected health, education, and other such intrinsic aspects of life and development. This book, as a whole, has made a modest attempt to analyse these multidimensional impacts of the pandemic and response of different institutions including Government and market in managing and mitigating its negative impacts.

Considering the evolving nature of the pandemic, the knowledge regarding its impact on lives, communities, and nations is far from complete. In this regard, this book, focussing on India, has attempted to obtain a substantive understanding regarding the impact of the pandemic on different sections of the society along with the societal response. The studies covered by the chapters use both quantitative and qualitative methods. While studies based on quantitative methods provide precise estimates, studies based on qualitative methods provide a more in-depth understanding of issues. Qualitative studies have attempted to understand the complexities and difficulties created by the pandemic.

The issues discussed in the chapters attempt to fill the knowledge gap in management of the pandemic or similar covariate shocks. Attempts have also been made in the chapters to provide direction to public policy to cope up with similar situations. The learnings from the book would be very much effective in managing further waves of the pandemic or any such public health disasters in future. This knowledge would not only attenuate the immediate deleterious impact of pandemic but also help in understanding and bridging gaps between different regions and sections of population.

1.2 The Pandemic and Unfreedoms

If development can be interpreted as expansion of freedoms (Sen, 1999), the crisis on account of a pandemic can be viewed as intensification of unfreedoms. The extent of the unfreedoms in the COVID-19 pandemic varied for different sections of the society. For instance, most of the formal sector, for its greater capacity, affordability, and compatibility, could adopt to the technology and shifted to online mode of operation and could sail over the worst periods of pandemic. However, many sectors in the informal economy that relied on physical movements of people and goods suffered huge losses of livelihood and income.

Like freedoms, unfreedoms are multiple and multidimensional (Sen, 1985a, 1985b). Inability to earn a livelihood was not the only unfreedom during the pandemic. Denial of rights to mobility, denial of education rights, inability to be adequately fed, inability to get treated for illness, and so on are also some of the many unfreedoms people faced during the pandemic.

These unfreedoms are not only linked but also feed on each other. And these interlinked unfreedoms can lead to catastrophe. Sen (1999, p.8), in his book *Development as Freedom*, illustrates from his own childhood experience, how during the Hindu-Muslim conflict times in Dhaka, a Muslim daily labourer, Kader Mia, had to venture into the Hindu neighbourhood in search of work, and in the process got knifed and killed. Kader Mia was extremely poor and his family had nothing to eat and this economic unfreedom coupled with violation of other freedoms associated with a riot-like situation led to the loss of his life and also his family further slipping into poverty and despair.

In the COVID-19 pandemic situation, there are many Kader Mias – scores of migrant labourers, domestic workers, slum dwellers, or the rural poor. The different chapters of the book bring out the plights of these vulnerable groups while analysing the roles of the different institutions and how these institutions have responded to the situation. A better management by the institutions, such as market, Government, private, civil society, and community-based organizations, can reduce threats fostered by the pandemic. In other words, the human capabilities to cope up with the shock is also dependent on how institutions facilitate human capability (Robeyns, 2005), both during normalcy and at the time of crises. Thus, not only the plights of different sections of the society during the pandemic are personal stories, but they are also reflections of institutional responses to absorb shocks, which this book attempts to unravel.

1.3. Policy Response

1.3.1 *Chaos and Inadequacy*

The role of an institution is to reduce uncertainty in human exchanges (North, 1995). One can think of Government to be the most important institution at the time of the pandemic, considering its size, scope, capacity, and outreach. Government's policy response to manage pandemic is crucial for behavioural change and providing succour to the vulnerable. Government as an institution can manage pandemics well, only when it can reduce uncertainty and shape exception so that people can plan and act accordingly. Inability to reduce uncertainty would lead to institutional failure.

Government's policy response to the pandemic has been analysed in Chapter 2 by Shyam Singh. The policy responses have been divided in three distinct periods: onset of COVID-19, the first wave, and then the second wave. Shyam Singh characterizes the public policies in these three periods by the nature of public policy response. At onset of COVID-19 policy response was reluctant and ad hoc, during the first wave it was ignorant and haphazard, and during the second wave it was graded and inadequate. Singh also identifies the policy chaos created by lack of coordination and multiplicity of responses from different apparatuses of the Government. He argues that the reason for such ad hoc and uncoordinated response is centralized planning and execution without much involvement of local communities.

The extent of coverage of Government initiatives has also been analysed in several chapters of the book. The household surveys by Surajit Das (Chapter 4) and qualitative study by Indranil De and others (Chapter 5) reveal that most of the households have received free ration through Government's public distribution system. However, De and others find that many of those who received free ration during the first wave of the pandemic did not get any such benefit during the second wave. Das criticizes Government's demand management policies as inadequate. He is also critical about meagre Government health expenses.

1.3.2 Political Economy and Justice

Government's response to the pandemic has been analysed from the political economy and social justice point of views in Chapter 3 by Hippu Salk Kristle Nathan and Indranil De. The key questions asked by the authors are whether the Government policies and activities have been able to address the plight of the poor and vulnerable, and whether the policies are justified in the context of existing inequality in the society. The theory of Rawls' distributive justice, particularly the difference principle and the elite capture and the political clientelism in policy formulation, are examined in the light of disaster unfolded by the COVID-19 pandemic. The authors examine nationwide lockdown, provision of health care, and vaccination through these theoretical lenses.

The analysis in Chapter 3 is very critical about the sudden announcement of lockdown on March 25, 2020. It led to migration of innumerable workers and their families from cities to their native places in the most inhospitable conditions. These workers were mostly engaged with informal activities. Public policy did not show due prudence and responsibility in managing such a crisis for the benefit of migrant workers although it demonstrated much more gradual and predictable policy initiatives for inbound international travellers. In Chapter 2, Singh characterizes the sudden lockdown as an ad hoc policy response.

Nathan and De argue that Government's differential response regarding migrant workers and inbound international travellers fails to hold Rawls' difference principle. The same principle fails to hold for health care provision and holds for vaccination. That access to health care suffered huge deficit in rural areas and quality of service was wanting in the areas where poorer and vulnerable section of society reside violates Rawls' difference principle. On the contrary, Government's policy of prioritizing older vulnerable people for vaccination and providing free vaccination adheres to Rawls' difference principle.

The pandemic has raised serious questions about the resilience of the institutional system of the country to absorb shocks of that magnitude. In Chapter 5, De and others find that market and factory mode of production failed miserably, affecting income and employment in both formal and informal sectors. Government's initiatives of providing food and non-food benefits did not reach the vulnerable. Sudden lockdowns affected small businesses severely. Schemes benefiting the vulnerable such as cash distributions were discontinued during the second wave. Overall, these institutional failures affected the non-poor along with the poor, but was much more damaging for the latter.

1.3.3 *Private Response to the Pandemic*

The role of companies in supporting COVID-19 management and supplementing resources has been discussed by Sudhir Kumar Sinha in Chapter 12. This chapter is particularly significant as corporate social responsibility (CSR) has been made mandatory by law in India. Sinha has argued for corporate philanthropy through CSR to meet moral and rational obligations of the corporate. He argues that CSR response in India is superficial and shallow, with a lack of intent to assist the vulnerable. He conceptualizes the self-serving nature of CSR spending by the corporates as conspicuous CSR. He is very critical about Government's nudge for urging corporates to contribute their mandatory CSR funds to PM CARES Fund, which is constituted by Government to mobilize resources to fight pandemic.

Voluntary organizations and non-Governmental organizations (NGOs) have been effective in making interventions and supporting the vulnerable. De and others have expounded the critical role played by NGOs in different parts of the country for not only proving immediate help for meeting food and non-food requirements of the communities but also for establishing market linkages and promoting alternative livelihood options.

1.3.4 *Inadequate Basic Infrastructure*

Access to water and sanitation and adequate physical space is essential to adhere to the public health recommendation of frequent hand washing, social distancing, and lockdown-induced restrictions amid COVID-19. Soumyadip Chattopadhyay, in Chapter 9, highlights that problems of insufficiency of water and sanitation as well as overcrowded and inadequate housing in Indian cities predate the pandemic. In 2018, 41% of urban households lived in inadequate houses (Roy and Meera, 2018). The subpar level of basic infrastructure imperils slums and informal settlements. It affects majorly specific groups including migrant labourers, the poor, and women and children. COVID-19 only exacerbated the existing inequalities in basic infrastructure. For example, buying water from private vendors at higher costs limited the use of water for needs like handwashing or accessing water through shared sources limited the scope for social distancing and isolation. Use of shared toilets without adequate water and soap not only constrained urban residents' capacity to adhere to basic hygiene requirements but also amplified the risk of transmission. NSSO (2019) data shows per person an available area of 9.90 square meters within houses; this further made it impossible for the inhabitants to maintain social distancing. This chapter also points to the inability of the conventional approaches of large-scale, centralized, and formal systems of infrastructure finance and operations in ensuring universal and affordable access to urban services.

1.4 Impact of the Pandemic

1.4.1 Income and Industry

The impact of pandemic on employment is investigated by Das in Chapter 4. A survey conducted over 15 states of India revealed that due to lockdown, on an average there was 61% and 54% slide in individual and family income, respectively. The average family expenditure per month came down by 11%. According to Das' calculations the unemployment rate rose by at least 187% in 2020–21 as compared to 2018–19. Furthermore, he uncovers substantial loss of demand for durable goods and services by urban upper middle class.

In Chapter 5, De and others argue that market and Government failed to smooth out income and consumption that were affected due to the pandemic. People were dependent on their social capital for smoothing out consumption. They procured credit from friends and relatives. One of the important income smoothing strategies that emerged during the pandemic was rural labour work in agricultural sector or the MGNREGS. Diversification of employment in traditional non-farm activities also emerged as an important income smoothing strategy. NGOs helped in income smoothing through establishment of market linkages and producing personal protective equipment such as mask locally.

The pandemic-induced lockdown devastated the business operations of many micro, small, and medium enterprises (MSMEs), especially the microenterprises in the country. Central and state Governments announced relief measures for MSMEs. In Chapter 7, Soumyadip Chattopadhyay and Partha Pratim Sahu, highlight low offtake of such schemes and higher coverage of such schemes for larger enterprises. Restarting businesses by MSMEs was further impaired by steep increase in raw material prices, lack of demand, unpaid dues, and lack of clarity in Government notifications. Accordingly, MSMEs have attempted to cope up with these challenges by operating with reduced capacity and workers, diversifying product and services, altering the marketing strategy by selling at reduced margin and exploring the e-commerce market, rescheduling bank loans, drawing on savings, and accessing support from informal sources.

1.4.2 Labour and Employment

According to ILO, globally more than 25 million jobs are at risk due to COVID-19 outbreak (ILO, 2020). It is estimated that four in five people (81%) of the global workforce of 3.3 billion people are currently affected by the lockdowns in various countries. In India, more than 40 crore informal workers might have been adversely affected by the COVID-19 outbreak. As per National Commission for Enterprises in the Unorganized Sector (NCEUS, 2007), informal employment accounts for 98% employment in agriculture, 75% in industry, 72% in services. It is not hard to understand that the nationwide lockdown has not only led to job loss, but also exposed millions of people to hunger, starvation, and death.

The latest report on the Periodic Labour Force Survey (2017–18) shows that about 57% of rural households derived their major income from self-employment activities and 25% had a major source of income from casual labour. Majority of these rural self-employed households are marginal cultivators and petty artisans, while in urban areas they are engaged in small shops, low-scale businesses, or petty economic activities. This segment of the working class lost their livelihoods during the pandemic-induced lockdown and they did not receive any legal protection.

In this book, two chapters, namely, Chapters 6 and 8, deal with the subject of impact of COVID-19 pandemic on informal workers. In Chapter 6, Kingshuk Sarkar discusses the difficulties faced by migrant informal sector workers during the pandemic-induced lockdown and also highlights the inadequacy of existing legal framework. In Chapter 8, Amrita Ghatak and Kingshuk Sarkar describe the difficulties faced by domestic workers during the lockdown in India in general and in cities of Ahmedabad and Kolkata in particular. This chapter also highlights lack of legal protection for domestic workers.

1.4.3 Health and Education

Health and education are fundamental aspects of personal and societal development. In Chapter 3, Nathan and De highlight that the government spending in health care in India is abysmally low, even lower than that of low-income countries. The severe shortfalls in health facility and health personnel in the rural areas have remained a great concern even in normal times. The COVID-19 pandemic exposed the vulnerability of rural health care system in India in two ways. First, it resulted in high mortality, particularly in the second wave. Second, it dampened the vaccination drive and will do so in future. The Government's underestimation of COVID-19 threats during the transition period of first and second waves made things worse. Also, the poor's low health awareness and vaccine hesitancy pose a challenge to the future course of actions.

While the entire health care administration and hospitals were busy in dealing with COVID-19 cases, the non-COVID-19 patients were ignored. In Chapter 10 of this book, Md. Sahidul Islam and Hippu Salk Kristle Nathan highlight the challenges faced by the non-COVID-19 patients. Through a primary survey the chapter shows non-COVID-19 patients delayed their treatment due to lockdown and suffered from high out-of-pocket expenditure in both medical head and non-medical needs such as commuting to hospitals via expensive private transport. This has led families to be caught in debt trap and has also affected the female population disproportionately, considering intra-household and intra-society gender disparity.

The impact of the pandemic on education is analysed in Chapter 11 of this book. The authors, Saswati Paik and Roshan M Samuel, make a qualitative assessment of impact of the pandemic on academic progress of school children, especially for those belonging to the socio-economically vulnerable groups. The closure of the schools not only deprived the children in education but also in nutrition due to the absence of midday meals provided by schools. The incapacity of schools where children of poor households study to shift to online education kept such children completely out of touch with study, leading to increase in child labour, child trafficking, and violence against children. The pandemic might have disrupted just two years of education, but, as Paik and Samuel argue in the chapter, it would have a generational impact.

1.5 Policy Implications

The findings and discussion of the book leave significant implications for Governmental and non-Governmental initiatives and policies to absorb the shock of COVID-19 pandemic or any such similar shock in future. These are both in the realm of pandemic management for its containment and regarding smoothing income and employment fluctuations, benefiting MSMEs, improving basic infrastructure and health care, and continuing schooling for the poor.

Singh suggests a more decentralized policy response and trust building efforts from Government could have avoided uneven and ad hoc responses across the country. He suggests mutual monitoring of citizens to rationalize administrative cost. Chattopadhyay suggests empowering city Governments and encouraging them to partner with grassroot organizations and informal service providers for better delivery of urban public services.

De and others suggest stronger intervention of NGOs and collective organizations to mitigate the damages of institutional failure. Sinha's work on corporate response to pandemic suggests that there should be separate policy and budgetary allocation for disaster management. This is markedly different from the current ad hocism and spend-centric approach of corporate philanthropy. Paik and Samuel highlight the need to revise the provision of age-appropriate admission in RTE 2009, and the immense need of promoting vocational education in schools and higher educational institutions in line with National Education Policy.

Invocation of Keynesian demand management policies to manage demand depression is strongly advocated by Das. He also suggests stepping up of expenditure on health services. Nathan and De also suggest a greater public spending on health care that can provide health services of adequate quantity and reasonable quality, specifically in rural areas. The authors also argue that this would foster the current vaccination drive and help Government to be better prepared to contain and manage any such virus in future. This would also prevent long-distance commuting of non-COVID-19 patients that posed severe challenges during lockdown as highlighted by Islam and Nathan.

The failure of market mechanisms and hauling of economic activities based on factory mode of production has impelled De and others to suggest income diversification away from factory mode of production to absorb a shock similar to the COVID-19 pandemic. On the other hand, acknowledging the need for new approaches in supporting the MSMEs in post-COVID-19 era, Chattopadhyay and Sahu urge for systematic collection of MSME data on business environment and bottlenecks to financial access and Government schemes. Simplifying access to formal finances along with their greater sensitization and recovery of unpaid dues is suggested to solve the problem of inadequate capital. Both Sarkar, while highlighting the issues of informal workers in general, and Ghatak and Sarkar, while doing the same for domestic workers in particular, emphasize on labour market reforms. The formalization of labour and stronger and more defined employer-employee relation is an imperative to reduce vulnerability of labour force.

1.6 End note

This book constitutes chapters that provide understanding of the institutional and governance issues faced by India amid COVID-19 pandemic and its adverse impact on the vulnerable sectors and groups. Not only did the pandemic have its ramification on the economy and livelihoods of people, but it also challenged the existing infrastructures and services including health care and education.

The chapters of the book show how different deprivations (unfreedoms) feed on each other as argued by Sen (1999). The lockdown (mobility unfreedom) impacted more severely the poor-informal workers, and microenterprises (economic unfreedom), who plunged further into the poverty trap with loss of livelihoods (for instance, loss of livelihoods for migrant labourers and domestic workers). Further, the mobility unfreedom fuelled the severity of the health unfreedom of households having non-COVID-19 patients and the education unfreedom of children who were in schools that did not have the capacity to adapt to technology to go online. Again, among such households, those who had economic unfreedom suffered the most in the COVID-19 era.

The existing institutional framework contributed to unfreedom of vulnerable populations due to lack of resilience of market and failure of Government. Lack of strong and defined employer-employee relation is a bane in the wake of lockdowns and lack of demand. The ad hoc and inadequate policy response of Government fails to free the vulnerable from uncertainties and hopelessness. The education policy of Government leaves much to be desired to adapt to the pandemic conditions and give marginalized children freedom to participate in the pursuit of human development.

The different institutions in the country including the state have responded to the pandemic. These institutions have different capacities to absorb and manage shocks. Their ability to reduce risk and stand out as a resilient institution is tested during this extraordinary time. While the book attempts to cover the major aspects of institutions and governance issues during this unprecedented pandemic within a limited scope of 12 chapters, it is selective in terms of analysing the adverse impacts on specific vulnerable groups.

On August 24, 2021 the WHO chief scientist Dr Soumya Swaminathan declared that India might have entered the endemic stage, where there would be ups and downs in the number of cases in various parts of the country, but the country would learn to live with the virus (BBC, 2021). That said, this book could not have been timelier considering preparedness required at the level of institutions as well as the public at large to meet such challenges.

References

BBC (2021). Covid-19: is India entering endemic stage of coronavirus? 26 August. Retrieved from https://www.bbc.com/news/world-asia-india-58302480.

Covid19India (2021). Cumulative cases in India. Retrieved from https://www.covid19india.org/

ILO (2020). ILO monitor 2nd Edition, Covid-19 and world of work- updated estimates and analysis. Retrieved from https://www.ilo.org/wcmsp5/groups/public/---dgreports/---dcomm/documents/briefingnote/wcms_740877.pdf, accessed on 25 August 2021.

NCEUS (2007). Report on conditions of work and promotion of livelihoods in the unorganised sector. National Commission for Enterprises in the Unorganised Sector, Govt. of India.

North, D. C. (1995). The new institutional economics and third world development. In *The New Institutional Economics and Third World Development* (pp. 31–40). Routledge.

NSSO (2019). *Drinking water, sanitation, hygiene and housing condition in India: NSS 76th Round*. New Delhi: Ministry of Statistics and Programme Implementation, Government of India.

OWID (Our World in Data) (2021). Data on daily confirmed Covid-19 cases in India. Retrieved from https://ourworldindata.org/

PLFS (2017–18). Periodic labour force survey 2017–18, Ministry of Statistics and Programme Implementation (MoPSI), Government of India, New Delhi. Retrieved from http://www.mospi.nic.in/publication/annual-report-plfs-2017-18.

Robeyns, I. (2005). The capability approach: a theoretical survey. *Journal of Human Development*, 6(1), 93–117.

Roy, D. & Meera, M.L. (2020). Housing for India's low-income households a demand perspective. *Working Paper 402*, ICRIER, New Delhi, December.

Sen, A. (1985a). *Commodities and Capabilities*. Amsterdam: North Holland.

Sen, A. (1985b). Well-being, agency and freedom. *The Journal of Philosophy*, LXXXII(4), 169–221.

Sen, A. (1999). *Development as Freedom*. Oxford University Press.

Part II

Challenges of COVID-19 for Institutions and Governance

2 Policy Response to Pandemic

COVID-19 SOPs and Guidelines

Shyam Singh

2.1 Introduction

The spread of COVID-19 has shaken the lives of people and the institutional ecosystem in India. New governance challenges were heaved towards the public institutions of various levels. These challenges go beyond health systems and institutions (Issac and Sadanandan, 2020). Whether it is contact tracing, managing the movements of migrant workers or vaccination, we witnessed a mix of innovations and chaos in the governance response. The central and state Governments issued standard operating procedures (SOPs) and guidelines regularly and revise them quite frequently. The frequent changes in the SOPs and the guidelines were the result of the fast reoccurrence as well as the severity of the pandemic in the specific states/districts and did not take into account the efficacy of the institutions in addressing the challenges. The guidelines were being released by multiple institutions simultaneously, including the Ministry of Home Affairs, the Ministry of Family Health and Welfare, the National Disaster Management Authority, the Indian Council of Medical Research, and National Centre for Disease Control, and so on. One can, though, argue that due to the dynamic nature of the pandemic, there was no time for assessing the efficacy of the institutions in implementing the SOPs. Institutions had to deal with newer sets of instructions and norms given to them almost every fortnight or even earlier. Due to the severity of the problem, guidelines were addressed to every level of the governance, namely: state, district, and panchayat, which presents a challenge for cross-sectoral coordination and also an opportunity to push for institutional change (Dutta and Fischer, 2021).

The effective and coordinated policy response to COVID-19 becomes important in the wake of the call that 'the rules of good public governance apply now than ever.'[1] The call for good governance during the pandemic emphasizes the need of public institutions to adapt to fast-changing scenarios and roll out innovative strategies without getting into bureaucratic sophistication. The business-as-usual method of governance would not yield the results that we expect in a short period of time. For example, policy analysis to predict the spread of the pandemic based on a traditional approach that would use tons of data is likely to fail if the analysts do not account for the dynamic human behaviour (Das,

DOI: 10.4324/9781003226970-4

2020). The institutions like district Governments and gram panchayats (GPs) are supposed to run such analysis, which they cannot take appropriate steps. In this chapter, the intent is to look at the two important issues: (1) variations and overlaps in the institutional norms suggested by the SOPs, and (2) if there was coordination and collaboration among various strata of governance. The chapter would keep a special focus on panchayats as the pandemic seem to hit rural areas significantly[2] during the second wave (April–June 2021).

Methodologically, the chapter is based on secondary data. The SOPs released by the central as well as state Governments right from the first lockdown imposed in the last week of March 2020 to different phases of unlocking and the second wave of the pandemic, that is, May 2021, have been analysed. The chapter compares the steps suggested in SOPs across three phases of the rollout of the pandemic in the country, and analyses the policy actions taken to respond to the challenges put forward by the pandemic. It is anticipated that the findings of this chapter would inform the policy responses towards the pandemic in particular and any disasters or covariate shocks in general.

2.2 Variations in Policy Response

The onset of the pandemic in India was quite rapid but not unexpected. The first case of COVID-19 was found in China in December 2019.[3] India witnessed its first COVID-19 case on January 27th, 2020 (Andrews et al., 2020). The COVID-19 cases in the country reached three digits on March 23rd and four digits on April 12th, 2020,[4] prompting the Government to impose the country-wide lockdown in instalments. Indian Government had got about three months to augment its resources and to devise pertinent strategies to fight the pandemic. The lockdowns gave them additional time. However, the lack of experience in dealing with a pandemic of such scale was exhibited from the initial policy response of the Government of India. While it was clear from the beginning that this disease may take the shape of a pandemic, we didn't see the governance preparedness to deal with the scale of the pandemic.

From the onset of the pandemic (January 2020) to the second wave of the outbreak (April-June 2021), the policy responses from the central and state Governments varied quite significantly. As the pandemic progressed, responses from Government were subjected to change to adapt to the new challenges posed by the virus and economy. The country's GDP contracted to a negative 24.4% in the second quarter of 2020 due to nationwide lockdowns. The contraction improved to a negative 7.4% in the third quarter of 2020 as the Government modified the policy responses.[5] This situation puts about 400 million people at the risk of slipping into poverty (Kugler and Sinha, 2020). These variations were incremental in building health infrastructure, providing social security support to the affected population, and providing stimulus to boost the economy. However, these responses were not adequate to mitigate the impact of the disease and were uneven across the states. Hence, it suggests a lack of coordination among the various public health agencies (Kar et al., 2021). In the next section, the discussion is based on the different policy approaches that the Indian Government adopted coinciding with the different phases of the spread of the pandemic in the country (Figure 2.1).

2.2.1 *Reluctant and Ad Hoc Approach*

In this section, the following three dimensions of policy response during the initial months of the pandemic in India are analysed: (1) lack of COVID-19 preparedness, (2) slow contact tracing, and (3) issue of migrant workers.

2.2.1.1 *Lack of COVID-19 Preparedness*

The human-to-human spread of COVID-19 apparently became a piece of public knowledge in December 2019, even though the WHO delayed its declaration (Jha and Jha, 2020). The Governments of various countries started taking precautionary measures. The time gap between the first case was detected in India, and the cases reaching three digits was close to two months.[6] In these two months, the major policy response to the pandemic was the screening of the passengers of international flights coming to India and advising citizens to avoid international travel. The Public health agencies started advising the citizens to use face masks when they venture out. However, this advice was revised several times that the face masks are unnecessary for the unaffected individuals to make it mandatory for everybody to make any public appearance outside the house (Martinelli et al., 2021). However, not much was done by the Government in the first two months of the onset of the pandemic in the country. India was not manufacturing even single personal protective equipment (PPE) in April 2020, and the number of COVID-19 testing labs, the most important health infrastructure to combat the pandemic, was one in the country in January and

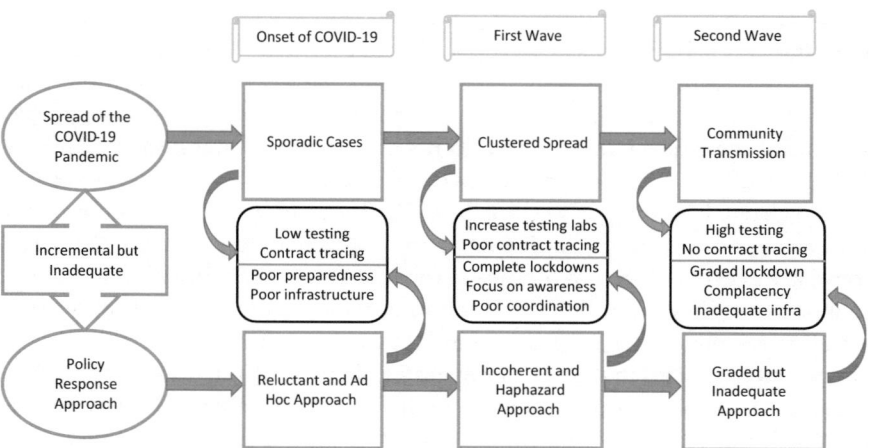

Figure 2.1 Variations in policy response approach during COVID-19 spread in India.

remained as it is till April 2020 (Jha and Jha, 2020). The low testing rate in the country during the initial time was a concern. With limited testing capacity, India was able to test only 1,400 samples a day during mid-March, and it went up to 6,500 samples during the lockdowns in May and June 2020 (Bharali et al., 2020). While the infections were increasing, the number of infections did not seem to be mounting due to low testing capacity.

The low preparedness of the health system in the country also hampered routine health practices. Rukmini (2020) presented an analysis of National Health Mission (NHM) data for March 2020. She found that NHM data did not report progress from about 75,000 health facilities in 75 districts due to the pandemic related restrictions and lockdowns. Rukmini (2020) accumulates various gaps in the health services due to pandemic: about 100,000 to 200,000 kids are estimated to miss various vaccines; unattended home birth deliveries are likely to go up in the absence of primary health services; and the number of inpatient and outpatient treatments are likely to reduce reduced (not because of lack of illness but due to lack of access to services). Therefore, the lack of preparedness in ensuring the citizens' access to health services during the pandemic is another setback for the citizens who were dealing with the pandemic anyway. This situation becomes serious, mainly when India's spending on health care services has historically been low. India spends about 3.6% of the GDP (out-of-pocket and public) on health, which works out to be about INR 200 per person (Mehra, 2020).

2.2.1.2 Slow Contact Tracing

The contact tracing during the initial time, when the benefits of the contact tracing could have been immense, was never a priority for the local health machinery. While the focus was being given to contact tracing initially, a few months into the pandemic, most of the states did not take it seriously (Saikia, 2020). This was being observed despite the clear protocol from the Government. The Government of India launched *Arogya Setu* app on 2nd April 2020 to use for contact tracing. However, despite the questions raised on the privacy and data security issues, the app has not been able to fuel the tracing efforts as people do not fill the requisite derails and do not update their travel history regularly (Clarance, 2020). The Government of India claims that about 114 million users were registered by the last week of May 2020, out of which 0.9 million users were advised for either quarantine or testing.[7] This number is meagre compared to what was expected out of the app as India has more than 550 million unique mobile users (Shashidhar, 2020). This is important to note that the health agencies were relying on the app for the physical contract tracing. Physical tracing is almost impossible given the size of the spread of the pandemic. Later, the studies suggested that contact tracing apps (not only in India but elsewhere) have largely been ineffective. A study that compares contact tracing apps in three countries (Italy, Germany, and Switzerland) found that the technology adopted in those apps for contact tracing is inaccurate (Gardner, 2020). Worldwide, only about

20% of people downloaded the app, and there is a chance of only about 4% of individuals coming into contact with another app user (Gardner, 2020).

2.2.1.3 Migrants Workers

The condition of migrant labour captured the highlight of the initial phase of the pandemic in India. When a series of lockdowns were imposed, migrant workers, with no means to live as there was no work due to lockdowns, started on a journey to their home states. Finally, the Indian Government allowed migrants to travel to their home states in the last week of April 2020. However, the arrangements made to help the migrant workers were not adequate. After a month of allowing migrants to travel, the Indian Railway, in the first week of June 2020, started 200 special trains to take the migrants to their homes. This initiative was considerably delayed. As per an estimate, about 10 million migrants left their place of work and went back to their villages, out of which about half a million either walked or rode the bicycle to reach their native places (Kugler and Sinha, 2020). The plight of the migrant workers was not merely economic but social too (Ranjan, 2021), as their joblessness impacted household welfare.

2.2.2 Incoherent and Haphazard Approach

India's policy response to the pandemic after March 2020 was, at best, ignorant and haphazard after the initial outbreak (January–March 2020). This was the time when the policy response should have been coordinated, informed and systematic. During the *Janta Curfew*[8] and thereafter the first instalment of full-fledged lockdown in the second half of March 2020, it was expected that that the pandemic would subsidize after the lockdown. In fact, there was an indication from the Government about 21 days are needed to break the chain of infection.[9] Perhaps, analysts were taking a clue from China, which was able to control the pandemic by the end of February 2020. Though, questions have been raised on the accuracy of the data provided by China. India went on to impose a series of lockdowns extending the hope that the country should be able to control the pandemic very soon. The Government of India imposed four country-wide lockdowns starting from March 24th to June 7th, 2020. However, the increase in daily infections continued (Figures 2.2 and 2.3). There was an absence of optimal lockdown strategies, which could have given optimal results in curbing the infections and flattening the curve and reducing the 'socio-economic cost' of the pandemic (Kantner and Koprucki, 2020). Optimal lockdown strategies recommend four locks down in four phases: a strict lockdown, reduced transition phase of the virus, a long period with full strength health infrastructure and stable virus prevalence, and achieving normalcy (Charpentier et al., 2020).

While we don't suggest that these four strategies would have been a success in bringing normalcy in the Indian context, however, the optimal strategies-driven lockdown could have provided benefits to manage the pandemic effectively. India's phases of lockdowns were devoid of such strategies and could not result

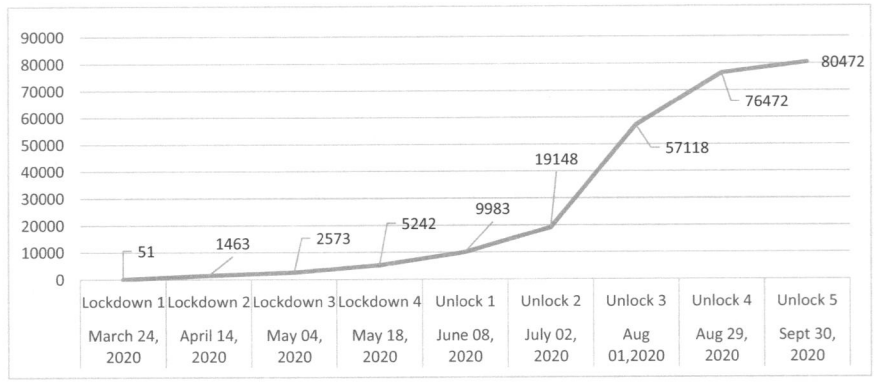

Figure 2.2 Daily COVID-19 cases on the given date.
Source: Data curated from PRS Legislative Research: https://prsindia.org/covid-19/overview [Accessed on 19th July, 2021].

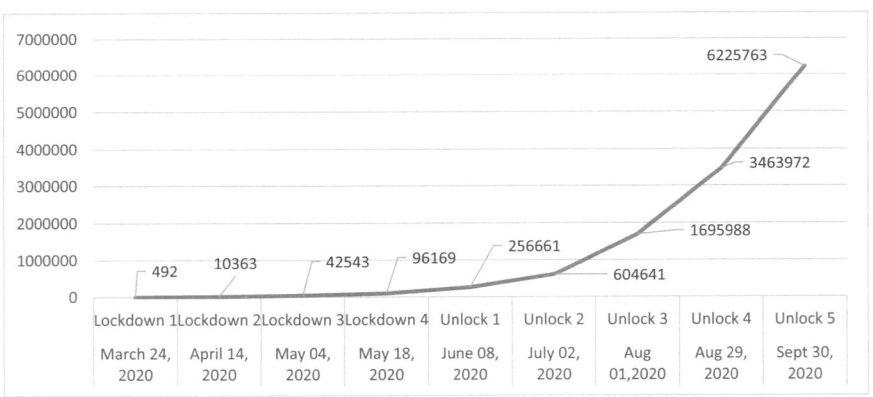

Figure 2.3 Cumulative COVID-19 cases on the given date.
Source: Data curated from PRS Legislative Research: https://prsindia.org/covid-19/overview [Accessed on 19th July, 2021].

in 'flattening of the curve'. 'Flattening the curve' indicates the spreading out the infections over an extended period of time, rather heaping the infections a small duration which may break the health care facilities (Herfurth, 2020). The Government had to initiate unlock under the pressure of economic meltdown (Kanitkar, 2020). The very reason that unlocks were initiated while the cases were surging up reflects a weak policy framing behind the lockdowns. While gradual unlocking could be a strategy to ease out the pressure on the economy, it should be adopted when daily cases reach a low threshold (Rawson et al., 2020). Though the partial benefit of the lockdowns in India was that the Government got some time to augment the health infrastructure while the infection rate was increasing at a slow pace (Paul, 2020), this was an unintended outcome. There was never any indication of this policy priority when the lockdowns were rolled out.

2.2.2.1 Poor Coordination among Public Agencies

Poor coordination among the various public agencies has been a perennial problem in the development trajectory of India. The bureaucracy avoids coordination among other agencies and departments mostly due to confidentiality (Peter, 2018). The coordinated policy response to COVID-19 is necessary; otherwise, all the states will produce the results which would be in sync with their natural development trajectory shaped by the existing capacities of the bureaucracy and civic culture. Some states with better coordination with the district and local Governments have produced better results during the first wave of the pandemic (Dutta and Fischer, 2021). But such instances are fewer. The major area where lack of coordination has been observed is the Centre-state relations. The lack of coordination was visible in handing the migrant labourers issues in the early phase of the pandemic (Aiyar and Krishnamurthy, 2020). Many states allowed migrants to leave their workplace, but several states, including the home states of some of the migrants, did not allow the entry of migrants. A similar scenario was observed during the managing oxygen supply in the second wave of the pandemic. In the times like these, there is a need for the Central Government to shift from 'command-and-control mechanism to 'Centre-state collaboration' to address the issue at hand (Aiyar and Krishnamurthy, 2020). The lack of co-ordination also exhibits that India has about 40 mobile apps launched by different states, municipalities, and law and order authorities to track and monitor the progress of COVID-19 response.[10] This situation leads to a muddled state where citizens may be needed to comply with the local requirements and may download several apps.[11]

2.2.2.2 Public Communications

One area where the Central Government did well was the public communication with respect to risk communication, including the COVID-19-appropriate behaviour that citizens should adopt. During the four episodes of lockdowns (March 24th–June 7th), the Central Government disseminated essential information through 86 media briefings, 71 COVID-19-specific information bulletins, and 1838 press releases.[12] The frontline workers at the local level were oriented not only in handing the COVID-19 cases but also the awareness drive so that citizens are well aware of do's and don'ts. Even the panchayats and frontline health workers have been given responsibilities to promote COVID-19-appropriate behaviour (Dutta and Fischer, 2021). The Ministry of Panchayati Raj, Government of India, has recorded the initiatives taken by panchayats in various states, shows that awareness and information dissemination is a regular feature of panchayats' involvement in COVID-19 Management.[13] The initial studies indicate the citizens are adequately aware of the pandemic related information and protocols (Kaushik et al., 2020; Singh et al., 2020).

2.2.3 Graded but Inadequate Approach

2.2.3.1 Handing Over to States

The experiences of the first wave of the pandemic presented the challenges and offered policy learning. The Central Government gave up the role of micromanager of the pandemic and gave states responsibility to spearhead the efforts by keeping local situation, availability of resources, and the scale of the pandemic into account. This step of the Central Government seems to address three issues, which are discussed in the following sections. First, states get more freedom to decide the extent of stringent measures (such as lockdowns) by keeping their economic health into account. States would be in a better position to carry the risk assessment as they are aware of the local context and citizens' behaviour. Second, if states lead the efforts, then the coordination among the public agencies gets relatively easier as the diversity of directions and the agencies reduce when managing pandemics shifts from the Central Government to states. Third, the Central Government was being accused, politically, of policy failure by the states ruled by the opposition parties. Hence shifting the responsibility of fighting the pandemic from the Central to states would also shift the blame if the pandemic could not be contained.

2.2.3.2 Cluster-Based Containment Strategy

One of the major policy changes that occurred post-first wave was reducing the reliance on the lockdown as a major strategy to fight the pandemic when reliable medicinal and vaccine protocols were absent. It was apparent from the series of country-wide lockdowns imposed during March–June 2020 that the lockdowns delay the spread but do not eliminate the pandemic. Lockdowns do not do any good to the economy as well. Hence, the Central Government shifted its strategy from imposing full-fledged lockdowns to a cluster containment strategy. The state Governments were asked to identify local clusters of cases and declare the clusters containment zones with restricted in and out mobility. This strategy was implemented to break the chain of transmission and blocking the spread to new areas. Though the containment strategy could not be effective in halting the pandemic, it allowed states and local Governments to continue with economic activities to avoid financial distress.

2.2.3.3 Graded Approach in Vaccination

Indian Government also speeded up with the vaccines providing them emergency use certificates. The Government provided a detailed operational guideline in the last week of December 2020 for the rollout of COVID-19 vaccination in the country.[14] The country-wide vaccination program started on January 16th, 2021. The first priority was given to frontline workers (health, essentials services, police personnel, etc.) and those above 60 years of age. Later the scope of vaccination was extended to individuals less than 50 years of age who have comorbidities and then opening it for everyone above 18 years of age (Kumar et al., 2021). There were multiple lacunes in rolling out the vaccines. India faced a substantial shortage of vaccines during April, May, and June 2021 due to poor planning and projections.[15] The Central Government gave states the responsibility to procure the vaccines as many states demanded that they be allowed to do so in the wake of a shortage of the vaccines. However, states were finding it difficult to procure the vaccines as various issues needed to be addressed by the national Government. These issues were related to exemptions sought by the vaccine companies to avoid any legal hassle and the diplomatic efforts that were needed to be launched to convince the countries to allow the export of the vaccine to India.[16] Hence, the Central Government took back the responsibility of COVID-19 vaccination from states, leaving scope for private hospitals to procure 25% vaccines. A better planning of vaccine rollout from the beginning could have yielded better results.

2.2.3.4 Inadequate Health Care Facilities

While India tried to augment its health infrastructure and resources to combat the pandemic throughout the first wave and post-first wave of the pandemic, it could never meet the demand during the second wave. This happened not because of the pace of the pandemic only, which failed all the expectations and estimations. The catastrophic gaps in the health systems in India were so deep that increased focus on filling the gap could not reach an adequate level. The Global Health Security (GHS) Index 2019[17] gives a snapshot of the pre-pandemic health readiness of the country. India stands at 57th rank (out of 195 countries) with an average mark of 46.5 (out of 100) in the GHS Index 2019. The country secured a better rank in rapid response (32) and health systems (36). It lagged severely in compliance with international norms (100), risk environment (103), and prevention (87). The rank in detection and reporting (67) is also worrisome.[18] The lower-middle-income countries like Indonesia, Georgia, Vietnam, Kenya, and Mongolia were doing better than India. Apart from the infrastructural gaps, incorrect projections of the spread of the second wave caught the public health agencies by surprise and unprepared (Koshy, 2021). The Government constituted expert group's projection of the second wave were left far behind by the actual number of infections. The projection predicted the peak of infection by one lakh; however, the actual number of infections went up to more than four lakhs.[19]

2.3 Multiple Sources of Response: An Analysis of SOPs and Guidelines

Lack of coordination among the public agencies, which is, anyway, an everlasting problem in the country's governance, caused the multiplicity of responses from different apparatuses of the Government. The lack of coordination and multiplicity results in ineffective delivery of services; hence, the agencies' productivity also comes under question (Afridi, 2017). Whether the system is decentralized or top-down, better coordination among the various Government agencies that deliver basic services is essential. In India's case of the COVID-19, several health agencies were found doing similar work without any coordinated monitoring (Figure 2.4). Figure 2.4 displays the multiple roles that different ministries and institutions played. It is not suggested here that only one actor could have done one role. It was required that different agencies have better coordination among themselves to ensure better disease management. Lack of oxygen supply, beds, and necessary medicines (Remdesivir, etc.) in the hospitals during the second wave of the pandemic is an apt example of the lack of coordination.

A review of SOPs and guidelines released by the public agencies indicate that MHA and MoHFW have released the greatest number of guidelines on similar subjects. While the ministries and departments were needed to carry out extraordinary functions during the pandemic, multiciliate functions and lack of coordination created chaos and confusion. For example, The Central Government was trying to ramp up the oxygen supply during the second wave of the pandemic. The state police stopped the tankers carrying the gas due to a lack of clear instructions and documents. Similarly, initially, there was no coordination with the private supplier of oxygen, and measures to stop the private contractor from hoarding the oxygen came very late. The Government could plug in these loose ends very late.

Another prominent example is the handling of migrants' issue. The Government started mapping their needs and searching for alternative employment

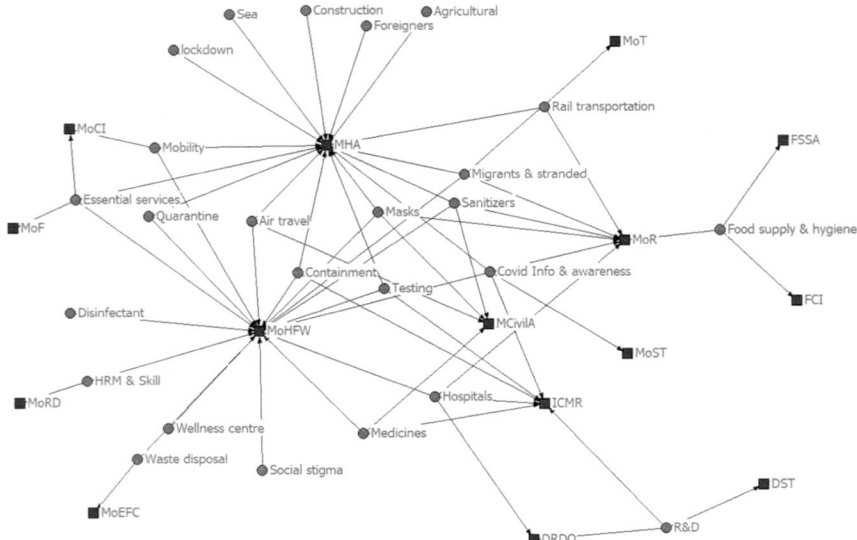

Figure 2.4 Multiplicity of functions across ministries/public institutions.

opportunities in their villages only after the issue attracted national attention. The relevant public development agencies had no plan until then, while migrant workers were addressed in the MHA, MoHFW, and Ministry of Railways guidelines.

The Central Government has constituted six empowered groups (taskforce) to coordinate the COVID-19 response. Later, in May 2021, these groups were reconstituted into ten groups to look after the various dimensions of COVID response: vaccination, oxygen supply, welfare measures, partnership with NGOs, testing, human resources, emergency capabilities, emergency management plan, and so on.[20] Despite the centrally located empowered groups and efforts of the concerned ministries, supply chain interruptions caused the shortage of raw material and lack of labour force; hence the supply of various essential economic services was disrupted.[21] During pre-COVID-19 times, companies were trying to supply the material very quickly, keeping them in the storage for zero time (or very less time), and hence minimizing the storage cost. This means that companies would not have sufficient inventory buffers to compensate the shortage during the pandemic-induced lockdowns (Roy, 2020). Restricted vehicle movement and shortage of labour added to misery[22].

Coordination is not merely needed among the public agencies. A synergy between public and private agencies would also be beneficial in difficult times. The role of a private actor is significant in providing the logistics and services for the most complex and world's biggest disease management initiative. The countries like Germany and South Korea have done significant work in this regard and have been able to restrict the adverse effects of the pandemic. In contrast, countries like the United States and Britain have suffered due to poor coordination and infrastructure (Mazzucato and Kattel, 2020).

2.4 Conclusion

The policy response to COVID-19 should have been like any natural disaster (Sharma et al., 2020) – planned approach, coordinated response, everyone knows what to do, information management, and so on. As a matter of normative governance principle, local Governments such as panchayats in rural areas and municipalities or municipal corporations in towns and cities should take a more active role to institutionalize the new norms. However, experiences suggest that disease response and management were centrally planned and executed, which resulted into uneven and ad hoc responses across different Indian states. We do not see any community action developing around disease management. Lack of community involvement creates service delivery issues. This learning was always known to the bureaucracy; still, the same was not put in action. There should have been an attempt to develop trust between the citizens and the administration. Mutual monitoring by citizens may have reduced adverse impacts of the pandemic and the administrative cost as well. The rollout of the COVID-19 pandemic in the country threw gigantic policy challenges, but we witnessed that not many policy innovations were brought to address these challenges. In times of unexpected attack by the outside factors (such as COVID-19), policy innovation becomes inherent. Existing capacities need to be complemented in innovative ways and more space should be provided to local institutions. Bringing local Governments in developing local resilience, awareness, managing the disease, and planning and executing the response would bring more fruitful results. This would also allow the local Governments to innovate in their response based on local conditions and resource availability.

Notes

1 OECD. Responding to COVID. Retrieved from https://www.oecd.org/governance/public-governance-responses-to-covid19/. Accessed August 5th, 2021.
2 Centre for Science and Environment, State of India's Environment 2021 in Figures. June 4th. Quoted from https://www.downtoearth.org.in/blog/pollution/state-of-india-s-environment-2021-people-and-planet-in-peril-75661 Accessed August 5th 2021.
3 World Health Organization. Coronavirus disease 2019 (COVID-19) Situation Report – 94. April 23rd 2020.
4 *Times of India*, Coronavirus Tracker. https://timesofindia.indiatimes.com/coronavirus Accessed April 20th 2021.
5 International Monitory Funds, Policy Tracker. https://www.imf.org/en/Topics/imf-and-covid19/Policy-Responses-to-COVID-19#I Accessed July 21st 2021.
6 *Times of India*, Coronavirus tracker, Available at https://timesofindia.indiatimes.com/coronavirus Accessed July 31st 2021.
7 Ministry of Electronics and IT, Government of India. Press Release. May 26th 2020. https://pib.gov.in/PressReleasePage.aspx?PRID=1626979 Accessed August 2nd 2021.
8 A voluntary curfew called by the Prime Minister of India on 22 March 2020, requesting the citizens to remain inside the home and avoid outside contacts.
9 *Economic Times* (E-paper). One year since a complete lockdown was announced, we look back on how India fought COVID. March 24th 2021. https://economictimes.indiatimes.com/news/india/one-year-since-a-complete-lockdown-was-announced-we-look-back-on-how-india-fought-covid/first-lockdown-announced/slideshow/81662838.cms Accessed July 20th 2021.
10 The Print. 40 COVID apps across India: Lack of coordination or needed for micro-management? June 4. Retrieved from https://theprint.in/talk-point/40-covid-apps-across-india-lack-of-coordination-or-needed-for-micro-management/435616/ Accessed July 31st 2021.
11 Ibid.
12 National Disaster Management Authority. COVID-19 impacts and responses: The Indian experience (Jan – May 2020). Retrieved from https://ndma.gov.in/sites/default/files/PDF/covid/COVID-19-Indian-Experience.pdf Accessed July 15th 2021.
13 Ministry of Panchayati Raj, Government of India, COVID-19 in India: States/UT level initiatives at the panchayat level. Retrieved from https://panchayat.gov.in/documents/20126/0/COVID-State+initiatives+at+the+GP+Level+03042020.pdf/12505a82-3c8f-c75a-fdae-5cbddd0ae58c?t=1585975029688 Accessed August 1st 2021.
14 Ministry of Health and Family Welfare, COVID-19 Vaccines: Operational Guidelines. https://www.mohfw.gov.in/pdf/COVID19VaccineOG111Chapter16.pdf Accessed 28 July, 2021.

15 *Financial Express.* Covid-19: Why India is facing vaccine shortage. May 10th 2021. https://www.financialexpress.com/lifestyle/health/covid-19-why-india-is-facing-vaccine-shortage/2248748/ Accessed July 29th 2021.
16 *Business Standard.* Centre steps in after foreign Covid-19 vaccine makers say no to state governments. 25th May 2021. https://www.business-standard.com/article/current-affairs/centre-steps-in-after-foreign-covid-19-vaccine-makers-say-no-to-state-govts-121052500002_1.html Accessed July 15th 2021.
17 It is a joint initiative of Nuclear Threat Initiative and the Johns Hopkins Center for Health Security, and was developed with The Economist Intelligence Unit. https://www.ghsindex.org
18 Global Health Security Index presents an assessment of health readiness in 195 countries. It can be accessed at https://www.ghsindex.org/country/india/
19 Livemint. Could not predict exact nature of COVID second wave: Scientists working on mathematical models. May 2nd, 2021. https://www.livemint.com/news/india/could-not-predict-exact-nature-of-covid-second-wave-scientists-11619944997986.html Accessed July 30th, 2021.
20 *Hindustan Times.* May 29th, 2021. https://www.hindustantimes.com/india-news/govt-reconstitutes-6-empowered-groups-into-10-to-tackle-covid-19-crisis-101622298616531.html Accessed July 30th, 2021.
21 EY. Managing the impact of COVID-19 on India's supply chains – Now, Next and Beyond. July 2020. https://assets.ey.com/content/dam/ey-sites/ey-com/en_in/topics/government-and-public-sector/2020/09/managing-the-impact-of-covid-19-on-india-supply-chains.pdf Accessed June 30th, 2021.
22 Ibid.

References

Afridi, F. (2017). Governance and public service delivery in India. International Growth.

Aiyar, Y. and Krishnamurthy, M. (2020). Covid-19: Centre and states must work together. *Hindustan Times* (e-version), April 1st. Accessed on July 30th, 2021. https://www.hindustantimes.com/analysis

Andrews, M. A., Areekal, B., Rajesh, K. R., Krishnan, J., Suryakala, R., Krishnan, B., Muraly, C. P., and Santhosh, P. V. (2020). First confirmed case of COVID-19 infection in India: A case report. *The Indian Journal of Medical Research* 151 (5): 490–492.

Bharali, I., Kumar, P., and Selvaraj, S. (2020). How well is India responding to COVID-19? July 2nd, Brookings. Accessed on June 13th, 2021. https://www.brookings.edu/blog/future-development/2020/07/02/how-well-is-india-responding-to-covid-19/

Centre. International Growth Centre. Accessed on July 30th, 2021. https://www.theigc.org/wp-content/uploads/2017/05/Afridi-2017-Synthesis-paper.pdf

Charpentier, A., Elie, R., Lauriere, M., and Tran, V. C. (2020). COVID-19 pandemic control: Balancing detection policy and lockdown intervention under ICU sustainability. Cornell University. arXiv:2005.06526.

Clarance, A. (2020). Aarogya Setu: Why India's Covid-19 contact tracing app is controversial. *BBC News*, May 15th. Accessed on June 13th, 2021. https://www.bbc.com/news/world-asia-india-52659520

Das, J. (2020). India's response to coronavirus can't be based on existing epidemiological models. *The Print*, April 6th. Accessed on June 23rd, 2021. https://theprint.in/opinion/indias-response-to-coronavirus-cant-be-based-on-existing-epidemiological-models/395275/

Dutta, A. and Fischer, H. W. (2021). The local governance of COVID-19: Disease prevention and social security in rural India. *World Development* 138: 105234. https://doi.org/10.1016/j.worlddev.2020.105234

Gardner, A. (2020). There's no evidence that contact-tracing apps are effective in containing Covid-19. *The Conversation at Scroll.in*, October 22nd. Accessed on June 12th, 2021. https://scroll.in/article/976492/theres-no-evidence-that-contact-tracing-apps-are-effective-in-containing-covid-19

Herfurth, H. (2020). What exactly does it mean to 'flatten the curve'? UAB expert defines coronavirus terminology for everyday life. The University of Alabama at Birmingham (UAB) News. Accessed on 18th August 2021. https://www.uab.edu/news/youcanuse/item/11268-what-exactly-does-it-mean-to-flatten-the-curve-uab-expert-defines-coronavirus-terminology-for-everyday-life

Issac, T. and Sadanandan, R. (2020). COVID-19, public health system and local governance in Kerala. *Economic and Political Weekly* 55 (21): 35–40.

Jha, A. K. and Jha, R. (2020). India's response to COVID-19 crisis. *India Economic Journal* 68 (3): 341–351.

Kanitkar, T. (2020). The COVID-19 lockdown in India: Impacts on the economy and the power sector. *Global Transition* 2: 150–156. https://doi.org/10.1016/j.glt.2020.07.005

Kantner, M. and Koprucki, T. (2020). Beyond just "flattening the curve": Optimal control of epidemics with purely non-pharmaceutical interventions. *Journal of Mathematics in Industry* 10: 23. https://doi.org/10.1186/s13362-020-00091-3

Kar, S. K. Ransing, R., Arafat, S. Y., and Menon, V. (2021). Second wave of COVID-19 pandemic in India: Barriers to effective governmental response. *EClinicalMedicine* 36: 100915. https://doi.org/10.1016/j.eclinm.2021.100915.

Kaushik, M., Agarwal, D., and Gupta A. K. (2020). Cross-sectional study on the role of public awareness in preventing the spread of COVID-19 outbreak in India. *Postgraduate Medical Journal*. https://doi.org/10.1136/postgradmedj-2020–138349

Koshy, J. (2021). Scientists see flaws in Govt-backed model's approach to forecast pandemic. May 4th. Accessed on August 17th, 2021. https://www.thehindu.com/news/national/government-backed-model-to-predict-pandemic-rise-and-ebb-lacks-foresight-scientists/article34479503.ece

Kugler, M. and Sinha, S. (2020). The impact of COVID-19 and the policy response in India. July 13th. Brookings. Accessed on July 20th, 2021. https://www.brookings.edu/blog/future-development/2020/07/13/the-impact-of-covid-19-and-the-policy-response-in-india/

Kumar, V. M., Pandi-Perumal, S. R., and Trakht, I. (2021). Strategy for COVID-19 vaccination in India: The country with the second highest population and number of cases. *npj Vaccines* 6 (6). https://doi.org/10.1038/s41541-021-00327-2

Martinelli L. et al. (2021). Face masks during the COVID-19 pandemic: A simple protection tool with many meanings. *Frontiers in Public Health* 8: 947. https://doi.org/10.3389/fpubh.2020.606635

Mazzucato, M. and Kattel, R. (2020). COVID-19 and public-sector capacity. *Oxford Review of Economic Policy* 36 (supp 1): s256–s269. https://doi.org/10.1093/oxrep/graa031

Mehra, P. (2020). India's economy needs big dose of health spending. *Livemint*. April 8th. Retrieved from https://www.livemint.com/news/india/india-s-economy-needs-big-dose-of-health-spending-11586365603651.html

Paul, V. (2020). Timely lockdown gave India an edge in war against coronavirus. *Indian Express*, July 28th. Accessed on July 1st, 2021. https://indianexpress.com/article/opinion/columns/india-coronvirus-lockdown-covid-19-spread-vacine-icmr-testing-vinod-paul-6526381/

Peters, B. G. (2018). The challenge of policy coordination. *Policy Design and Practice* 1 (1): 1–11. https://doi.org/10.1080/25741292.2018.1437946

Ranjan, R. (2021). Impact of COVID-19 on migrant labourers of India and China. *Critical Sociology* 47 (4–5): 721–726.

Rawson, T., Brewer, T., Veltcheva, D., Huntingford, C., and Bonsall, M. B. (2020). How and when to end the COVID-19 lockdown: An optimization approach. *Frontiers in Public Health* 8: 262. https://doi.org/10.3389/fpubh.2020.00262.

Roy, D. (2020). Covid-19 exposes Indian industry's supply chain vulnerabilities. *BusinessLine*, 1st April. Accessed August 18th, 2021. https://www.thehindubusinessline.com/opinion/covid-19-exposes-indian-industrys-supply-chain-vulnerabilities/article31224928.ece

Rukmini, S. (2020). How covid-19 response disrupted health services in rural India. *Livemint*, April 27th. Accessed on May 17th, 2021. https://www.livemint.com/news/india/how-covid-19-response-disrupted-health-services-in-rural-india-11587713155817.html

Saikia, A. (2020). Covid-19: As cases surge in India, most states abandon contact tracing. July 13th. Accessed on April 30, 2021. https://scroll.in/article/967223/covid-19-as-cases-surge-in-india-most-states-abandon-contact-tracing

Shashidhar, K. J. (2020). Arogya Setu App and its many conflicts. Observer research foundation. Accessed on July 19th, 2021. https://www.orfonline.org/expert-speak/aarogya-setu-app-many-conflicts-67442/

Sharma, G. D., Talan, G., and Jain, M. (2020). Policy response to the economic challenge from COVID-19 in India: A qualitative enquiry. *Journal of Public Affairs* 20 (4): e2206.

Singh, A. K., Agrawal, B., Sharma, A., and Sharma, P. (2020). COVID-19: Assessment of knowledge and awareness in Indian society. *Journal of Public Affairs* 20 (4): e2354. https://doi.org/10.1002/pa.2354

3 The Dichotomies of Management and Governance in the COVID-19 Pandemic

A View from Rawls' Difference Principle and Political Economy Perspective

Hippu Salk Kristle Nathan and Indranil De

3.1 The Pandemic and the Rich-Poor Divide

A disaster that does not distinguish between the 'haves' and 'have-nots' makes the latter more vulnerable because of their lack of capacity – financial, infrastructural, and social. The COVID-19 pandemic is not an exception to this. The novel corona virus disease (COVID-19) was reported from China in December 2019 (WHO, 2021), and by 24 June 2021 there were close to 180 million cases and 3.9 million deaths on account of COVID-19 worldwide (JHU, 2021). With 220 countries and territories being affected by COVID-19 till date (Worldometer, 2021), there is hardly any region left which has not been invaded by COVID-19 virus.

The virus does not distinguish between rich and poor (Günther, 2020; Tuncer, 2020), but like many other ailments, the protection from the virus is not equally easy or difficult for rich and poor (Günther, 2020). Poverty, as it is understood, is a manifestation of several layers of inequality (Ray, 1998). The rich not only have a greater economic endowment but tend to live in safer house in a better locality having a superior infrastructure in terms of several facets of living standards such as greater access to safe water and sanitation, cooking fuel and electricity, and transport and communication. This is true about better education and health care service infrastructure too. Also, people with low socioeconomic status are also endowed with less social capital for the benefit of their health (Uphoff, Pickett, Cabieses, Small, & Wright, 2013).

The rich-poor divide in terms of health is visible in the mortality-morbidity gap (Tripathi & Nathan, 2016). In a subjective indicator like self-reported morbidity, the poor report better health condition whereas the better-off report worse health status; however, in an objective assessment like mortality the poor are worse off, leading to a situation called 'dying in silence' (Tripathi & Nathan, 2016). Sen (2002) has suggested that the self-perception of health or 'internal view of health' is dependent on social experiences, and poor and disadvantaged people failed to report illness because of poor health care infrastructure and

DOI: 10.4324/9781003226970-5

health awareness resulting in low perception of health. Therefore, the poor, in general, due to lack of affordability to health care and lack of awareness, remain as silent sufferers of low health attainments. A lesser medical facility on one hand and a greater constrains to access the same on the other add to the disadvantageous situation of the poor.

The symptom of 'dying in silence' gets amplified in the COVID-19 pandemic situation because of the enhanced risks of COVID-19 mortality under the comorbidity condition (Sanyaolu et al., 2020; Wang, Li, Lu, & Huang, 2020). Also, the poorer society is not endowed with enough resources to meet the huge challenge posed by the pandemic. In other words, poor countries lack the capacity to respond to threats of COVID-19 and poor individuals lack the choices and risk their lives by coming out to the streets, making them vulnerable in the process (Charles, 2020; Vilasanjuan, 2021). For instance, in Kenya, for more than 50 million population has only 537 ICU beds and 256 ventilators (Barasa, Ouma, & Okiro, 2020). Similarly studies from Latin America shows pandemic is resulting in increase of inequality in the region and the poorest are three times more likely to die than the richest (Charles, 2020).

Given this backdrop, this chapter looks into the Indian Government's response in terms of its governance and management of the pandemic with respect to three aspects – lockdown, provision of health care, and vaccination drive. It analyses how these responses were distinct between different segments of society – rich and poor, formal and informal, urban and rural, and well-connected and ill-connected. The analysis is carried out using Rawls' difference principle and political economy perspective.

The rest of the chapter is organized as follows. Section 3.2 briefs Rawls' difference principle and a minor amendment to it for its application to the current study. Section 3.3 gives the political economy framework, and the context to elite capture and political clientelism. Section 3.4 presents and analyses the three measures undertaken by the Government to meet the challenges posed by the pandemic – lockdown, provision of health care, and vaccination drive under the lenses of difference principle and political economy framework. Section 3.5 gives the concluding remarks.

3.2 Rawls' Difference Principle

John Rawls is considered as one of the most influential political philosophers of last century (Dombrowski, 2001; Freeman, 2003; Nagel, 2003; Brooks, 2006; Ryan, 2006; Cilne, 2013; Wolfe, 2020). Rawls (1993) has put forward two principles of justice that can serve as guidelines for basic institutions to realize the values of liberty and equality. The two principles are (Rawls, 1993, pp. 5–6) (i) each person has an equal claim to a fully adequate scheme of *equal basic rights and liberties*; (ii) social and economic inequalities are to satisfy two conditions: (a) they are to be attached to positions and offices open to all under conditions of *fair equality of opportunity*; and (b) they are to be to the *greatest benefit of the least advantaged* members of society.

The second condition of the second principle is referred to as the 'Difference Principle'. The difference principle is lexically inferior to first condition of second principle (equality of opportunity could not be sacrificed for greater social and economic equality) and the second principle in turn is inferior to the first principle (equal basic liberties could not be sacrificed for greater equality of opportunity or greater social and economic equality) (Reiff, 2012). The difference principle concerns the absolute position of the least disadvantaged and permits and recommends that level of inequality in the society which would lead to maximize the absolute position of least advantaged (SEP, 2017).[1]

Most of the criticisms of difference principle lies with justifying the socio-economic inequality for the greatest benefit to the least advantaged (difference principle would allow socio-economic inequality), and with the assumption that lesser degree of inequality would make the least advantaged worse-off. Greater inequality at all conditions may be not acceptable from the normative point of view just because it leads to higher benefits to the most disadvantaged. For the purpose of this chapter, we have considered an amended version of difference principle, which restricts its scope to provision of opportunities by the social political institutions where inequality is introduced to provide the greatest benefits to the least advantaged and the same can be validated by taking any two groups. In Figure 3.1 below we give the logical flow of Rawls' principles in provision of opportunities. A society can choose which of the provisions can be provided equally and which are the ones provided unequally to benefit the disadvantaged.

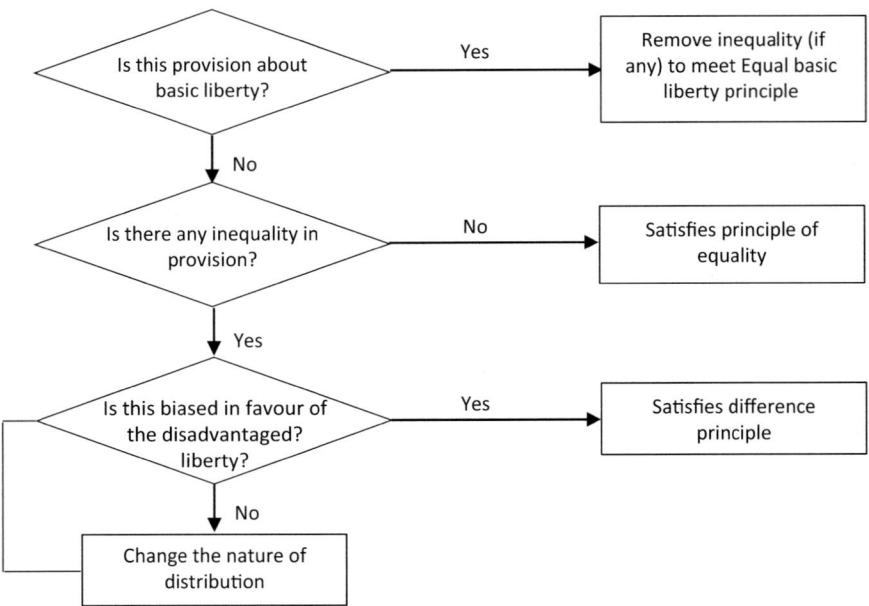

Figure 3.1 Schematic sketch for test for inequality of provision as per amended Rawls' theory of justice.

This would make the rationale of difference principle strictly egalitarian in the sense of Sen's flute example, where the child who does not have any toy to play ends up getting the flute as against the child who has made the flute or the child who knows how to play it (Sen, 2006). This way difference principle explains, for instance, the affirmative action clearly, which otherwise not easy to derive from Rawls' theory of justice (Nagel, 2003; Mathew, 2015). Also, it is worth noting here that the dichotomies like rich and poor, urban and rural, well-connected and ill-connected can be mapped to the advantaged-disadvantaged situation described above.

3.3 Elite Capture and Political Clientelism

In a majoritarian democracy, public policy should ideally depend on the majority decision. In other words, public policy would protect and promote the interest of the majority. The problem of such public policy decision-making process is that the gains of the policy are accrued to one group, which is typically the larger in size, at the cost of others (Butler, 2012).

In India, the level of inequality is very sharp with a small group economically much well-endowed as compared to the masses. According to National Sample Survey Organization 66th Round (2009–10), the average monthly per capita consumption expenditure (MPCE), an indicator of economic wellbeing, was 456% and 878% higher for the highest decile of MPCE class as compared to the lowest decile in rural and urban India, respectively (Figure 3.2). Furthermore, MPCE was higher by 106% and 152% for the 10th (highest) decile as compared to 8th decile, respectively, for rural and urban areas. Hence, there is stark divide between the richer 20% and the poorer 80% of the population. India being democratic, one would expect, public policies benefitting poorer majority can be devised at the cost of richer minority.

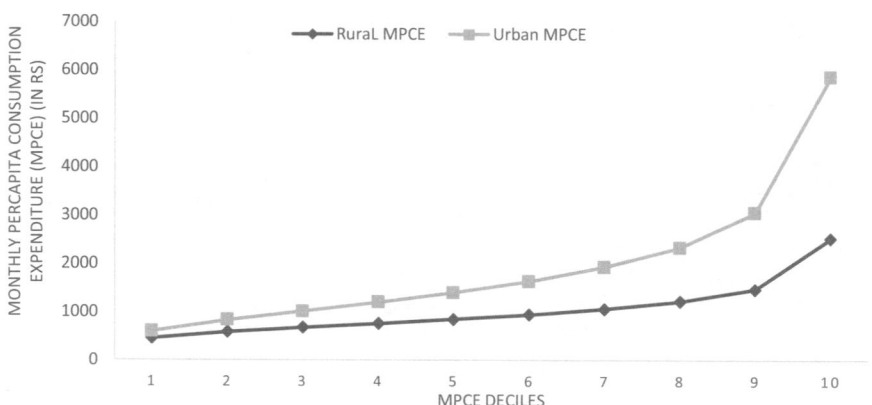

Figure 3.2 Distribution of households by monthly per capita consumption expenditure (MPCE).

Source: National Sample Survey Organization, 66th Round (2009-10).

However, it is not that straight forward. Despite poorer section constituting the majority, the poor may not get the benefits of public policy vis-à-vis the rich. Poor may not be able to influence public policy such that the cost of public action is shifted to the rich. This is due to the presence of interest groups, which are small groups empowered with resource (money) and intrusive ability due to political connections (Butler, 2012). Due to the influence of interest groups, public policy may serve the richer by ignoring the poorer. Public policy can benefit interest group, who has a say in public policy, at the cost of poor majority. In this process of public choice exercised through public policy, the gains are concentrated to the small interest group and the cost is spread across vast majority (see Figure 3.3). This system may not lead to collective dissent by the majority as the per capita cost ascribed to the majority would be very low and hence majority would ignore such policy bias against them. This is called *rational ignorance* (Downs, 1957; Lopez de Leon & Rizzi, 2014).

The influence of powerful minority in crafting favourable public policy decision at the cost of vast majority, who are poor and powerless, is called *elite capture*. Public policy can be influenced by elite in many ways. Policies can be devised in favour of elites. Also, public actions may desist implementation of pro-poor public policy, or it may go even against pro-poor policies. Moreover, there may be parallel policies: one benefiting rich, and the other benefitting the poor. But, the benefits to the rich would be much higher than the benefits to the poor.

Elite capture in public policy may lead to formal-informal dichotomy in public policy formulation and actions. The rationale of such dichotomy is the lower socio-economic status of poor in India. The activities that the poor are engaged with are mostly classified as informal and the activities that the rich engaged with are mostly considered as formal. Formal sector gets the benefit of social protection and security of employment, while the informal sector gets no such benefit. As a result, informality is equated with instability and formality with stability (Tranberg Hansen & Vaa, 2004; van Assche, Beunen, & Duineveld, 2014). However, there is hardly any well-defined criteria to differentiate between

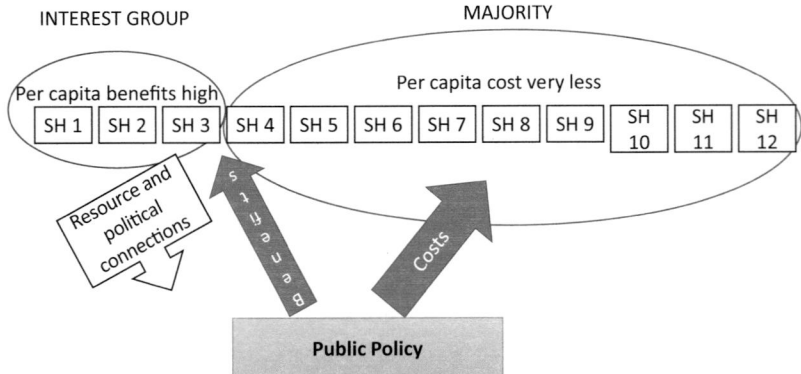

Figure 3.3 Public policy formation.

formality and informality (Roy, 2009; Schindler, 2014). The distinction between formality and informality is largely negotiated (Schindler, 2014) and the informality work under a set of negotiated rules (Banks, Lombard, & Mitlin, 2019). It makes formal-informal hierarchy a norm (Roy, 2005), with informal sector relegated in the hierarchy although its contribution is very high, both in the economy and employment.[2] Due to the elevated position of formal sector, public policy benefiting it is assumed to be justified in spite of the greater importance of informal sector in overall economy. Moreover, the benefits remain within a small interest group of people and hence per capita benefit is highly tangible. On the contrary, public policy on informal sector is ignored due to its lower status. Due to the sheer size of the group, benefits provided to the informal sector may be insufficient on per capita basis (and therefore easily dispensable) unless the amount of benefit provided is very high. A similar argument can be built between other dichotomies as well – poor and rich, rural and urban, ill-connected and well-connected.

But the important question is that how Government keeps the interest of the poor, who are a very large voter. Government may provide direct and tangible benefits to the individuals to gain political support. This process is *political clientelism*, whereby public benefits are privatized against political support. In this system politicians create a patron-client relationship with the citizens (Keefer & Khemani, 2005). Clientelism is discretionary granting of available public resources and services in exchange of political subordination (Heredia, 1997; Kitschelt & Wilkinson, 2007).

3.4 Pandemic Management and Governance – An Indian Case

Indian's public policy response to the COVID-19 pandemic reveals contrasts while dealing with different groups of population. We analyse three phenomena: lockdown, provision of health care, and vaccination drive.

3.4.1 Lockdown

The Government announced nationwide lockdown on 25 March 2020 (Hebbar, 2020). This suddenly restricted the movement within the country. However, the greater threat of spread of pandemic was from inbound international travel, which continued till 16 March 2020, when passengers from or through UAE, Qatar, Oman, and Kuwait were mandated a 14-days of quarantine (Business Standard, 2020). Travel from member countries of the European Union, the European Free Trade Association, Turkey, and the UK were totally prohibited only on 18 March 2020 (Business Standard, 2020); however, this was preceded by a decision taken on 11 March 2020 to ban foreigners entry to India from 13 March 2020 (*The Wire*, 2020) giving an indication of total prohibition. On 17 March 2020 passengers from Afghanistan, Philippines, and Malaysia were prohibited (India Today, 2020). Further, all inbound international flights were suspended from 22 March 2020 (Dey & Sinha, 2020). These series of decision show there is some sort of gradualist approach while imposing bans and this must have given some travellers to find time to take appropriate decision. However, the same did not hold true for the nationwide lockdown, which was announced the very previous evening (Hebbar, 2020). This directly impacted the migrant workers in the informal sector.

Lakhs left cities to their natives due to loss of employment and fear of uncertainty. The return of these migrant workers to their natives continued for next few months. Without any warning and any transportation option available, they walked hundreds of kilometres along the highways to reach their native places after the lockdown was announced. Some of them took resort to unusual, unsafe means of transport, starting from bicycle to being stuffed in carrier trucks or insider the drum of concrete mixer paying hefty money and being on empty stomachs (Singh, 2020; Yadav, 2020). The media carried innumerable plights of migrant workers including that of the 15-year girl who cycled 1200 kilometres carrying his injured father for eight days (Jyoti & Dey, 2020). Only after 1 May 2020, that is, 39 days after announcing lockdown, the Indian railways (Government operated) started its operation to take the migrant workers from cities to their natives through Shramik special trains (PIB, 2020). The arrangement was no match as compared to the need for transportation. The migrants spent days in front of railway station with their family with a hope of getting some decent means to transport to travel back to their natives. Because of their lack of digital knowledge, they faced huge difficulties in booking tickets which was available online only. The situation for the inbound international travellers was different. The first evacuation mission of Indian citizens was carried out by Air India flights (Government operated) from Wuhan, China on 31 January and 1 February 2020 (WION, 2020). Starting on 7 May 2000, Indians were evacuated from foreign countries through different phases under Vande Bharat Mission (*The Hindu*, 2021).

This difference of response from Government for Indians abroad and migrant workers fails the test of Rawls' difference principle. The former group is clearly privileged and more capable, whereas the latter is more vulnerable. Similarly, some of the formal sectors which could adapt to technology could sustain the lockdown. Whereas most of the informal sector, which heavily relies on physical transactions suffered adversely with severe loss of livelihoods and income for which there was hardly any contingency arrangement by the Government. Had it gone by the difference principle, the inequality of arrangements should have been biased towards the disadvantaged section of the society, rather than favouring the advantaged group.

However, the explanation of this action is plausible from a political economic angle. The negligence of informal sector in public policy and action is very much akin to a-formal public actions conceptualized by Goodfellow (2019). A-formal is a form of political informality driven by rules that are unclear or non-existent. This negotiable system creates opportunity for political exploitation and manipulation. Indian Government initiated transportation of workers through

Shramik special trains only after hue and cry on the plight of migrant workers became major political issue. There was no prior planning to deal with mass return-migration. The public voice to make arrangements for transportation did not lead to overwhelming Government response. The arrangements made were inadequate and insufficient. Although the demand for public action to manage the chaos is for the majority poor but still public policy did not satisfy the need. This is due to the low de facto political power or bargaining strength of the poor to influence the public policy at large (see Acemoglu, Johnson, and Robinson (2005) for de facto political power).

3.4.2 Provision of Health Care

India's public expenditure on health care hovers around 1% of India's GDP and it is lower than low-income countries of the world. For instance, in 2016, for India, which is a lower middle-income country, the public spending on health was at 1.17%, whereas the same for countries classified as low-income countries works out to be on an average 1.57% (Dutta, 2019). If we add private expenditure to it, India's total health expenditure as a share of GDP in 2018 was 3.54%, whereas the corresponding figure on an average for low-income countries was 5.23% (World Bank, 2021a). The lack of health care expenses in India, particularly, the public spending, has traditionally made India's poor more vulnerable.

There is an urban-rural divide in health care infrastructure in India. In rural areas there is a shortfall of health facilities: 24% sub-centres (SCs), 29% primary health centres (PHCs), and 38% community health centres (CHCs) (MHFW, 2020a). Also, there is lack of human resources in health sector in rural areas. There is a shortage of 66% male workers in the SCs; 23% nursing staff, 46% ANM (Auxiliary Nurse Midwife) workers, and 72% of health assistants in the PHCs and 76% of specialists (79% surgeons, 70% obstetricians and gynaecologists, 78% physicians, and 78% paediatricians) in the CHCs (MHFW, 2020a). Moreover, there are shortage of 56% radiographers in CHCs, and 25% pharmacists and 49% lab technicians in PHCs (MHFW, 2020a). Urban areas do not face such severe shortages like rural areas (see data for urban health centres in MHFW (2020a)). Similarly, in terms of availability of beds urban areas are better off with 64% share, with rural areas having 36% of the share. This translates to availability of beds per 10,000 population as 10.8 in urban areas, and the corresponding figure in the rural areas is 3.3 (calculated from National Health Profile 2020 data and assuming 65% of India's 1.38 billion population lives in urban areas).

Due to health care shortfalls, in terms of testing services, weak surveillance system, and overall poor medical care, rural areas are not equipped to contain COVID-19, particularly in northern densely populated and underserved states such as Uttar Pradesh and Bihar (Kumar, Nayar, & Koya, 2020). In the second wave this vulnerability of rural areas got exposed. A State Bank of India (SBI, 2021) research released on 7 May 2021, showed the share of new cases coming from rural district increased to 48.5% in May from 36.8% in March 2021. A Down To Earth (2021) study showed that in May 2021, rural districts accounted for majority (53%) of cases and majority (52%) of deaths. Also, in terms of share of new cases, by May 2021, rural, semi-rural, semi-urban, urban areas accounted for 35%, 30%, 22%, and 13% of the new cases, respectively (Radhakrishnan, 2021). There are several other media reports indicating high mortality from specific rural districts of Maharashtra, Haryana, Gujarat, Uttar Pradesh and Bihar, with visuals of mass burials sites in riverbed and corpses floating in the river Ganga in those districts of Uttar Pradesh and Bihar (Chakrabarty & Suri, 2021). The report of cases and deaths on account of COVID-19 can be an under estimation in rural areas considering lack of testing facility on one hand and testing hesitancy by the villagers on the other (Chakrabarty & Suri, 2021; Thakur, 2021).

The solutions to meet the challenges of pandemic in rural India is to bridge the shortfalls in physical and human resources in rural health care sector and to bring in urban-rural parity (Kumar, Nayar, & Koya, 2020, Chakrabarty & Suri, 2021). This would ensure better health care in rural areas in regular non-pandemic times as well. Considering lower affordability and higher out-of-pocket health expenditure in rural areas, the Rawls' difference principle would argue for greater provision of health facilities and human resources in rural areas. Also, even without invoking this normative argument, for a democracy like India, where poor in rural areas are the majority of voters, non-provision of better quality of health care to them is puzzling. However, this happens, because of the short-run political objectives of prioritizing private transfers and subsidies over provision of broad public goods for electoral gain (Keefer & Khemani, 2004). Such political tradition along with social fragmentations among poor (that provides fertile ground for political clientelism), and lack of information on quality of public services among the poor contribute towards low prioritization of improvement on public goods in general (Keefer & Khemani, 2004).

One of the first condition to ensure better provision of public goods is to commit for higher expenditure for setting up the public goods and ensuring maintenance of quality. This is true for all public goods, and health is not an exception to this.

As a way forward, India needs to increase public health expenditure, particularly targeting rural areas. China did the same in the last two decades. The World Bank (2021b) shows at the turn of the century both China and India had near to 1% share of GDP as domestic general Government health expenditure. India has been languishing at the same level, whereas China has slowly increased the same to more than 3% (see Figure 3.4).

3.4.3 Vaccination

On 11 March 2020 the World Health Organization declared coronavirus as a global pandemic (WHO, 2021). Owing to both high infectiousness and contagiousness of COVID-19 and its symptomatic uncertainty, and rapid spread (Li et al., 2020), it's long realized that 'no one is safe unless everyone is safe' (Padilla, 2021). Currently, 18 vaccines are in use and of which eight are in Phase IV (Shrotri, Swinnen, Kampmann, & Parker, 2021), which is the phase

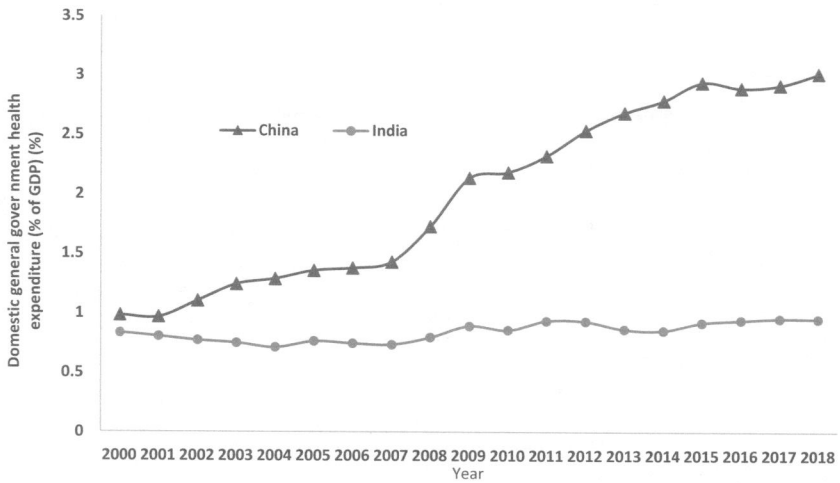

Figure 3.4 Domestic general Government health expenditure (% of GDP) – India, China.
Source: World Bank (2021b).

where studies on the vaccine go on after the efficacy and safety of the vaccine tested and the vaccine is approved and licensed and made to use (CDC, 2021).

Figure 3.5 gives the progress of COVID-19 vaccination in world and some selected countries including that of India. The rich-poor divide is vividly evident with the fact that though globally 22.6% population have got at least one dose vaccination, only 0.9% population in low-income countries have got at least one dose (OWID, 2021).

Clearly, the global distribution of vaccination fails to satisfy Rawls' difference principle. From the available data on premarket purchase commitments for COVID-19 vaccines from leading manufacturers to recipient countries, it is found that as of 15 November 2020, there was purchase commitments of 7.48 billion doses (or 3.76 billion courses) and more than half of it (51%) of these doses have gone to high income countries having less than one-seventh population (14%) (So & Woo, 2020). More than 10% of the reserved doses, that is, 800 million were booked by the United States which has a population of 330 million; similarly, Japan, Canada, and Australia, put together though have 200 million population, have pre-booked one billion doses (Kuhen, 2021). This skewed distribution has led to a situation, where it is estimated that one-quarter of global population will not get vaccination until 2022 (So & Woo, 2020).

India's vaccination drive started on Jan 16, 2021 with two types of vaccines, namely, Covaxin by Bharat Biotech International Ltd. and Covishield by Serum Institute of India Ltd (Bagcchi, 2021). India's initial plan for vaccination drive has been outlined by the Ministry of Health and Family Welfare (MHFW, 2020b). The first recipient of vaccines were to be the health workers and front-line workers, and old people (age above 50 years). Among old people, the priority

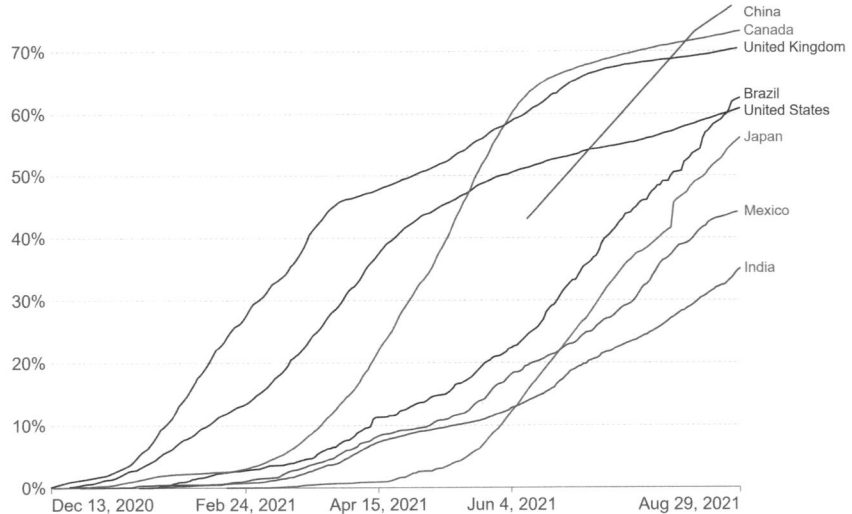

Figure 3.5 Share of the total population that received at least one vaccine dose.
Source: OWID (2021).
Note: Data for China available since 10 June 2021.

would be given to those above 60 years of age. The next in line were people with age below 50 years but having comorbidities, which makes them more vulnerable. The remaining population would be considered next. The phasing of roll out of vaccines would depend on pandemic situation, disease epidemiology, and vaccine availability (MHFW, 2020b). The plan was to vaccinate 300 million people (10 million health worker, 20 million frontline workers, and 260 million elderly more than 50 years, and 10 million less than 50 years with co-morbidities like diabetes, hypertension, cancer, and lung diseases) (MHFW, 2020b; Bagcchi, 2021). Beginning with January 2021, as planned the vaccine was extended to elderly with more than 60 years and those who are more than 45 years and having comorbidities on 1 March 2021.

However, the vaccine rollout took a different course afterwards. On 1 April 2021 the vaccine was made open to all above 45 years and on 1 May 2021 made open to all adults (MHFW, 2021). This change of plan can be viewed from two different perspectives. First, this made the more vulnerable elderly people relatively deprived. Between 3 May and 5 June 2021 there were more first doses administered to people in the age group 18-44 years than people more than 60 years (Lloyd-Sherlock et al., 2021). This is so, even there are more than three times population above 60 years yet to be vaccinated than the doses given to 18–44 years (Lloyd-Sherlock et al., 2021; PIB, 2021). By doing this, India caused large number of avertable deaths (Lloyd-Sherlock et al., 2021). This view is in line with Rawls' difference principle, assuming the younger are less vulnerable than older.

An alternative view to this was that the surge of cases in the second wave and with younger people becoming hospitalized with severe symptoms, made the Government change its original plan (BBC, 2021). Also, it was primarily the younger population which used to make the bulk of the movements post lockdown after the first wave. So, in this sense, younger people were not less deserving for vaccination.

On a separate note, Government's decision to provide vaccine free of cost in public health centres confirms to Rawls' difference principle, assuming poorer are the major beneficiaries of such centres.

However, the crux of the problem lied in India's slow vaccination. With less cases for a few months before the second wave, the Government presumed it had beaten the pandemic (*The Lancet*, 2021). The complacency was so much so that the then health minister Dr Harsh Vardhan had remarked that India is at the end game of the COVID-19 pandemic (*Economic Times*, 2021). India did not realize the extreme urgency to vaccinate its denizens and exported 66 million (of which approximately 36 million are commercial exports) vaccines to 95 countries between 20 January 2021 and 22 April 2021, post which there is no export (MEA, 2021). As per the official statement of India at the UN General Assembly on 26 March 2021 India had exported more vaccines than given to own people (Haidar, 2021; *Outlook*, 2021). This was done for all the good reasons including extending a helping hand to the neighbours and poorer countries and also for the larger purpose of global vaccine equity, but this also indicates vaccine hesitancy at domestic front on one hand and underestimation by the Government of vaccination urgency for our citizens on the other.

The immediate concern to contain second wave and minimize the impact of a possible third wave is to have the universal vaccination drive (SBI, 2021). The data on vaccination doses showed an urban-rural divide. By May 2021, the shares of population having at least one dose were in rural, semi-rural, semi-urban, urban areas were 13%, 15%, 19%, and 30%, respectively (Radhakrishnan, 2021). In terms of fully vaccinated, 2.6% share in rural population were vaccinated, whereas the corresponding figure in urban areas was 7.7% (Radhakrishnan, 2021). This urban-rural divide in vaccination can be attributed to the digital divide as well as vaccine hesitancy (Chakrabarty & Suri, 2021). Also, the lack of health facility and personnel in rural areas as highlighted earlier weakens the vaccination drive in villages.

3.5 Concluding Remarks

This chapter conducts case study on three different aspects of pandemic management and governance. These are (a) sudden lockdown and lockdown-induced displacement of people, (b) access to curative health care including availability of beds and oxygen, and (c) access to vaccination as a preventive health care. The chapter has made use of secondary data available in the public domain for analysis. We evaluated the above-mentioned cases from the point of view of Rawls' distributive justice, specifically, the difference principle. The difference principle allows deviation from fair equality of opportunity when the inequality leads to the greatest benefit of the least advantaged member of the society. An example of difference principle is the Government of India's policy towards vaccination drive prior to the second wave. It allowed only people above 60 years and those above 45 years having comorbidities. These people fall in the category of the most vulnerable so deserved to be the right side of an unequal attention. However, with regard to lockdown the Government has treated the vulnerable informal sector adversely as compared to the economically better-off formal sector. This would violate the difference principle.

We have also used the political economy framework to explain the differential actions of the Government for different sections of the society. For example, rich has been treated differently than poor so as formal sector as compared to informal sector. At the juncture of lockdown during the first wave of COVID-19 pandemic in India, the Government allowed the Indian nationals, who were the importers of the virus, to fly into the country. However, it did not make arrangements for scores of the migrant workers to move back to their native. Strange but true, a democracy can afford to ignore the large number of voters because of endogenous institutions (institutions are of the affluent, for the affluent, and by the affluent) and political clientelism (votes of the poor are bought in exchange of public goods controlled and marketed by the affluent). The authors believe understanding of these notions not only provide explanations for the Government actions but also gives clues towards making course corrections.

Notes

1 For further applications and critiques on difference principle, see, Gordon (1973), Nagel (1973), Pen (1974), Goldman (1976), Nielson (1980), Shaw (1992), van Parijs (2003), Brennan (2007), Read (2011), Wyatt (2011), Gainer (2012), Reiff (2012), Demir (2018), Koller (2018), Lister (2018), and Young (2018) among others.
2 The Gross Value Added by unorganized (informal) sector is more than 50% in recent years in India. According to Periodic Labour Survey 2017–18, 90.7% of the workers are informal.

References

Acemoglu, D., Johnson, S., & Robinson, J. A. (2005). Institutions as a fundamental cause of long-run growth. In P. Aghion & S. Durlauf (Eds.), *Handbook of Economic Growth* Vol (1st ed.) (pp. 385–472). Amsterdam: North Holland.

Bagcchi, S. (2021). The world's largest COVID-19 vaccination campaign. *The Lancet Infectious Disease*, 21(3), 323. doi: 10.1016/S1473-3099(21)00081-5

Banks, N., Lombard, M., & Mitlin, D. (2019). Urban informality as a site of critical analysis. *The Journal of Development Studies*, 56(2), 223–238. doi: 10.1080/00220388.2019.1577384

Barasa, E.W., Ouma, P.O., & Okiro, E.A. (2020). Assessing the hospital surge capacity of the Kenyan health system in the face of the COVID-19 pandemic. *PLoS One*, 15(7), e0236308. doi: 10.1371/journal.pone.0236308

BBC (British Broadcasting Corporation) (2021). India's Covid vaccine shortage: The desperate wait gets longer. May 01. Retrieved from https://www.bbc.com/news/world-asia-india-56912977

Brennan, J. (2007). Rawls paradox. *Constitutional Political Economy*, 18(4), 287–299. doi: 10.1007/s10602-007-9024-2

Brooks, T. (2016). *Rawls and Law*. New York: Routledge.

Business Standard (2020). Mandatory quarantine for passengers from UAE, Qatar, Oman and Kuwait: Health Ministry. March 17.

Butler, Eamonn (2012). *Public Choice: A Primer*. London: Institute of Economic Affairs.

CDC (Centers for Disease Control and Prevention) (2021). Vaccine testing and the approval process. Retrieved from https://www.cdc.gov/vaccines/basics/test-approve.html

Chakrabarty, M., & Suri, S. (2021). Winning the COVID-19 battle in rural India: A blueprint for action, special report, Observer Research Foundation.

Charles, M. (2020). Disease of the rich, killer of the poor. How Covid-19 brought Latin America to its knees. *The Telegraph*. Retrieved from https://www.telegraph.co.uk/global-health/science-and-disease/coronavirus-in-latin-america/

Cilne, E.M. (2013). *Confucius, Rawls and the Sense of Justice*. New York: Fordham University Press.

Demir, A. (2018). Marxist critiques of the difference principle. In M. Knoll, S. Snyder, & N. Şimsek (Eds.), *New Perspectives on Distributive Justice - Deep Disagreements, Pluralism, and the Problem of Consensus* (pp. 487–504). Berlin: De Gruyter.

Dey, S., & Sinha, S. (2020). Covid-19: Govt bans all international flights to India from March 22 to 29. *Times of India*. March 20. Retrieved from https://timesofindia.indiatimes.com/india/govt-bans-all-international-flights-to-india-from-march-22-to-29/articleshow/74720923.cms

Dombrowski, D.A. (2001). *Rawls and Religion – The Case for Political Liberalism*. New York: State University of New York Press.

Down To Earth (2021). State of India's environment in figures: Rural India worst hit by COVID-19 second wave, June 04.

Downs, A. (1957). *An Economic Theory of Democracy*. New York: Harper and Row.

Dutta, S.S. (2019). India's public expenditure on health less than lower income countries: Government data. *The New Indian Express*. November 01. Retrieved from https://www.newindianexpress.com/nation/2019/nov/01/indias-public-expenditure-on-health-less-than-lower-income-countries-government-data-2055553.html

Economic Times (2021). We are in the endgame of Covid-19 pandemic in India: Harsh Vardhan, Health News. March 08.

Freeman, S. (2003). *The Cambridge Companion to Rawls*. Cambridge: Cambridge University Press.

Gainer, M. (2012). Assessing happiness inequality in the welfare state: Self-reported happiness and the Rawlsian difference principle. *Social Indicators Research*, 114(2), 453–464. doi: 10.1007/s11205-012-0155-0

Goldman, A.H. (1976). Rawls's original position and the difference principle. *The Journal of Philosophy*, 73(21), 845–849. doi: 10.2307/2025405

Goodfellow, T. (2020). Political informality: Deals, trust networks, and the negotiation of value in the urban realm. *Journal of Development Studies*, 56(2), 278–294.

Gordon, S. (1973). John Rawls's difference principle, utilitarianism, and the optimum degree of inequality. *Journal of Philosophy*, 70(9), 275–280. doi: 10.2307/2025008

Günther, I. (2020). Why social distancing is a big challenge in many African countries, Provided ETH Zurich, April 20. Retrieved from https://phys.org/news/2020-04-social-distancing-big-african-countries.html

Haidar, S. (2021). What went wrong with India's vaccine diplomacy? *The Hindu.* April 23. Retrieved from https://www.thehindu.com/news/national/worldview-with-suhasini-haidar-what-went-wrong-with-indias-vaccine-diplomacy/article34394622.ece

Hebbar, N. (2020). PM Modi announces 21-day lockdown as COVID-19 toll touches 12. *The Hindu.* March 24. Retrieved from https://www.thehindu.com/news/national/pm-announces-21-day-lockdown-as-covid-19-toll-touches-10/article31156691.ece

Heredia, B. (1997). Clientelism in flux: Democratization and interest intermediation in contemporary Mexico. Working Paper. Mexico: CIDE (Centro de Investigaci'ony Docencia Econ'omicas).

India Today (2020). Coronavirus: India bans entry of passengers from Afghanistan, Philippines, Malaysia, March 17. Retrieved from https://www.indiatoday.in/india/story/coronavirus-travel-advisory-afganistan-phillipines-malaysia-1656323-2020-03-17

JHU (Johns Hopkins University) (2021). Covid-19 dashboard, last updated 6/24/2021, 6:51 PM. Center for Systems Science and Engineering, JHU. Retrieved from https://www.coronavirustraining.org/live-map

Jyoti, D., & Dey, S. (2020). The tragic lessons of Covid migrant crisis. *Hindustan Times.* March 24. Retrieved from https://www.hindustantimes.com/india-news/the-tragic-lessons-of-covid-migrant-crisis-101616529601176.html

Keefer, P., & Khemani, S. (2004). Why do the poor receive poor services? *Economic and Political Weekly*, 39(9), 935–943. Retrieved from https://www.epw.in/journal/2004/09/special-articles/why-do-poor-receive-poor-services.html

Kitschelt, H., & Wilkinson, S. I. (2007). Citizen–politician linkages: An introduction. In H. Kitschelt & S.I. Wilkinson (Eds.), *Patrons, Clients, and Policies: Patterns of Democratic Accountability and Political Competition* (pp. 1–49). Cambridge: Cambridge University Press.

Koller, P. (2018). A defense of the difference principle beyond Rawls. In M. Knoll, S. Snyder, & N. Şimsek (Eds.), *New Perspectives on Distributive Justice - Deep Disagreements, Pluralism, and the Problem of Consensus* (pp. 469–488). Berlin: De Gruyter.

Kuhen, B.M. (2021). High-income countries have secured the bulk of COVID-19 vaccines. *JAMA*, 325(7), 612. doi: 10.1001/jama.2021.0189

Kumar, A. Nayar, K.R., & Koya, S.F. (2020). COVID-19: Challenges and its consequences for rural health care in India. *Public Health in Practice*, November, 1: 100009. doi: 10.1016/j.puhip.2020.100009

Li, Y.-D., Chi, W.-Y., Su, J.-H., Ferrall, L., Hung, C.-F., & Wu, T.-C. (2020). Coronavirus vaccine development: From SARS and MERS to COVID-19. *Journal of Biomedical Science*, 27(1),104. doi: 10.1186/s12929-020-00695-2

Lister, A. (2018). The difference principle, capitalism, and property-owning democracy. *Moral Philosophy and Politics*, 5(1), 151–172. doi: 10.1515/mopp-2017-0012

Lloyd-Sherlock, P., Kandiyil, N.M., McKee, M., Perianayagam, A., Venkatapuram, S., Pathare, S., ... Ghosh, S. (2021). Pandemic lessons from India: inappropriate prioritisation for vaccination. *British Medical Journal*, 373, n1464. doi: 10.1136/bmj.n1464

Lopez de Leon, F.L., & Rizzi, R. (2014). A test for the rational ignorance hypothesis: Evidence from a natural experiment in Brazil. *American Economic Journal: Economic Policy*, 6(4), 380–398. doi: 10.1257/pol.6.4.380

Mathew, D.C. (2015). Rawlsian affirmative action: A reply to Robert Taylor. *Critical Philosophy of Race*, 3(2), 324–343. doi: 10.5325/critphilrace.3.2.0324

MEA (Ministry of External Affairs) (2021). Made-in-India COVID19 vaccine supplies so far, Vaccine Supply, MEA, Govt. of India. Retrieved from https://www.mea.gov.in/vaccine-supply.htm

MHFW (Ministry of Health and Family Welfare) (2020a). Rural Health Statistics 2019–20, Statistics division, MHFW, Govt. of India.

MHFW (2020b). Covid-19 Vaccines – operational guidelines (updated on 28 Dec 2020), MHFW, Govt. of India.

MHFW (2021). Near to Home COVID Vaccination Centres (NHCVC) for elderly and differently abled citizens, MHFW, Govt. of India. Retrieved from https://www.mohfw.gov.in/pdf/GuidanceNeartoHomeCovidVaccinationCentresforElderlyandDifferentlyAbledCitizens.pdf

Nagel, T. (1973). Rawls on justice. *The Philosophical Review*, 82(2), 220–234. doi: 10.2307/2183770

Nagel, T. (2003). John Rawls and affirmative action. *The Journal of Blacks in Higher Education*, 39. Spring, 82–84. doi: 10.2307/3134387

Nielson, K. (1980). Rawls and the left: Some left critiques of Rawls' principles of justice. *Analyse and Kritik*, 2(1), 74–97. doi: 10.1515/auk-1980-0105

Outlook (2021). We exported more Covid-19 vaccines than what we used: India at UN. *Outlook*. March 27. Retrieved from https://www.outlookindia.com/website/story/india-news-we-exported-more-covid-19-vaccines-than-what-we-used-india-at-un/378411

OWID (Our World in Data) (2021). Share of people who received at least one dose of COVID-19 vaccine. Retrieved from https://ourworldindata.org/explorers/coronavirus-data-explorer

Padilla, T.B. (2021). No one is safe unless everyone is safe. *Business World*. February 24.

Pen, J. (1974). A theory of justice by John Rawls. *Challenge*, 17(1), 59–63. doi: 10.1080/05775132.1974.11470037

PIB (Press Information Bureau) (2020). Ministry of railways details on Sharamik specials. May 27. Retrieved from https://pib.gov.in/PressReleasePage.aspx?PRID=1627231

Radhakrishnan, V. (2021). Vaccination in rural India trails urban areas even as cases surge. *The Hindu*. May 18. Retrieved from https://www.thehindu.com/news/national/vaccination-in-rural-india-trails-urban-areas-even-as-cases-surge/article34589734.ece

Rawls, J. (1993). *Political Liberalism*, expanded edition, Colombia Classics in Philosophy. New York: Colombia University Press.

Ray, D. (1998). *Development Economics*. Princeton, NJ: Princeton University Press.

Read, R. (2011). Why the ecological crisis spells the end of liberalism: Rawls' "Difference Principle" is ecologically unsustainable, exploitative of persons, or empty. *Capitalism Nature Socialism*, 22(3), 80–94. doi: 10.1080/10455752.2011.593893

Reiff, M.R. (2012). The difference principle, rising inequality, and supply-side economics: How Rawls got hijacked by the right. *Revue de Philosophie Economique*, 13(2), 119–173. doi: 10.3917/rpec.132.0119

Roy, A. (2005). Urban informality: Toward an epistemology of planning. *Journal of the American Planning Association*, 71, 147–158. doi: 10.1080/01944360508976689

Roy, A. (2009). Why India cannot plan its cities: Informality, insurgence and the idiom of urbanization. *Planning Theory*, 8, 76–87. doi: 10.1177/1473095208099299

Ryan, C. (2006). Rawls on negotiating justice. In A.K. Schneider and C. Honeyman (Eds.), *The Negotiator's Field Book* (pp. 75–80). Washington DC: American Bar Association.

Sanyaolu, A., Okorie, C., Marinkovic, A., Patidar, R. Younis, K., Desai, … Altaf, M. (2020). Comorbidity and its impact on patients with COVID-19. *SN Comprehensive Clinical Medicine*, 2, 1069–1076. doi: 10.1007/s42399-020-00363-4

SBI (State Bank of India) (2021). Economic disruptions gain momentum as cases surge: Opportunity for administrative reforms? *Ecowrap*, FY 22, 8. 07 May.

Schindler, S. (2014). Producing and contesting the formal/informal divide: Regulating street hawking in Delhi, India. *Urban Studies*, 51(12), 2596–2612. doi: 10.1177/0042098013510566

Sen, A. (2002). Health: Perception versus observation. *British Medical Journal*, 324(7342), 860–861. doi: 10.1136/bmj.324.7342.860

Sen, A. (2006). What do we want from a theory of justice? *The Journal of Philosophy*, 103(5), 215–238. doi: 10.2307/20619936

SEP (The Stanford Encyclopedia of Philosophy) (2017). Difference principle, distributive justice. Retrieved from https://plato.stanford.edu/entries/justice-distributive/#Difference

Shaw, P. (1992). Rawls, the lexical difference principle and equality. *The Philosophical Quarterly*, 42(166), 71–77. doi: 10.2307/2220449

Shrotri, M., Swinnen, T., Kampmann, B., & Parker, E.P.K. (2021). An interactive website tracking COVID-19 vaccine development. *Lancet Glob Health*, 9(5), e590–e592. doi: 10.1016/S2214-109X(21)00043-7

Singh, D. (2020). Lockdown: Truck drivers make big bucks transporting stranded migrants. *India Today*. May 12. Retrieved from https://www.indiatoday.in/india/story/lockdown-truck-drivers-make-big-bucks-transporting-stranded-migrants-1677298-2020-05-12

So, A.D., & Woo, J. (2020). Reserving coronavirus disease 2019 vaccines for global access: Cross sectional analysis. *British Medical Journal*, 371, m4750. doi: 10.1136/bmj.m4750

Thakur, A. (2021). Proof that Covid is now a rural pandemic in India. *Times of India*. May 12. Retrieved from https://timesofindia.indiatimes.com/india/proof-that-covid-is-now-a-rural-pandemic-in-india/articleshow/82569846.cms

The Hindu (2021). Vande Bharat becomes one of top civilian evacuations. April 21. Retrieved from https://www.thehindu.com/news/national/vande-bharat-becomes-one-of-top-civilian-evacuations/article34361996.ece

The Wire (2020). India bans entry of foreigners for a month, WHO declares coronavirus a 'Pandemic'. March 12. Retrieved from https://thewire.in/health/india-visa-suspended-entry-of-foreigners-ocis-covid-who-corona-global-pandemic

Tranberg Hansen, K., & Vaa, M. (Eds.). (2004). *Reconsidering Informality: Perspectives from Urban Africa*. Oslo: Nordic Africa Institute.

Tripathi, T., & Nathan, H.S.K. (2016). Dying in silence: A study on mortality-morbidity gap in India. Paper presented at the Human Development and Capability Association 2016 Annual Conference on 'Capability and Diversity in a Global Society' held at Hitotsubashi University, Tokyo, Japan during September 1–3. Retrieved from https://hd-ca.org/es/publications/dying-in-silence-a-study-on-mortality-morbidity-gap-in-india

Tuncer, F.F. (2020). The spread of fear in the globalizing world: The case of COVID-19. *Journal of Public Affairs*, 20(4), e2162. doi: 10.1002/pa.2162

Uphoff, E.P., Pickett, K.E., Cabieses, B., Small, N., & Wright, J. (2013). A systematic review of the relationships between social capital and socioeconomic inequalities in health: A contribution to understanding the psychosocial pathway of health inequalities. *International Journal for Equity in Health*, 12, 54. doi: 10.1186/1475-9276-12-54

van Assche, K., Beunen, R., & Duineveld, M. (2014). Formal/informal dialectics and the self-transformation of spatial planning systems: An exploration. *Administration & Society*, 46(6), 654–683. doi: 10.1177/0095399712469194 van Parijs, P. (2003). Difference principles. In S. Freeman (Ed.), *The Cambridge Companion to John Rawls* (pp. 200–240). Cambridge: Cambridge University Press.

Vilasanjuan, R. (2021). A virus for the rich and for the poor? Retrieved from https://www.isglobal.org/en/healthisglobal/-/custom-blog-portlet/virus-rico-virus-pobre/90649/0

Wang, B., Li, R., Lu, Z., & Huang, Y. (2020). Does comorbidity increase the risk of patients with COVID-19: Evidence from meta-analysis. *Aging*, 12(7), 6049–6057. doi: 10.18632/aging.103000

WHO (World Health Organization) (2021). Listings of WHO's response to COVID-19. Retrieved from https://www.who.int/news/item/29-06-2020-covidtimeline

WHO (2020). Virtual press conference on COVID-19 – 11 March 2020. Retrieved from https://www.who.int/docs/default-source/coronaviruse/transcripts/who-audio-emergencies-coronavirus-press-conference-full-and-final-11mar2020.pdf?sfvrsn=cb432bb3_2

WION (World Is One News) (2020). Air India raises Rs 6 crore bill for evacuating 647 from coronavirus epicentre Wuhan, March 04. Retrieved from https://www.wionews.com/india-news/air-india-raises-rs-6-crore-bill-for-evacuating-647-from-coronavirus-epicentre-wuhan-284283

Wolfe, C.J. (2020). John Rawls: Reticent socialist by William A Edmundson. Book Review. *The National Catholic Bioethics Quarterly*, 20(4), 844–845. doi: 10.5840/ncbq202020474

World Bank (2021a). Current health expenditure (% of GDP) – India, World Health Organization Global Health Expenditure database.

World Bank (2021b). Domestic general government health expenditure (% of GDP) - India, China, World Health Organization Global Health Expenditure database. Retrieved from https://data.worldbank.org/

Worldometer (2021). Countries where COVID-19 has spread. Retrieved from https://www.worldometers.info/coronavirus/countries-where-coronavirus-has-spread/

Wyatt, C. (2011). *The Difference Principle Beyond Rawls*. London: Bloomsbury Publishing.

Yadav, S (2020). Coronavirus lockdown, despair packs migrant workers from U.P. into a concrete mixer truck. *The Hindu*. May 2. Retrieved from https://www.thehindu.com/news/national/other-states/coronavirus-lockdown-despair-packs-migrant-workers-from-up-into-a-concrete-mixer-truck/article31491203.ece

Young, J. (2018). Justice, equity, and distribution: Adam Smith's answer to John Rawls's difference principle. In M. Knoll, S. Snyder, & N. Şimsek (Eds.), *New Perspectives on Distributive Justice - Deep Disagreements, Pluralism, and the Problem of Consensus* (pp. 505–522). Berlin: De Gruyter.

Part III

Impact of COVID-19 on Livelihood and Income of People

4 Some Aspects of Impact of Lockdown in India and the Way Forward

Surajit Das

4.1 Introduction

This chapter attempts to assess the impact of COVID-19-induced lockdown on the income and employment opportunities of common people in India. It seeks to find out a solution of severe demand depression in terms of larger Government expenditure on health and that for the employment generation for solving the humanitarian crisis and also for ensuring faster recovery of the aggregate level of activity in the economy. It also tries to point out the possible route to finance the required fiscal stimulus on the face of huge revenue shortfall and argues for the need of a Keynesian policy direction at the aggregate level.

In order to understand the impact of COVID-19-induced lockdown on the income, expenditure, expected income and that on saving and indebtedness of common people in India, we conducted a survey in 15 States among 3,142 households. The implementation of the Pradhan Mantri Garib Kalyan Yojana (PMGKY) has also been assessed based on the answers of the respondents (Section 4.2). Possible impact of lockdown on the aggregate employment during the year 2020–21 has also been attempted to estimate (Section 4.3) in absence of any other reliable data. Another survey with 500 households has been conducted among the urban upper middle-class people in and around Delhi to assess the impact of lockdown and income loss of this section of population on the demand for commodities and services from 7 sectors including automobile, furniture, electronic items, real estate, domestic tourism, surgery, and organisers/supplier in family get-togethers (Section 4.4). The fiscal situation of 2020–21 has also been analysed in this paper (Section 4.5). The situation of credit-deposit ratio of Indian banks along with that of the foreign exchange reserve of the Reserve Bank of India (RBI) and the movements of Bombay Stock Exchange Sensex have also been discussed (Section 4.6). The situation of combined government health expenditure in India has also been examined (Section 4.7) along with the need for an universal employment guarantee programme in the country. The current paper ends with some policy conclusions for faster recovery of the economy.

DOI: 10.4324/9781003226970-7

4.2 The Ground Level Situation: Survey Report

To understand the impact of COVID-19-induced lockdown on the people of India at the ground level, we conducted primary survey in 15 states in the year 2020–21. It was not possible to visit the states during the lockdown because of the health risk and other logistic difficulties. Telephonic surveys were conducted in 13 states including Bihar, Odisha (Cuttack city), Delhi, Gujarat, Haryana, Kerala, Union territory of Ladakh, West Bengal (North Bengal), Sikkim, Telangana, Tripura, Uttarakhand, and Uttar Pradesh. We could visit Goa and Assam in the months of November 2020 and January 2021 after opening up. The surveys took place in different time periods for different states starting from June 2020 to January 2021. The total sample size was 3,142 households comprising a total of 14,472 people. The sample size varied widely from state to state and that was also true for the sample characteristics. Degree of lockdown varied widely state to state and the timings of the surveys and the nature of sample households were also different; it is not possible to do a state-wise comparison based on our data. However, the combined picture of all 15 states would give us some insights about the ground level situation following the COVID-19-induced lockdown in the country during 2020–21. It is important to mention here the caveat that the sampling technique was not robust and it was based on availability and convenience. This is a common limitation in these kinds of surveys under pandemic but it may not necessarily be a representative sample. However, it would definitely give us some picture of the ground level situation, which may be a partial picture and may not be a general picture of an economy of 135 crore population but it definitely throws some light on the ground level situation, in absence of any other more reliable data on this at the aggregate level.

There were 2,260 Hindu families (72%), 565 Muslim families (18%), 179 Christian families (5.7%), 118 Buddhist families (3.75%), and 20 families from other religious backgrounds in our sample of total 3,142 households. As far as the broad caste categories are concerned, there were 1,160 families from unreserved castes (37%), 975 families (31%) from other backward castes (OBC), 650 families (20.8%) from scheduled castes, and 287 scheduled tribe families (9%) in our sample from 15 states in India. The caste category of the rest 70 families was unknown. Almost 80% (2,500) respondents were male and 20% (636) respondents were female in our sample. We have got six respondents from the third gender as well. The respondents were from diverse occupational backgrounds mostly involved in the unorganised/informal sectors.

We have got information on both their pre and post-lockdown income during the respective survey periods from 2,466 respondents. Out of them almost 50% (1,209 respondents) have reported absolutely zero income during the lockdown. The average monthly income of these 2,466 respondents was Rs. 20,536 before the lockdown that came down to only Rs. 7,962 during the lockdown period. Therefore, the average income of these respondents came down by 61% due to the lockdown. Information about the family income was received for 2003 families. Their average family income was Rs. 28,075 before the lockdown. It came down to Rs. 12,859 during the lockdown registering a fall of almost 54.2%. 936

families out of 2003 families (46.7%) for which the information about family income was available, reported zero income during the lockdown. As far as the family expenditures are concerned, information about both pre and post lockdown expenditure of the sample households is available for 2,225 families. The average monthly family expenditure of these families was Rs. 14,309 which, came down to Rs. 12,708 registering a fall of around 11%. The family size varies widely – the per capita average monthly expenditure came down from Rs. 3,680 to Rs. 3,310 (i.e. by 11%) for the 2000 sample families due to the lockdown. Many have reported that there has been an increase in expenditure during lockdown because of the rise in prices of the essential commodities. The expenditure could not be brought down proportionately as compared to the fall in income for the sample households. So, people had to manage either with their past savings or they had to borrow from their relatives, friends, local money lenders and from other sources. We have got information for 2,294 households about their formal or informal loans. Till the time of survey, 1,033 households (almost 50%) have reported increase in their indebtedness due to the lockdown. Rest of them could somehow manage with their past savings. For very few people (particularly the Government employees) there was no income drop due to the lockdown.

Information about the expected income in next six months from the time of survey was available for 2,921 respondents. As many as 732 respondents (25%) have said that they have no idea about this and the future stream of income is extremely uncertain. Most of the other respondents were expecting significantly lower income in the coming six months as compared to their pre-lockdown incomes. As high as 46% of the respondents in our sample (out of 2,421 respondents for which this information was available) suspected that their expected income would be 40% of their pre-lockdown income, on an average. 3,124 respondents answered the question whether an urban employment guarantee scheme is required in India or not. More than two-third (2,127 respondents 68%) respondents have said there is definitely a need for such a programme in the current situation and the rest 32% have said that either they do not know or they are do not think that there is a need for having such a programme in place.

Promise for free ration, cash transfer in Jan-Dhan accounts and free cylinders of cooking gas was made initially in PM Garib Kalyan Yojana (https://www.india.gov.in/spotlight/pradhan-mantri-garib-kalyan-package-pmgkp) and later it was made part of the Atmanirbhar Bharat Abhiyan package. But the implementation of these schemes varied widely state to state. Collating the available information from all 15 states, it was found that as high as 27% of the sample families (who needed it) did not get any free ration whatsoever. Twenty-two households in our sample did not want free ration and the rest of the families (72%) got at least some ration (may be much lower than the original entitlement) free of cost during the lockdown months. Otherwise, there would have been famine in the country on the face of drastic income fall because of the lockdown, particularly that of the poor and vulnerable section population in the country (which is quite large in India). However, 74% of the sample families either did not have Jan-Dhan account or they have not received any money in that account. Only

789 respondent families (25%) have received some money in Jan-Dhan account out of total 3,142 sample families across 15 states in the country. There was no information available regarding this for 30 families in our sample. Less than 23% families (710 out of 3,142) have reported to receive free gas cylinders during the lockdown and 77% have not. Information regarding this was not available for 19 families. This was the state of affairs at the ground level as far as our sample survey is concerned.

4.3 The Unemployment Situation in 2020–21

In absence of data for unemployment rate of 2020–21, it has been attempted to have an assessment of the fall of employment opportunities at the aggregate level, following lockdown, with the help of provisional estimate of sectoral GDP for 2020–21 and the past data of employment. As far as the data on employment-unemployment is concerned, that is available for the year 2018–19 from the periodic labour force survey (PLFS). According to this data, the labour force participation rate, the worker-population ratio and the unemployment rates were 37.49%, 35.30%, and 5.83%, respectively. If we assume the population for the year 2018–19 to be 133 crore (based on projection using the 2011 census data), then the total size of the labour force was around 49.95 crores in India. The size of the workforce was around 47.03 crores and the aggregate unemployment was around 2.91 crores in 2018–19. Given these rates, in 2020–21, the population would have been 136 crores and the size of the labour and workforce would have been approximately 51 crores and 48 crores producing around 3 crore unemployment at the aggregate level in India. If we look at the sectoral distribution of the aggregate workforce in 2018–19 (Periodic Labour Force Survey), we see that 42.5% of employment was in the agriculture, forestry, and fishing sector; 0.4% in mining and quarrying sector; 12.1% in manufacturing sector; 0.6% in the sector called electricity, gas, water supply, and other utility services; 12.1% in the construction sector; 18.5% in the trade, hotel, transport, communication, and services related to broadcasting; 2.3% in the financial, real estate, professional services; and 11.6% in the public administration, defence, and other services.

The provisional estimate of GDP for the year 2020–21 tells us that there has been negative 7.3% growth in 2020–21 over 2019–20 in real terms (NSO Press release dated 31st May, 2021) due to the COVID-19-induced lockdown. Therefore, the unemployment is also expected to rise in 2020–21 due to the lockdown. If we assume that the unemployment rate would have been the same as 2018–19 in the year 2020–21 in absence of the lockdown and the sectoral shares of the workforce would have remained the same, then the sectoral employment numbers would have been as the following. It is assumed that the unemployment rate and the sectoral shares of employment remained the same in 2019–20 as they were in 2018–19. The sectoral growth rates in 2020–21 over 2019–20 for the above-mentioned eight sectors have been taken from the provisional estimate of gross value added (GVA) released by the National Statistical Office (NSO) press release dated 31st May 2021 (Table 4.1).

Table 4.1 Sector-wise employment without lockdown and GVA growth in 2020–21

Sl. No.	Sector	Estimated employment (in crores)			% GVA growth in 2020–21
		2018–19	2019–20	2020–21	
1.	Agriculture, forestry, and fishing	19.98	20.21	20.43	3.6
2.	Mining and quarrying	0.20	0.20	0.20	−8.5
3.	Manufacturing	5.67	5.74	5.80	−7.2
4.	Electricity, gas, water supply, and other utility services	0.26	0.27	0.27	1.9
5.	Construction	5.69	5.75	5.82	−8.6
6.	Trade, hotel, transport, communication, and services related to broadcasting	8.72	8.82	8.92	−18.2
7.	Financial, real estate, and professional services	1.06	1.08	1.09	−1.5
8.	Public administration, defence, and other services	5.44	5.50	5.56	−4.6
	Total	**47.03**	**47.56**	**48.08**	**−6.2**

Source: PLFS 2018–19 and NSO Press release dated 31st May, 2021.

It is evident from the above table that the trade, hotel, transport, communication, and services related to broadcasting has been affected the most registering a negative growth rate of –18.2% followed by the construction sector (–8.6%), the mining quarrying (–8.5%) and the manufacturing sector (–7.2%) in 2020–21 (PE). Now, if we assume that the average sectoral labour productivities remained the same during 2020–21 as they were in 2019–20, then the sectoral employment numbers would change in the same rates in which the sectoral GVAs have changed during 2020–21. So, we can have an idea of 2020–21 aggregate sectoral employment by multiplying these sectoral growth rates with the sectoral employment numbers of 2019–20. Generally, the average sectoral labour productivity goes up every year and the sectoral employment does not grow proportionately with the annual sectoral growth rates of the GVAs. It is obvious that we assume the labour productivity to increase in 2020–21, the unemployment would be even higher. However, even if we assume the sector-wise labour productivities to remain unchanged in the lockdown year, the sectoral employment would change according to the growth rates of the sectoral GVAs.

Many have argued that the data on informal sector has not been incorporated in the provisional estimates of GDP and the unorganised informal sector has been more severely affected due to lockdown, the actual sectoral GVA numbers for the year 2020–21 are likely to be even lower (Das, 2020a). However, even if we assume that the provisional estimates are reliable, the employment growth rate is likely to be negative 5.85% as compared to the aggregate employment of

2019–20. It is important to mention here that the agricultural sector is a residual sector of the economy characterised by substantial disguised unemployment and under employment (Sen, 1973). 3.6% annual growth in agriculture does not mean that the agricultural employment would grow by 3.6% within a year. If we assume the agricultural employment to remain the same in 2020–21 as it was in 2019–20 at the aggregate level, the total employment in 2020–21 is likely to be 44.78 crores in the country in the lockdown year of 2020–21. This is 6.87% less than the expected employment in the same year if the COVID-19-induced lockdown would not have happened. Even if we consider 3.6% growth in agricultural employment in 2020–21 as compared to that in 2019–20, this reduction in aggregate employment, including all the 8 sectors mentioned above, would be 5.36% of the aggregate employment of 2019–20. Therefore, the unemployment has been at least doubled in the lockdown year of 2020–21 in India (Table 4.2).

Table 4.2 suggests that the unemployment rate is likely to be 12.3% in 2020–21 as compared to 5.83% according to the PLFS 2018–19 registering a 211% rise in unemployment rate. Even if we consider 3.6% annual growth in agricultural employment in 2020–21 (which is unlikely to happen), the unemployment rate would be 10.9% with a 187% jump within a year. Total unemployment in the year 2020–21 is likely to be 6.3 crore as compared to less than 3 crores in the previous year. Even if we assume some employment growth in agricultural sector in 2020–21 but less than 3.6%, the aggregate unemployment is likely to be at least double in 2020–21 as compared to the previous year or as compared to the hypothetical situation if the lockdown would not have happened in 2020–21. It is important to remember here that the composition of the Indian workforce is such that more than half of it is self-employed (52%), one-fourth is casual and contractual labourers (25%) and only less than one-fourth (23%) is salaried employees including the private and the public sector employees in India (Das 2020b). Now the income of majority of self-employed people and casual workers have drastically come down due to the lockdown even if they have got some job or could reopen their small businesses. In the data, they may look employed but actually many of them were partially employed or employed with zero income

Table 4.2 Estimated size of the labour force, workforce, and unemployment in India

Year	Labour force	Employment	Unemployment	Unemployment rate
2018–19	49.94	47.03	2.91	5.83
2019–20	50.51	47.56	2.95	5.83
2020–21 without lockdown	51.06	48.08	2.98	5.83
2020–21 with agriculture	51.06	45.50	5.55	10.87
2020–21 (Provisional estimates)	**51.06**	**44.78**	**6.28**	**12.30**

Source: Author's Calculations.

during the lockdown (Anand & Thampi 2021). It is needless to say that if the actual GVA or GDP numbers happen to be lower than these provisional estimates, the estimated unemployment would rise further.

4.4 Squeeze in Demand from the Upper-Middle Class

It is quite evident from section 2 that the income and purchasing power of common people in India fell drastically due to the COVID-19-induced lockdown in India in 2020–21. It was not only true for the people with average monthly income of rupees 20 thousand or so engaged primarily in the unorganised informal sector of the economy, however, it was also true for the urban upper middle class families with monthly income of rupees two and half lakhs. Another google form based survey (in English) was conducted in and around national capital region (NCR) of Delhi in July 2020 among 501 households. A 25% reduction of average monthly family income was recorded from pre-lockdown to post lockdown period, whereas a reduction of 19%–20% was observed in the average monthly family expenditure of these households. Almost 10% households of this income class in our sample became indebted during the lockdown as the fall in income exceeded fall in expenditure. Others could manage either by reducing their saving or by consuming part of the past savings. The questionnaire also inquired the households about their expected monthly family income over the next six months. About 45% of the respondents reported that they expected a fall in the income compared to their pre-lockdown income. Among those, roughly 16% expected a fall in income by more than 50%.

Out of the total 501 households in the sample, 166 had a plan for purchasing automobiles, 154 had a plan of buying some furniture, 209 had plans for procuring some electronic items, 141 families were thinking of booking some property or flat or residential house, 408 households had plans for some domestic travel,

Table 4.3 Postponement of consumption decision due to the lockdown

	Industry	Yes (out of 501)	Happened/ purchased/ visited	Postponed by 3 months	Postponed by 6 months	Postponed by 1 year	Postponed by more than 1 year
1	Automobile	166	23 (14%)	41 (25%)	32 (19%)	16 (10%)	54 (33%)
2	Furniture(s)	154	25 (16%)	40 (26%)	37 (24%)	12 (8%)	40 (26%)
3	Electronic Item(s)	209	63 (30%)	55 (26%)	32 (15%)	15 (7%)	44 (21%)
4	Property/Flat/ House	141	14 (10%)	32 (23%)	30 (21%)	11 (8%)	54 (38%)
5	Travel within India	408	15 (4%)	32 (8%)	97 (24%)	112 (27%)	152 (37%)
6	Surgery	149	36 (24%)	18 (12%)	9 (6%)	19 (13%)	67 (45%)
7	Get-together	283	61 (22%)	16 (6%)	66 (23%)	63 (22%)	77 (27%)

Source: Goyal and Das (2021).
Note: The percentages in parentheses denote the numbers as proportions of initial demand.

149 families had plan to undergo some surgery and 283 households had plans for some get together (marriage, etc.) during the first three months of lockdown (i.e. April, May and June 2020) in 2020–21. Only 14% of those households which had a plan to purchase automobiles, could buy them according to the plan. The percentages are 16%, 30%, 10%, 4%, 24%, and 22% for furniture, electronic items, property, domestic travel, surgery, and get-togethers, respectively. The others had to postpone the plans by 3 months or by 6 months or by 1 year or even more (see Table 4.3 for details).

The maximum number of households had a plan for domestic travel and tourism followed by number of families with a plan for a get-together, followed by families with plans for purchase of electronic/electrical consumer durables, automobiles, furniture, surgery and that for buying some property, house, or flat in our sample. As far as the postponement is concerned, it was also highest in travel and tourism within India followed by booking of properties, automobiles, furniture, family gatherings, surgery, and electronic items. The demand for automobile sector is likely to come down by 43%, that for the furniture sector by 34% and that of the electronic/electrical consumer durables by 28% in 2020–21. According to our survey results, the demand for the property/flat/house is likely to reduce by 46%, that for the domestic travel by 64%, that for surgery by 58% and that for the family functions at least by 49% in 2020–21 due to the lockdown in India. This is bound to cause an economic recession coupled with huge rise in unemployment in the country. The questionnaire also inquired the households about their expected monthly family income over the next six months. About 45% of the respondents reported that they expected a definite fall in the income compared to their pre-lockdown income. Among those, around 16% of the respondents expected a fall in the family income by more than 50% due to the COVID-19-induced lockdown.

4.5 The Fiscal Situation: Union Budget 2021–22

The fiscal deficit (revised estimate) is likely to be 9.5% in 2020–21 for the Union Government alone, as compared to that of 3.4% in 2018–19 and 4.6% in 2019–20 (Union Budget 2021–22). The fiscal deficit of all the state Governments taken together is also likely to rise in 2020–21 primarily because of the revenue shortfall caused by the COVID-19-induced lockdown. Therefore, the aggregate fiscal deficit to GDP ratio is likely to be around 13% of GDP in 2020–21. The data on state Governments' fiscal deficit is yet to come for all the states. However, it is important to note that the rise in fiscal deficit has happened mainly because of the negative growth rate and economic depression in 2020–21. Because of the depression, income of people and profit of majority of the business class have suffered badly. As a result of that the income and profit tax revenues of the union Government was not buoyant. Because of lack of purchasing power, uncertainty and the lockdowns, the aggregate consumption of various goods and services was low. The GST and other indirect tax collections were also lower, which has affected both central and the state exchequers. As a result of all these, the revenue shortfall of the combined Government has been huge in 2020–21. Also, when we calculate the fiscal deficit to GDP ratio, if the denominator grows at a negative rate, the ratio is bound to rise. The rise in the Government expenditure as proportion of the expected GDP of 2020–21 before the lockdown was not substantial in 2020–21. Interestingly, till December 2020, in first three quarters of 2020–21 financial year, the Union Government's total expenditure was exactly 75% (Rs. 2,280,147 crore) of what was budgeted for the entire year (Controller General of Accounts https://cga.nic.in/). Therefore, there was absolutely no increase in expenditure including the Atmanirbhar Bharat Abhiyan package. There have been increases in some expenditures at the cost of cuts in some other expenditures keeping the aggregate expenditure intact. Obviously, there would be some rise in the expenditure-GDP ratio because of the fall in GDP and not because of the rise in the expenditure. The fiscal deficit increased primarily due to the revenue shortfall in a lockdown year. Total receipt of the union Government including revenue receipts and disinvestment has been only 50% of what was budgeted for the entire year, in the first three quarters of 2020–21 (Source: Controller General of Accounts, Government of India).

Following the economic depression in 2020–21, it was expected that the Government would plan for an expansionary fiscal policy. It may appear that the large fiscal deficit to GDP ratio would play a role of fiscal stimulus under depression. However, lower tax-GDP ratio is relatively less effective than the higher expenditure-GDP ratio in stimulating the economy. Moreover, given any degree of progressivity in the direct and indirect tax structure, stimulus in terms of tax cuts would aggravate inequality in the country. Given the fact that the poorer section of population suffered relatively more because of this exogenous shock (Basole *et al.* 2021), the inequality is likely to go up anyway. If the Government spends more money in pro-poor manner, the Government expenditure and investment multiplier in enhancing the level of activity and employment would be higher as the propensity to consume is relatively higher for the poor.

For the current year (i.e. 2021–22), the union Government has set a disinvestment target of Rs. 1.75 lakh crore (almost equal to 1% of GDP and 4% of combined Government expenditure in India) on the face of huge revenue loss (Union Budget 2021–22). The aggregate expenditure of the Union Government is set to reduce by more than 2% of the Gross Domestic Product (GDP) of the country (Das 2021a). The Government exchequer is in extremely tight situation so much so that the Government could not pay the dearness allowances (and the arrears) for its own employees since January 2020. The ministry of finance, on record, has said that the central Government is not in a position to give the due compensations to the states on account of revenue loss in goods and services tax collection and so on and so forth (Press Trust of India: The Hindu 20th July 2021). However, naturally there are huge protests against the selling of the important public sector units for ever. Moreover, this negative capital expenditure should not be treated as revenue receipts (which is formally called non-debt capital receipts) in calculation of the fiscal deficit. As far as the aggregate demand is concerned, mere handover of the PSUs from the Government to the private hands would not help in increasing aggregate (public plus private) investment and hence it would not make an iota of difference in the aggregate demand. There is one crucial ethical question involved – whether the current Governments can sell the public sector assets accumulated over time using the tax payers' money of the previous generations.

The huge exogenous negative shock of lockdown has caused the unemployment to rise in an unprecedented manner and incomes of employed people, excepting a small proportion of the aggregate workforce in the country, have also come down substantially. This has led to a situation of severe demand depression at the aggregate level. The Keynesian demand management policy suggests that the Government should boost the aggregate demand in the economy through expansionary fiscal policy under a demand constrained situation in order to ensure larger employment and output. Larger export can surely boost demand; however, our export destinations are also in bad shape due to the pandemic and the demand for our exportable crucially depend on the demand from those countries. The domestic private investment rate would not increase until there is profitable opportunity in the market, which, in turn, depends on the income and purchasing power and consumption demand of the common people in the country. Therefore, only the expansionary fiscal policy can bring the economy out of this vicious trap and ensure faster recovery. If employment and growth recover at a faster rate, the fiscal deficit and public debt as proportion of GDP would automatically come down because of the rise in the denominator of the ratio. Again, with faster recovery, the revenue receipts would also be buoyant in the Government exchequer, which would also help in reducing the fiscal deficit to GDP ratio in the near future. Alternatively, if the Government follows the path of fiscal conservatism on the face of a revenue loss, the future fiscal deficit to GDP ratio may actually rise despite expenditure cuts because of the lower growth and lower future revenue receipts and the economy would take longer time to recover. Lot of people would suffer from unemployment and reduced income for a longer period of time. In the union budget for the year 2021–22, it has been proposed that the total expenditure of the central Government as proportion of GDP would be reduced by more than 2 percentage points from 17.7% in 2020–21 (Revised Estimate) to 15.6% of GDP in 2021–22 (Budget Estimate: Union Budget 2021–22). Clearly, the policy direction is to reduce fiscal deficit to GDP ratio by expenditure cuts and disinvestments. However, this is nothing but fiscal conservatism under a severe demand depression.

4.6 The Credit Deposit Ratio, Forex Reserve, and BSE Sensex

The Atmanirbhar Bharat Abhiyan package was full of measures taken to infuse liquidity into the system by reducing the reserve ratios and measures to encourage credit in easier terms without collateral and with Government guarantees and so on and so forth. In fact, the actual expenditure enhancement was around 1% of GDP out of this 10% of GDP worth of package to boost the economy (Das

2020c). Total potential additional liquidity subject to demand was 4.8% of GDP and credit with Government guarantee, particularly for the farmers and small and medium enterprises, was more than 3% of GDP. Together they constitute 7.8% of GDP or more than three-fourth of the Atmanirbhar Bharat Abhiyan, which was announced in May 2020. Interestingly, the credit deposit ratio of all the commercial banks taken together started falling immediately after the announcement of lockdown was made in end of March in India. It continues to fall up to end of September from more than 76% to less than 72%. Then it remained below 73% till the end of financial year 2020–21 and it has started falling again since then (see Figure 4.1 below). Even after credit encouragements by the Government, the credit-GDP ratio could not recover because of lack of demand in the market. Currently, the repo rate is just 4%, the cash reserve ratio is also 4% and the statutory liquidity ratio is 18%. Despite that the banks are found to invest in Government and other approved securities around 30% of their deposits. The investment in Government securities has increased from less than 36% of total credit offtake in end-March 2020 to more than 43% in end-September despite much less rate of return on Government because of lack of demand for credit in the market.

The BSE Sensex has continuously increased from March 2020 to July 2021 – the share market depicts absolutely no sign of any crisis throughout this period. Both foreign and domestic investments have taken place in Indian share markets. The Bombay Stock Exchange has registered a phenomenal increase in Sensex from 30 thousand to over 50 thousand during this period. The foreign exchange reserves with the Reserve Bank of India (RBI) have increased from Rs. 38 lakh crores to more than Rs. 46 lakh crores during the same period (Figure 4.2). This idle asset is worth more than 23% of our GDP. The rate of return on this asset is very nominal. The increase in this asset is also more than 4% of GDP during

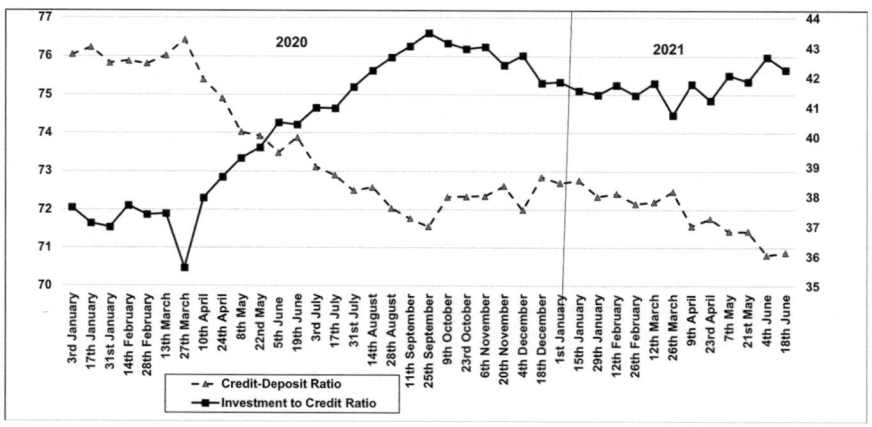

Figure 4.1 Credit-deposit ratio and investment to deposit ratio in India (In %)
Source: Weekly Statistical Supplements, Reserve Bank of India, GoI.
Note: The investment to credit ratios are plotted along the secondary axis.

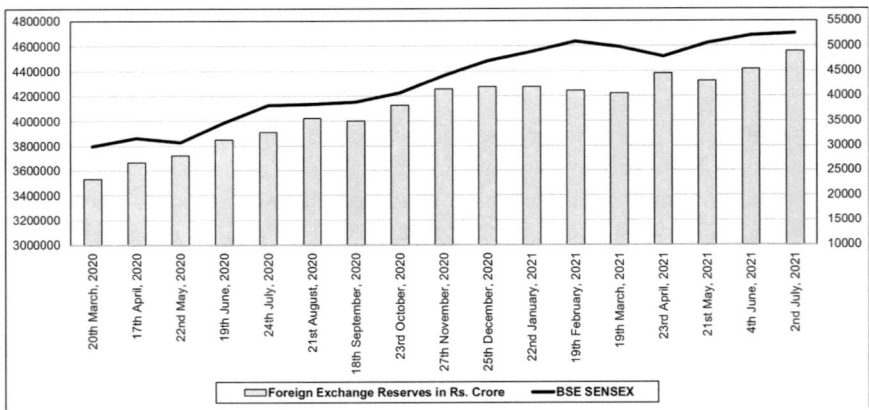

Figure 4.2 India's foreign exchange reserve (in rupees crore) in India and BSE Sensex.
Source: Weekly Statistical Supplements, Reserve Bank of India, and Bombay Stock Exchange.
Note: The BSE Sensex is plotted along the secondary axis. The forex reserve is measured in terms of Rupees crore.

the period mentioned above. Therefore, the RBI is absolutely in a comfortable position to lend some money to the Government to finance its fiscal deficit at some discounted rate under the ongoing crisis. It would not cause demand-pull inflation under a demand depression. Moreover, it would not put much additional pressure on the exchequer if the money is borrowed at some discounted rate from the central bank. Most importantly, the required fiscal stimulus can be financed in order to ensure faster recovery of employment and growth.

4.7 State of Health Expenditure in India

COVID-19 crisis has shown us the lacuna of health infrastructure in the country in more glaring manner. The Government expenditure on health as proportion of GDP is one of the lowest in India – excluding the expenditure for water supply and sanitation it is less than 1% of GDP (World Development Indicators, The World Bank). As on 10th August 2021, the reported number of COVID-19 deaths is third highest in India after the United States and Brazil (World Health Organisation, https://covid19.who.int/table). There are lot of unreported deaths in the country because of lack of testing at an affordable rates to all. 80% of our population is poor for all practical purposes. So, the unregulated private health care system is simply not affordable to most of them. The proportion of out of pocket expenditure health is also one of the highest in this country. Therefore, the direct intervention in the health sector is absolutely essential in a country like India.

In the year 2004, in National Common Minimum Programme (NCMP) of the union Government, the goal was set to increase the combined

Government expenditure on health to 2%–3% of GDP(https://web.archive.org/web/20050315235132fw_/http://pmindia.nic.in/cmp.pdf). Unfortunately, it is still less than 1% of GDP in the country even after 17 years and it is still not a priority of the Governments of different tiers in India. Given that the poorer section of population avail the Government health services more, the Government expenditure on health has huge multiplier effect and enormous forward and backward linkages. This expenditure, by default, is pro-poor in nature and it would enhance the purchasing power of the poorer sections of population by reducing their out-of-pocket expenditures on health. Therefore, a substantial rise in the Government health expenditure would help in faster economic recovery. Moreover, it would save the lives of poor people by providing quality treatments without any cost or with a marginal cost affordable to all. Most of the country Governments in the world spend more than 3% of their GDP on health and it is below 1% of GDP in India (World Development Indicators, The World Bank). It must be enhanced substantially sooner than the later.

Health is also crucially dependent on the nutrition, which, in turn, is dependent on people's purchasing power and income. People's income has suffered badly under the COVID-19-induced lockdown and unemployment rate has also gone up like anything. It is extremely important to ensure universal employment of last resort programme under such a situation. We have Mahatma Gandhi National Rural Employment Guarantee Scheme (MGNREGS) for the rural areas. But unemployment has gone up suddenly not only in the rural areas but also in the urban areas as well. There is a need expand this employment guarantee scheme the urban areas as well. The average wage rate is only Rs. 202 per day under this scheme, which also should be made equal to the state-wise minimum wage norms to ensure more purchasing power in the hands of poorer section of population. As of now, there is a cap of 100 days of work in a year per family. That cap should be removed at least for the time being until the employment situation becomes normal. This universal employment of last resort scheme would help in enhancing the purchasing power of the poorest of the poor on the face of rise in unemployment and fall in income. This would also have enormous multiplier effect (because of the higher consumption propensity of this income class and also because of their composition of consumption basket full of wage goods or necessities) in reviving growth and employment rate in the economy. From the point of view of community health also, this measure would be extremely useful for improving almost all the average health indicators in the country for improving our human development ranking (which was already very low and it has gone down further in the recent past). Poor people of India would be able to lead a relatively better life.

4.8 Policy Conclusions

If we summarise the above arguments, we observe that the income of common people suffered badly due to the COVID-19-induced lockdown in India. The unemployment rate is likely to be double due to the lockdown. As a result of massive fall in purchasing power of people and increase in uncertainty vis-à-vis the future stream of income, the demand for various sectors suffered severely. This calls for the need of Keynesian demand management policies under a demand depression. On the other hand, the fiscal deficit has increased enormously as a proportion of GDP mainly due to the revenue loss. The Government is found to take a conservative position and planning to cut down expenditure and to disinvest various public sector units in order to reduce the fiscal deficit. The credit-deposit ratio of all the commercial banks taken together is not improving because of lack of demand at the aggregate level. Interestingly, the share market continuously boomed even under lockdown and the foreign exchange reserve of the RBI has increased enormously. Also, there is a dire need to enhance Government health expenditure in the country particularly on the face of COVID-19 crisis. The Government should spend more money also on the employment generation and the poverty alleviation schemes.

The policy direction that emerges from the above discussion is as the following. Clearly, there are two vicious cycles. First, because of the income and employment loss, people have lost their purchasing power at the aggregate level due to the COVID-19-induced lockdown. As a result of this, the aggregate demand for goods and services has come down. This, in turn, is making most of the businesses less profitable. As a result, the investment demand and the employment opportunities are not rising following the depression caused by this huge exogenous shock. This means again lower income of people at the aggregate level, lower purchasing power, and lower aggregate demand. There is another vicious cycle of public finance. Lower income, lower purchasing power, lower consumption demand, and lower profit have reduced the revenue receipts of the Government. As a result, the fiscal deficit to GDP ratio has gone up and the Government expenditure is not rising. Because of this, the economy would not get the required fiscal stimulus for faster recovery. The future revenue receipts would also be lower creating lower fiscal space in the days to come.

The way out seems to be a big push to the economy to get rid of both these vicious traps. It has to be a demand-side push by enhancing the Government expenditure substantially particularly in the areas of health and employment guarantee with greater multiplier effects. The size of the additional Government expenditure has to be more or less equal to the size of the negative income shock that the economy has faced in terms of income and employment loss due to the lockdown. Then the recovery would be faster, the employment and GDP would grow. The credit-deposit ratio would improve as investments become profitable. The stream of future revenue receipts in the Government exchequer would also be buoyant. The fiscal deficit to GDP ratio would automatically come down. This would definitely require a huge fiscal deficit on top of the already high fiscal deficit. This can be financed through monetisation using part of the excess idle foreign exchange reserve of the RBI. This would not cause any demand-pull inflation, because of excess liquidity in circulation, under the huge demand depression. There can be cost-push inflation led by the higher oil price and so on. However, if income-contracting monetary policy is undertaken to control that kind of inflation in the present context, the nominal income of people would reduce, further aggravating the ongoing crisis. The demand-side economists must be given a patient hearing in order to overcome the crisis sooner than the later.

Acknowledgements

The author is indebted to Preksha Mishra, Kanika Goyal, Kirti Jain, Vaishali, Melba J. Fernandes, Shaikh Sameer M., Soni T. L., Manjoor Ali, Atibhi Sharma, Pooja Kukreti, Parma Chakravartti, Saqib Khan, Adina Ara, Anuj Vijay Bhatia, Abdul Hannan, M. U. Farooque, Sabarni Chowdhury, Athary Janiso, Prakash Kumar Shukla, Madhubrata Rayasingh, Shantanu Mishra, Kaveri Choudhury, Oli Borah, and Kiran Lamba for their research support and help.

References

Anand, I. & A. Thampi (2021) – "Do PLFS numbers underestimate the pain of lockdown?", *The Hindustan Times*, Available at https://www.hindustantimes.com/business/do-plfs-numbers-underestimate-the-pain-of-lockdown-101629229850220.html, August 18.

Basole, Amit *et al.* (2021) – "State of working India 2021: One year of covid-19", *Azim Premji University*, Available at https://cse.azimpremjiuniversity.edu.in/wp-content/uploads/2021/05/State_of_Working_India_2021-One_year_of_Covid-19.pdf as viewed on 25th August 2021.

Das, S. (2020a) – "What GDP numbers didn't tell", *Telangana Today*, Available at https://archive.telanganatoday.com/what-gdp-numbers-didnt-tell?fbclid=IwAR31MhNwCnH9QKmWNqhirwRYwyu8QyjsIZHT5xIt9VbK8hlKfKZZusWXAN8, 5th September.

Das, S. (2020b) – "Coronavirus lockdown may lead to famine: Possibly worse", *Newsclick*, Available at https://www.newsclick.in/Coronavirus-COVID-19-Nationwide-Lockdown-Impact-Famine?fbclid=IwAR28WqhbTDqEsZlrMAmaNFfPRO43tYyQM0W-9CWcZ9ahYHYuGcaE8iTJyeZw, 25th March.

Das, S. (2020c) – "Understanding the Atmanirbhar Bharat package numbers", *Vikalp*, Available at https://vikalp.ind.in/2020/05/understanding-atmanirbhar-bharat/?fbclid=IwAR0Ydf42Q2IiZotD89AJBJuYhWisWdJQwDtqPLRvqrFtLVSpBTkJZb-2v4bE, 19th May.

Das, S. (2021a) – "A contractionary budget under demand depression is not good news", *Newsclick*, Available at https://www.newsclick.in/A-Contractionary-Budget-Under-Demand-Depression-Good-News?fbclid=IwAR16T1yFaQexrT1dXmaByTV8Vq347X-kyvdbktvtTdG5LlSxKRkEduBBv09c, 3rd February.

Periodic Labour Force Survey 2018–19 unit level data of the Government of India, Available at mospi.nic.in

Press Trust of India (2021) – "₹81,179 cr. due to states as GST compensation for FY21", *The Hindu*, Available at https://www.thehindu.com/business/Economy/81179-cr-due-to-states-as-gst-compensation-for-fy21/article35415850.ece as viewed on 10th August 2021.

Sen, A. K. (1973) – "Dimensions of unemployment in India", Convocation address, Indian Statistical Institute, Calcutta, 31st December, Available at http://library.isical.

ac.in:8080/xmlui/bitstream/handle/10263/5126/amartya%20sen%20speech.pdf?sequence=1&isAllowed=y as viewed on 4th August 2021

Union Budget 2021–22 (2021), Government of India, Available at https://www.indiabudget.gov.in/ as viewed on 10th August 2021.

WHO Coronavirus (Covid-19) Dashboard, World Health Organisation, Available at https://covid19.who.int/table as viewed on the 10th August 2021.

World Development Indicators of The World Bank, Available at https://data.worldbank.org/indicator/SH.XPD.CHEX.GD.ZS as viewed on the 10th August 2021.

5 Income Shocks and Resilience of Economic Institutions
Role of Collective Organizations

Indranil De, Mubashshir Iqbal, and Rooba Hasan

5.1 Introduction

COVID-19 pandemic has hit hard the economy worldwide. The world GDP of 2021 is projected to be 6.5 percentage points lower than in the pre–COVID-19 projections (IMF, 2020). IMF (2020) estimates suggest that the global economy is likely to contract by 4.9% in 2020. By the same estimates, Indian economy is likely to contract by 4.5%. The impact of the slowdown would be most severe on the low-income households and the recovery would be very slow and gradual. In this backdrop of current economic shock induced by the pandemic, it is interesting to understand the coping strategies of households involved in disparate economic activities. The coping strategies would largely depend on the institutional structure of the economic system, as institutions are developed to reduce the uncertainty in human exchange (North, 1995). This chapter attempts to look at the coping strategies in the wake of income shocks due to two major waves of COVID-19 pandemic during 2020–21 in India. Instead of providing estimates of loss of employment, income, or savings, it provides impact of pandemic on the nature of these losses across different livelihood activities. The chapter also examines resilience of the economic structures for the livelihood activities and the abilities to absorb shocks. It critically looks into the role of different institutions including market, Government, and collective organizations in absorbing the shocks.

The first COVID-19 case in India was detected on 30th January 2020.[1] Initially it was confined within few metropolitan cities, but it gradually spread across different regions of India. According to Ministry of Home Affairs, Government of India, more than 30 million are affected by the disease and more than four lakhs lost their life (by 2nd August 2021).[2] The pandemic has not only put excess pressure on the medical facilities of the country but also affected livelihood activities. It is especially due to the halting of economic activities after announcing lockdown by the Government from 25th March, 2020. Although unlocking started from 1st June, economic activities remained sluggish due to norms of social-distancing and other restrictions as mandated by the Government. The sudden and unprecedented slide in economic activities has resulted in an acute income shock.

DOI: 10.4324/9781003226970-8

Households devise strategies to cope up with severe idiosyncratic and covariate shocks leading to high consumption volatility having negative impact on both rural and urban households, although the extent of impact is different between the two regions (Günther and Harttgen, 2009). Households who are at the upper end of the income distribution are less affected due to better access to insurance mechanisms (Skoufias and Quisumbing, 2004). But rural households often bear idiosyncratic risk, along with covariate risk (Townsend, 1995). These risks are tackled through consumption smoothing and / or income smoothing activities (Morduch, 1995). These coping strategies may be very costly for the households in low-income countries – high cost of credit has to be borne, and expected profits has to be sacrificed for lower risk because of the incapacity of the households to take high risks. There are evidences from South India that consumption smoothing is affordable for well-off farmers but not for small farmers and landless labourers who face constraints in borrowing (Morduch, 1995).

Spatial distancing, popularly known as socio-distancing, is one of the most important strategies to contain the COVID-19 pandemic (Abel and McQueen, 2020). It is likely to disrupt all activities which require people to conglomerate, as in factory mode of production. If factory mode of production is affected, then it would affect the process of capital accumulation and growth through division of labour and economies of scale (Smith, 1776). Other models of production, such as self-employment, are likely to get affected lesser as they may not need conglomeration and production may continue at the household level by engaging family labour.

The coping strategies to absorb shocks are primarily driven by market mechanisms and Government initiatives. However, there are several instances of market failure, especially in credit and insurance in less developed countries (Besley, 1994). Failure of commission and omission in Government intervention is also well pervasive (Krueger, 1990). However, the role of NGOs in such situations is less studied. In this context, this chapter examines the role of voluntary sector and collective organizations for absorbing shocks and bridge the institutional gaps created by market and Government failures.

5.2 Coping Strategies

Ravallion and Chaudhuri (1997) argue that in Indian villages there is very limited evidence of intra-village sharing of income risk and therefore there is hardly any consumption insurance for the households. Poor households balance income and expenditure to reconcile assets and liabilities when economic prospects are grim (Harris-White et al., 2013). There are informal credit institutions that have emerged to support households to smooth out consumption in the context of missing formal credit and insurance markets (Besley, 1995). These non-market institutions provide credit as a substitute of insurance when market opportunities for risk sharing are limited.

The households can reduce risk and smooth out income by diversifying farming activities. In Ethiopia, agrarian shocks impact agricultural income negatively but to cope up with the loss of earnings in agriculture, non-agricultural earnings needed to increase by equal amount (Porter, 2012). Diversification in as many as five distinct livelihood activities has been considered as strategy to manage economic shock by the rural households in Zimbabwe (Mutenje et al., 2010). Cattle selling has been used as insurance in Africa and Asia for long time (Rosenzweig and Wolpin, 1993; Udry, 1995).

Savings is one of the important instruments to cope up with income shocks and smooth out consumption. Zimbabwean Households, especially the lower income ones, cut their expenses and increased savings as precautionary behaviour to tide over economic shocks induced by rainfall variability (Ersado et al., 2003).

Cutting consumption expenditure is one of the strategies of households to cope up with shocks. Households in lower income bracket showed higher propensity to cut expenditure when rainfall variability increases (Ersado et al., 2003). This cut in expenses may include market and non-market food and non-food items. Evidence from Brazil suggests that unemployment shock significantly increases the probability of children entering to the labour force, dropping out of school, and failing in school advancement (Duryea et al., 2007).

Collective organizations such as micro finance institutions (MFIs) also have important role in consumption and income smoothing (Zeller, 1999). However, the literature on the role of different types of collective organizations including NGOs in income and consumption smoothing is scanty. Most of the literature discusses about role of market in consumption and income smoothing. However, market may fail in less developed countries. This chapter attempts to fill the gap of by investigating the role of collective organizations in smoothing of consumption and income in the wake of Government and market failures.

5.3 Government Response to the Pandemic in India

India's fight against the COVID-19 pandemic was initiated by imposition of lockdown or restrictions on economic and social activities. The unlocking was initiated from 1st June in two phases where all activities were allowed barring functioning of cinema halls, bars and gyms. Different restrictions were imposed on functioning of public transport (Abhishek et al., 2020). Essential services were maintained during all the phases.

The Government of India also made announcements for distribution of payment to women, the poor, senior citizens, and farmers under *Pradhan Mantri Garib Kalyan Yojana* (PMGKY) package.[3] One component of this package, *Pradhan Mantri Garib Kalyan Ann Yojana* (PMKAY), is meant to distribute 5 kilogram (kg) wheat or rice per person along with 1 kg pulses per household to 800 million poor Indians. This is over and above of the existing amount of subsidised food grains distributed through the public distribution system (PDS). Under the PMGKY package, the Government provided cash transfers for refilling gas cylinders; the scheme is known as *Pradhan Mantri Ujjwala Yojana* (PMUY). Furthermore, direct cash transfer of Rs. 500 to women was announced under *Pradhan Mantri Jan Dhan Yojana* (PM-JDY). An advance pension of three months for senior citizens, disabled persons, and widows along with a grant of Rs. 1,000 was also initiated under National Security Assistance Program (NSAP). These transfers were made through a 'zero balance' account, known as *Jan Dhan* account. Funds were also transferred to small and marginal farmers under *Pradhan Mantri Kisan Samman Nidhi* (PM-KISAN), which is an income support programme launched by central Government in 2018. The Government employment generation programme, Mahatma Gandhi National Rural Employment Guarantee Scheme (MGNREGS) offers 100 days of guaranteed wage-employment to adult members to enhance their livelihood security. The wage rate in MGNREGS was increased, although by a meagre amount of Rs. 20.[4]

5.4 Methodology and Data

The study has been conducted through 19 in-depth telephonic interviews with adult individuals and six interviews with key informants of collective organizations across India. We have attempted to cover all regions of India in selecting individuals and location of work of collective organizations. We have selected individuals from different occupations and organizations with different primary focus areas of work from all regions of India. We have conducted seven interviews in the northern region, three from the southern region, two from the eastern region, one from the north-eastern region, and six from the western region of the country. The main occupations of the individuals are teaching, weaving, trading, driving, and farming.

The survey individuals belong to different ethnic groups. Eight are Hindus and the rest are Muslims and Christians. Furthermore, 10 out of 19 individuals are from Scheduled Caste (SC), Scheduled Tribe (ST), and Other Backward Castes (OBC), categorized by the Government as socially backward caste. The other nine individuals are from general caste or upper caste. The details of the sample individuals selected for in-depth interviews are given in Table 5.1.

We have also conducted in-depth telephonic interviews with the key informants of seven NGOs and collective organizations across different parts of the country. Three of them are from eastern India, two are from northern India, and one each from eastern and southern India. These NGOs work in different areas like livelihood promotion, and women and child welfare. Two voluntary organizations working for Delhi riot victims were also surveyed. The details of these organizations are given in Table 5.2.

The survey of individuals and the NGOs have been conducted twice. All the individuals and NGOs have been surveyed in June-July 2020 just after the first wave of the pandemic. A repeat survey was conducted on some of the individuals and NGOs in June 2021 after the second wave of the pandemic. The individual numbers 5, 6, 7, 16, and 17 in Table 5.1 and NGO numbers 2, 5, and 6 in Table 5.2 were included in the repeat survey. The other individuals and NGOs or collective organizations could not be included in the repeat survey as either they could not be contacted, or they did not respond.

Table 5.1 Selected sample individuals for in-depth interview

No.	Gender	Age	Religion	Caste/Ethnicity	Education level	Occupation	Place of residence	Region
1	Female	40	Muslim	OBC	High School	sewing	Northeast Delhi, Delhi	Northern
2	Female	34	Hindu	General	Graduate Studies	teacher	Yamuna Nagar, Haryana	
3	Male	30	Muslim	General	High School	garment trader	Northeast Delhi, Delhi	
4	Female	28	Muslim	General	Graduate Studies	professional developmental/ child therapist	Southeast Delhi, Delhi	
5	Female	60	Hindu	SC	Illiterate	Housemaid	Bageshwar Town, Uttarakhand	Southern
6	Male	30	Muslim	OBC	Graduate	Business (wood)	Bageshwar Town, Uttarakhand	
7	Male	65	Muslim	General	High School	Business (shoes)	Bageshwar Town, Uttarakhand	
8	Male	55	Christian	General	High School	Lorry driver	Palissery, Ernakulam, Kerala	
9	Female	48	Hindu	OBC	Illiterate	Agricultural labourer	Nambiyur, Coimbatore, Tamil Nadu	
10	Female	30	Hindu	OBC	High School	Cocopeat cottage industry worker	Ponnegoundanur, Coimbatore, Tamil Nadu	
11	Female	34	Hindu	General	High School	Weaver	Phulia, Nadia, West Bengal	Eastern
12	Male	37	Muslim	OBC	High School	Migrant worker	Keri, Gomia Bokaro, Jharkhand	
13	Male	52	Christian	ST	High School	Farmer	Makhao, Churachandpur, Manipur	North -eastern
14	Male	45	Buddhist	SC	Primary School	Petty tea shop (physically challenged)	Pali, Maharashtra	Western
15	Male	21	Muslim	General	High School	Call centre executive	Mehsana, Gujarat	
16	Female	40	Hindu	SC	High School	Maid in school	Pune City, Maharashtra	
17	Male	25	Muslim	General	Graduate Studies	Optometry professor	Anand Town, Gujarat	
18	Male	20	Hindu	SC	Primary School	Fishing	Khorwad, Anand, Gujarat	
19	Male	38	Hindu	General	High School	Farming	Himatnagar, Sabarkantha, Gujarat	

Table 5.2 Description of NGOs and collective organizations surveyed

No.	Institution	Area of specialization	Place of survey	Region
1	Human Welfare Foundation and Society for Bright Future	Delhi Relief and Rehabilitation Project – for the Victims of Delhi Pogrom 2020	New Delhi	Northern
2	Indian Red Cross Society (IRCS)	Provide relief in times of disasters/ emergencies and promotes health & care of the vulnerable people and communities.	Bageshwar district of Uttarakhand	
3	SEWA Bharat	Livelihood for informal sector women	Phulia, Nadia, West Bengal	Eastern
4	Aga Khan Rural Support Programme (AKRSP)	Livelihood development and social issues.	Bihar- Samastipur, Muzaffarpur, and Vaishali	
5	Pragati	Social welfare and education	Navrangpur and Koraput districts of Odisha	
6	Kutch Mahila Vikas Sangathan (KMVS)	Women empowerment and women livelihood	Kutch district and Bhuj city of Gujarat	Western
7	Kudumbashree	Micro Finance	Kerala	Southern

Survey has been conducted through in-depth semi-structured interviews. The qualitative data collected through interviews has been processed through data reduction technique. Data reduction is one of the central objectives of qualitative data analysis, consisting of few distinct but interconnected steps (Robson, 1993). Informal labels were assigned to the information obtained from our transcript of interviews. These labels were then categorized according to the importance and relevance of information for the study. Then we arrived at broader themes by clubbing the similar categories. At the next stage, to conceptualize the data, inter-connections were established between these categories or themes of study. Finally, results and interpretations were derived to realise the objectives of the study.

5.5 Results from Interviews

The individual interviews reveal the distribution of economic activities in formal and informal sector, financial stress, and coping strategies of households. It also provides an understanding about failures of market and Government and the role of non-market and non-Government organizations such as NGOs and collectives. We have discussed the results of initial phase of interviews conducted in 2020 first and then the results of repeat interviews in 2021.

5.5.1 *First Wave of Pandemic 2020*

5.5.1.1 *Impact on Employment*

People engaged with both formal and informal sectors were affected in the pandemic. It impacted people from all walks of life, and from all age groups. A high school passed male, who migrated from Gujarat state to Delhi to take a call centre job, found himself unemployed in the pandemic. He lost his job without any compensation or advance notice. A 40-year-old woman from Pune, who works in a reputed international school, has been reimbursing half of her monthly salary to her employer since the lockdown. A 25-year-old assistant professor in the Optometric department of a private paramedical college in one of the small towns in Gujarat has not received salary from April 2020. A 28-year-old lady from Delhi, working as professional Child Therapist/Developmental Psychologist, experienced a pay cut of 50% in the initial two months, and later 65% in the month of June 2020.

The loss of earnings for those engaged with the informal and semi-formal sector is equally conspicuous. A migrant worker who returned from Kerala to his native village in Jharkhand has no income in his native place. Similarly, the young lady working in cocopeat cottage industry in Coimbatore, Tamil Nadu has no income since the beginning of lockdown. The small tea stall in a village of Maharashtra is closed and the owner has no income. An elderly woman from Bageshwar, Uttarakhand lost almost all work as a household maid, only to retain two of them. A 52-year-old man from Manipur who earns his livelihood by paddy cultivation with masonry work as a secondary source of income has lost all sources of additional income.

Both the large and small business owners have lost income in the same district due to the pandemic. The negative impact of lockdown for large business owners is also high; they need to retain some of their staff without whom it is difficult to resume work. The small-time shoe retailers are purchasing products at 1.5 times higher prices, but selling at the same prices (often at the maximum retail price stipulated by the Government) as earlier.

The pandemic has impacted both the demand and supply side of the economy. Demand for the products are less due to tumbling purchasing power of households. In addition, demand is less as people are not willing to visit markets. Moreover, as transport costs have increased, people from nearby villages are making fewer visits to the nearest towns. On the supply side, due to shortage of inputs and increasing labour cost, prices of products have increased. In Jharkhand, gas cylinders are made available in black-market at a price as high as Rs. 5,500–6,000, which is at least eight times higher than the market price. Labour cost of loading and unloading has increased all over. Moreover, the mode of business has also changed. Previously retailers used to buy products in credit. After lockdown, they have to make payment upfront or in advance.

5.5.1.2 *Extent of Financial Stress*

The loss of income ranges from as low as 30% to 100%. The sales of the owner of large woodworking business in Uttarakhand reduced from Rs. 7–8 lakhs per month to Rs. 1 lakh per month post lockdown. The loss of family income of the development psychologist in Delhi is around Rs. 75,000 during the last three months. Similarly, the BPO executive from Delhi lost his monthly salary of Rs. 25,000 from April 2020. The migrant worker from Jharkhand to Kerala lost Rs. 45,000–60,000 during the three months since lockdown. A lorry driver from Kerala lost around Rs. 45,000 during the last three months and his son, who was laid off temporarily from his company, lost his monthly salary of Rs. 9,000. The loss of income of the small tea stall owner is relatively less in absolute amount at Rs. 3,000 per month. Half of the family income has been lost for the man from Manipur.

Interestingly the drop in income is relatively less for those who work as agricultural labourers. The monthly wage earnings of the lady who works as agricultural labour in Coimbatore, Tamil Nadu reduced from Rs. 6,000 per month to Rs. 4,000–5,000. The earning of Rs. 20,000 of cocopeat cottage industry worker halted completely, but her husband is able to manage to earn Rs. 4,000 only through agricultural labour work.

Till 24 February 2020, a 40-year-old lady from Shiv Vihar, New Delhi earned her livelihood by sewing frocks. Her husband used to arrange fodder with the help of his camel cart from Loni, Uttar Pradesh (Delhi-Uttar Pradesh border) to nearby areas of northeast Delhi. From these sources, she used to earn around Rs. 500 per day whereas her husband's three-day haul (required to complete the whole process) used to raise an income of Rs. 1,500 every third day. Two brothers, again from Shiv Vihar, used to earn Rs. 35,000–40,000 per month before the riots. Currently, all of them have no income.

The severity of the impact is highest for those who were under some other crisis even before the pandemic. For the victims of the February 2020 Delhi riot, the pandemic is an additional crisis. It has only increased their vulnerability.

5.5.1.3 *Coping Strategies*

In response to the income shock the households have reduced their expenditure on average by 50% and that too on items having long term implications, such as health and education. The migrant to Delhi who lost his income in the city and did not get any work back at his home town in Gujarat is unable to buy insulin and other medicines for his diabetic mother. The man (respondent 14 in Table 5.1) from Maharashtra whose small-time tea stall has been closed is unable to pay fees for children's education. He had to buy vegetables of degraded quality to reduce expenses.

The major consumption smoothing strategy of the households is taking credit from friends, relatives and institutions. Those who have not taken credit and hence not in immediate financial stress, have given credit to friends and relatives such as the psychotherapist from Delhi. She is uncertain about the recovery any soon. The man from Manipur who does not have any savings, have taken loan of Rs. 50,000 to deal with the loss of family income. A woman from Nadia district of West Bengal has taken a loan of Rs. 16,000 from a self-help group (SHG). The riot victim lady from Delhi has borrowed Rs. 15,000 from friends to cope up with financial distress.

Income smoothing strategies appear to be better for those who either work or willing to work as labourers or own their own means of production. Working as wage labourers in agriculture or MGNREGS work is one widely acknowledged coping strategies for the rural households. Most of the households have job card required for getting work in MGNREGS, but not all. For example, one woman from Coimbatore district has a job card, while the other woman from the same district does not have one. The loss of wage is also less for those working as agricultural labourers or those who can take such work.

The woman from Pune is contemplating to take up stitching work in the town. The woman in the village of Coimbatore has also planned to smooth out their income stream by working in petty activities like coconut leaf stick making. The psychotherapist from Delhi is contemplating to launch a self-owned online counselling platform for income smoothing. The family of weavers from Nadia district of West Bengal has earned an additional income of Rs. 500–600 per month by selling directly products of a reputed brand in local area.

Savings is one of the important fallback options. These savings have been used to meet daily expenses, although savings have implications for long-term investments in human capital. The psychologist from Delhi planned to use her savings of Rs. 40,000 for initiating an online counselling platform. The woman from Coimbatore who works as agricultural labourer is less anxious as she has enough savings to face future vagaries. The weaver from Nadia district of West Bengal has saved Rs. 20,000 by selling sarees (traditional Indian female dress) few months back. These sarees were sold in an exhibition in Rajasthan (western part of India) with the help of SEWA Bharat, an NGO. The riot victim brothers from Delhi faced special difficulty as they ran out of savings due to dowry paid for marriage before lockdown.

The coping strategies are even more difficult for those devastated by Delhi riots. The woman from Shiv Vihar (where the riot broke out) ran away to save her and her children's life without taking any belongings. She had arranged food and shelter in exchange of her own and daughter's jewellery, which they were wearing at the time they fled. The brothers from Shiv Vihar who were managing a garment business ran away by motorcycle, leaving the stock of 195 pieces of jeans, cash of around Rs. 20,000, jewellery, and other valuables in their house. Later they were informed that their home was completely looted and burned to the ground. These people have very little resource left to cope up with the pandemic.

The ability to cope up with the crisis crucially depends on the skills and social network of the individuals. The large woodworking business owner in Uttarakhand could not sack some of the employees as they were skilled in woodwork.

The optometric skills and business networks of the young man from Gujarat helped to take orders over phone and deliver at home. Nevertheless, just having skills may not resolve problems. The migrant from Jharkhand, who had worked as a piece-rate labourer for preparing and repairing revolving chairs in Kerala, did not find any employment opportunity in his native place. He had expected to double his income at the least in the near future in Kerala, where he had had all the contacts. But he did not have the requisite network to produce and sell products developed out of his skills in his native place. The network of friends and relatives helped individuals to manage credit. The riot victims could withstand the shock just because of the support they received from friends and relatives. The local NGOs also developed a database and helped the victims. Thus interconnection and information are very important enablers to cope up with the shock.

5.5.1.4 Market Failure

One of the major effects of the pandemic and subsequent lockdown is market failure. The major reason behind market failure is mismatch between demand and supply of labourers. Men and women are willing to take labour work for livelihood and tide over the crisis. But they are hardly getting any avenues to sell their labour, especially in the non-farm sector. The riot victim lady and her husband are unable to find work in Delhi. However, those who are in villages are able to find or expecting to get work in agriculture or MGNREGS. On the other hand, there is excess demand for labourers in the economy. The large woodworking businessman from Bageshwar, Uttarakhand is unable to get labourers for loading and unloading of wood and final products as the labourers have gone back to their homes with the onset of lockdown. The shoe shop owner also complained that that the suppliers are providing goods at 1.5 times higher price as the cost of transportation has increased; and labourer shortage is one of the contributors of increase in supply price.

The pandemic has led to failure of product markets and consequent suspension of other income generating activities. Perishable products like fish and vegetables could not be transported due to disruption of supply chain. The fishing folk from Anand district of Gujarat revealed that earlier fishes and prawns used to be transported to Delhi at premium price. But due to disruption of supply chain they have to sell in local market at a very cheap rate. Even vegetables could not be sold to the wholesale markets by farmers in Sabarkantha district of Gujarat due to supply chain disruptions. The middlemen (Mahajans) are unable to buy sarees from the weavers in West Bengal as they are unable to transport these goods to the urban centres. However, this does not mean the there is any deficit in people willing to provide transportation services. The lorry driver from Ernakulum district of Kerala is out of service and willing to resume work as soon as possible.

5.5.1.5 Government Intervention and Failure

The Government support in the pandemic is varied; it appears to be better in rural areas or small towns as compared to metropolitan areas. The psychologist and

BPO employee in Delhi has not received help from any Government programme. However, families in Delhi, Pune, Bageshwar town, village of Maharashtra, and Manipur have received free rations from PDS. The riot victim's family was supported by the free ration as stipulated by Government. Their daughters received stipulated Rs. 500 per month in their *Jan Dhan* account. Free gas cylinder, as promised by the Government, has not been received by most of the families. Only in Nadia district of West Bengal the prescribed amount for gas cylinder was received through *Jan Dhan* account. In Jharkhand, although food grains were freely available from PDS, gas cylinders were sold in the black market at an exorbitant price of Rs. 5,500–6,000/cylinder. Almost all have not heard about *PM Garib Kalyan Yojana*.

A few households have MGNREGS job card or *Jan Dhan* account. Among those who have *Jan Dhan* account, most households have not received any Government transfers. The surveyed individuals have not received benefits that were promised to them. For example, Rs. 5,000 announced for the migrant workers by Jharkhand state Government has not been received by the potential beneficiary. He has also registered for *Krishi Credit Pariyojana* and expects to receive Rs. 2,000, but haven't had any luck till date. The non-payment of the promised amount of compensation by Government is most inimical and hurting for Delhi riot victims. The promised compensation of Rs. 3,000 per person has not been received yet by the lady whose house was looted. Only Rs. 25,000 out of the compensation of Rs. 500,000 was received by the brothers we interviewed as their house was burnt.

Government support or compensation can act as a saviour while coping with crises and shocks. The small-time tea seller in Maharashtra and his brother receive a monthly pension of Rs. 1,000 each as both of them are handicapped. This helps to meet the very basic needs as their tea shop is closed. Those who have received free food grains in villages could sustain income shock, many without borrowing. With Government support and availability of agricultural labour work, women from Kerala have not even drained their hard-earned savings. Having MGNREGS job card and other Government support provide some hope of meeting their daily expenses. Those who do not have these support systems are in despair as they would exhaust their savings very soon.

5.5.1.6 *Intervention by NGOs and Collectives*

One of the major initiatives to smooth out consumption is the organization of community kitchens in different parts of the country. It was first initiated by a state Government run self-help group (SHG) Kudumbashree in Kerala. The objective was to provide food to the daily wage earners, migrant workers, and the poor and destitute.[5] Indian Red Cross Society (IRCS) in Uttarakhand, Aga Khan Rural Support Program (AKRSP) in Bihar, Pragati in Odisha, and Kutch Mahila Vikas Sangathan (KMVS) in Gujarat provided food grains and other basic necessities to the vulnerable sections of the population. The local Government and NGOs worked in tandem to identify vulnerable people. AKRSP, KMVS, and other NGOs launched awareness programmes to sensitise people regarding the new norms of social distancing and other practices to contain the COVID-19 pandemic. Collective organizations' role was crucial in providing succour to the families affected by the riot. Human Welfare Foundation (HWF) and Society for Bright Future (SBF), working with riot victims, provided essentials such as food ration, masks, sanitizers, and other essential commodities to the underprivileged and destitute and migrant workers at a significant scale.

NGOs have played a very important role in income smoothing of the families in coping with the difficulties. The nature of support and target group depends on the activities and people that the NGOs deal with in general. The help received from an NGO by the weavers in Nadia district of West Bengal has multiple implications. The woman from a weaver's family had attended workshop on financial literacy organised by SEWA Bharat. This training helped her to better plan and manage income and expenditure. Moreover, when sarees produced by her family were not purchased by local middle-men (*mahajan*), they were sold through an online platform, Anubandh, developed by SEWA Bharat to provide direct marketing facility to the weavers. The women expressed that they think that marketing is the only initiative which can help them sell their stock soon. To sell existing stock of sarees, SEWA Bharat collaborated with an online wholesale retail brand, India Kraft. The women were also involved in the production of masks, that are purchased by SEWA itself at Rs. 8 to Rs. 10 per piece. Other women were involved in logistics if they lacked requisite skills for mask production.

Aga Khan Rural Support Program (AKRSP) initiated preparation of masks in SHGs during lockdown. Although movement was highly restricted during lockdown, AKRSP in coordination with the block development officials arranged raw materials for preparation of masks. These masks were purchased by AKRSP at 5 rupees per mask. Till 1st July nearly 500 women associated with the SHGs were engaged with mask preparation. To impart skills for rehabilitation of the return migrants AKRSP was preparing a list with their details with the help of SHGs.

Pragati, in Odisha, also made efforts to sell vegetables, food grains and other perishable farm produce in the markets. They did do through farmer producer organization (FPO), a collective of farmers. They liaised with Government officials for requisite permission for transportation of goods. They also supported farmers by distributing seeds for millet, paddy and vegetable cultivation. In a similar manner Kutch Mahila Vikas Sangathan (KMVS), supported the SHGs under their preview in mask making. They linked the SHGs to organizations needing mask and also provided raw materials if needed.

Human Welfare Foundation (HWF) and Society for Bright Future (SBF) are planning to provide e-rickshaw (local transport vehicle) to the husband of woman we interviewed. He lost his camel and hence cannot earn from camel cart. Under Delhi Relief and Rehabilitation Project (DRRP), the NGOs distributed e-rickshaw, three- and four-wheeler cart, sewing machine, vegetable stock, cycle, grains stock, utensils, two wheelers, seat cover preparation machine with stabilizer, and so on for reviving income generation activities of the riot victims. They also took initiatives for renovation, reconstruction, and restart of commercial establishment. The establishments affected by riot were supported by assistance in repairing the computer centre, restarting paper folding unit, repairing soda shop, restarting grocery shop, and renovating restaurant.

5.5.2 Second Wave of Pandemic 2021

5.5.2.1 Impact on Employment

The onslaught of the pandemic continued to impact people from all the sectors, as in case of first wave. The lady who used to work as a maid in a reputed school in Pune has lost her job and does not expect to get reinstated in next one year. She is struggling to make a living by stitching clothes. However, due to lockdown and other problems she is not getting enough orders. On the other hand, the lady from Bageshwar who used to work as a housemaid has been able to resume her work in few houses after a hiatus.

The assistant professor in the paramedical college could retain his job due to continuation of online classes, although at half his original salary. He also runs a business of spectacles but it is in the downside in spite of getting new orders due to lack of resources to buy raw materials. It appears that the pernicious effect of the pandemic is lesser for the formal sector, but it is still considerable. The salaries are also disbursed in an interval of two to three months. Some teachers were also forced to resign from their institutions.

The businessmen engaged with woodworking from Uttarakhand have fired almost all of their workers as they are unable to pay salaries. Their business has gone down considerably due to lack of demand for furniture. They have been able to retain only two workers for sawing of wood. Fortunately, they could remain open as their business is registered under small industries (*Laghu Udyog*).

Lockdown has led to a huge loss for the shoe shop owner from Uttarakhand. He ordered shoes to meet the seasonal demand but could not sell due to lockdown. The concern is that shoes lose quality and firmness in three months. New designs also arrive to the market in a short period.

5.5.2.2 Coping Strategies

The school maid from Pune had to cut spending as her family could no longer depend on husband's earning of Rs. 10,000/month. Her husband closed his Provident Fund Account (social security) and withdrew money for fulfilling their daily needs. The housemaid from Bageshwar had to take up the work as maid in two more houses to compensate the loss of earnings of family members. Her husband and son had experienced a considerable loss of earnings as painter. They are now able to get only 10% of the orders of normal times. The shoe shop owner in Uttarakhand drew down savings, taken loan from friends and relatives, and even deferred payment to wholesalers to meet daily expenses.

5.5.2.3 Government Intervention and Failure

The school maid from Pune and housemaid from Bageshwar received free monthly ration (10 kg rice and 10 kg wheat grains) from PDS. However, from last two months before the interview (June 2021) the school maid did not receive free ration. She has never received free gas or any other benefit from PDS or govt. The housemaid from Bageshwar and her husband used to get pension from Government under *Vridha Pension Yojana*. But from last four months they have not received any pension. Government failure to provide committed support that one is supposed to get particularly during shock can cause enormous stress.

Local political clientelism has acted as discriminatory force in the lockdown period. The shoe shop owner reported that shopkeepers having good political contacts were able to open partially. Others were under the threat of a fine amounting to Rs. 1,000, if shop is found open by police. They chose to remain closed.

Lack of prior information regarding lockdown has been cited as one reason that affects business, especially affecting planning for procurement of raw materials, which becomes unusable after some time. There was demand to wave off Goods and Services Tax (GST) temporarily to provide subsidized transport facility to revive business.

5.5.2.4 Intervention by NGOs

The school maid and housemaid reported some NGOs helped by providing cereals, oil, pulses, and other food items last year but this year similar support was absent. Indian Red Cross, working in various blocks of Bageshwar, is raising its funds from public, newspaper advertisements, advertisements in social media like Facebook, WhatsApp, and so on. Red Cross and KMVS is still providing food kits to the villagers. Red Cross has evolved a mechanism with the Gram Pradhan (village headman) to identify the needy. KMVS provided cash support of Rs. 3,000 per family to about 700 families and Rs. 1,000 per family to 70 families from different towns of Kutch district. Both Red Cross and KMVS has distributed safety and monitoring equipment. Red Cross provided the safety equipment in regions where COVID-19 positive cases are high and transportation is difficult. The NGO has worked with hospitals and informed the chief medical officer in Government to conduct testing in highly affected and secluded regions. The NGOs also conducted vaccination awareness campaign. KMVS provided tele-medicine and e-consultation support for COVID-19 patients. They established quarantine centres for COVID-19 patients. To motivate the community to observe COVID-19 appropriate behaviour they tried to identify credible influencers from amongst the community. They also campaigned for appropriate behaviour through community radio, social media, and volunteers.

KMVS continued its efforts in providing support to women for making and marketing masks. Pragati, an NGO in Odisha, made efforts to analyse farmer's problems during the pandemic rather than simply distribution of food or equipment. They found that major problems of farmers is supply of inputs and selling outputs. They worked with a farmer producer organization (FPO) for crop planning, purchase of inputs, and selling output. Pragati has provided revolving fund to the FPO. The NGO also supported labourers and migrants by providing funds at 0% interest rate. They also provided loan to medium farmers at 5%–6% rate of interest.

5.6 Discussion and Conclusion

The COVID-19 pandemic has halted economic activities and constrained the economy from both demand and supply sides. The market mechanism failed both in product and labour markets. The pandemic has also raised question on resilience of the factory mode of production. Employment in factory or organizations which require people to conglomerate was severely affected due to the norm of social-distancing. Diversification of economic activities is likely to smooth out the income of the vulnerable households. However, the households may be able to absorb the shock only if they are able to diversify from factory model of production to other modes requiring less agglomeration, such as self-employment.

The weakness of market as an institution in less developed nations has become more glaring during this pandemic. It is interesting to note that even those employed in formal sector are facing loss of employment and income, while many those who are engaged with the informal sector, such as agriculture and self-employment, are better poised to retain their employment and income. Harriss-White (2013) also observed that households having self-employed members were better protected against shocks than those engaged in the manufacturing sector. The dominant idea that formality leads to stability and informality leads towards volatility (Tranberg Hansen and Vaa, 2004; Van Assche et al., 2014) stands up to scrutiny in the wake of evidence of loss of income and employment in formal sector during crises like a pandemic. Hence, informal sector and informal arrangement may be considered a very important part of developing resilient economic institutions.

Given the failure of market and formal institutions it is incumbent on the Government to buttress the vulnerable population for consumption and income smoothing. The Government has taken many initiatives by providing free food grains, pluses and gas cylinders, but many vulnerable families are not able to access due to Government's failures of commission and omission. Moreover, apart from food grains, other essentials were not provided by the Government during the second wave of the pandemic. Furthermore, cash distribution through pension schemes was discontinued during the second wave. No prior announcement before declaring lockdown has also affected business.

The NGOs and collective organizations bridged the gap created by Government and market failure. The NGOs have distributed food kits and medical support to the vulnerable. They played an important role in identifying and verifying the potential beneficiaries. The local Governments may also help the NGOs to identify the potential beneficiaries. They have also been seen activate to usher behaviour change by identifying influencers and working through local level connections. Hence, the non-market and non-Government institutions has demonstrated their importance in consumption smoothing exercise and containing the pandemic. NGOs have made arrangements to plan for alternative economic activities, arranged inputs for production (especially during lockdown and supply chain disruptions) and linked producers with the markets through different initiatives. The training provided by them have helped women to absorb shocks through better financial planning. Thus, they have been able to give fillip to employment opportunities other than those based on factory mode of production.

The efforts of NGOs in linking institutions have proven to be useful. The role played by SEWA Bharat in developing platform to link larger market, and liaising with Government by Pragati to link input and output market with local economy bears testimony of usefulness of NGOs in this regard. AKRSP and HWF and SBF have contributed in developing alternative livelihood activities. Thus already acquired skills may be utilized gainfully through self-employment and new skills can be acquired in future.

The role of non-market and non-Government organizations in consumption and income smoothing has long been ignored by the mainstream neo-classical economic theory. In systems, where market and Government failures are common, role of NGOs and collective organizations become imperative to fill the gaps created by institutional failure. It is all the more important when the shock is driven by social or political disturbances. People non only losses their livelihood but also their basic belongings in ethnic clashes. Hence, it requires planning and execution at micro level along with trust building, which these organizations are able to do in a better manner. Hence, non-market and non-Government institutions and informal sector should be included in developing resilient economic institutions.

Notes

1 Data available on https://pib.gov.in/PressReleaseIframePage.aspx?PRID=1601095, Accessed 2nd August 2021
2 Data available on https://www.mohfw.gov.in/, Accessed 2nd August 2021
3 See https://pib.gov.in/PressReleasePage.aspx?PRID=1608345, Accessed 2nd August 2021
4 Exchange rate: 1 USD = Rs. 75.18
5 More information can be found at https://www.kudumbashree.org/pages/830, Accessed 2nd August 2021 and https://www.who.int/india/news/feature-stories/detail/responding-to-covid-19---learnings-from-kerala, Accessed 2nd August 2021

References

Abel, T., & McQueen, D. (2020). The COVID-19 pandemic calls for spatial distancing and social closeness: Not for social distancing! *International Journal of Public Health*, 65, 231.

Abhishek, B., Gupta, P., Kaushik, M., Kishore, A., Kumar, R., Sharma, A., & Verma, S. (2020). India's food system in the time of COVID-19. *Economic and Political Weekly*, 55(15), 12–14.

Besley, T. (1994). How do market failures justify interventions in rural credit markets? *The World Bank Research Observer*, 9(1), 27–47.

Besley, T. (1995). Nonmarket institutions for credit and risk sharing in low-income countries. *Journal of Economic Perspectives, 9*(3), 115–127.

Duryea, S., Lam, D., & Levison, D. (2007). Effects of economic shocks on children's employment and schooling in Brazil. *Journal of Development Economics, 84*(1), 188–214.

Ersado, L., Alderman, H., & Alwang, J. (2003). Changes in consumption and saving behavior before and after economic shocks: Evidence from Zimbabwe. *Economic Development and Cultural Change, 52*(1), 187–215.

Günther, I., & Harttgen, K. (2009). Estimating households vulnerability to idiosyncratic and covariate shocks: A novel method applied in Madagascar. *World Development, 37*(7), 1222–1234.

Harriss-White, B., Olsen, W., Vera-Sanso, P., & Suresh, V. (2013). Multiple shocks and slum household economies in South India. *Economy and Society, 42*(3), 398–429.

IMF (2020). World Economic Outlook. International Monetary Fund, June 2020, https://www.imf.org/en/Publications/WEO/Issues/2020/06/24/WEOUpdate-June2020, Accessed on 26th September, 2021.

Krueger, A. O. (1990). Government failures in development. *Journal of Economic Perspectives, 4*(2), 9–23.

Morduch, J. (1995). Income smoothing and consumption smoothing. *Journal of Economic Perspectives, 9*(3), 103–114.

Mutenje, M. J., Ortmann, G. F., Ferrer, S. R. D., & Darroch, M. A. G. (2010). Rural livelihood diversity to manage economic shocks: Evidence from south-east Zimbabwe. *Agrekon, 49*(3), 338–357.

North, D. C. (1995). The new institutional economics and third world development. In: *The New Institutional Economics and Third World Development*, Harriss, J., Hunter, J. & Lewis, C. (eds). London: Routledge, pp. 17–26.

Porter, C. (2012). Shocks, consumption and income diversification in rural Ethiopia. *Journal of Development Studies, 48*(9), 1209–1222.

Ravallion, M., & Chaudhuri, S. (1997). Risk and insurance in village India: Comment. *Econometrica: Journal of the Econometric Society, 65*(1), 171–184.

Robson C (1993). *The Real World Research – A Resource for Social Scientists and Practitioner Researchers*. Oxford: Blackwell Publications.

Rosenzweig, M. R., & Wolpin, K. I. (1993). Credit market constraints, consumption smoothing, and the accumulation of durable production assets in low-income countries: Investments in bullocks in India. *Journal of Political Economy, 101*(2), 223–244.

Skoufias, E., & Quisumbing, A. R. (2004). Consumption insurance and vulnerability to poverty: A synthesis of the evidence from Bangladesh, Ethiopia, Mali, Mexico and Russia. *European Journal of Development Research, 17*(1), 24–58.

Smith, A. (1776). *An Inquiry into the Nature and Causes of the Wealth of Nations: Volume One*. London: printed for W. Strahan; and T. Cadell, 1776.

Townsend, R. M. (1995). Consumption insurance: An evaluation of risk-bearing systems in low-income economies. *Journal of Economic Perspectives, 9*(3), 83–102.

Tranberg Hansen, K., & Vaa, M. (Eds.). (2004). *Reconsidering Informality: Perspectives from Urban Africa*. Oslo, Norway: Nordic Africa Institute.

Udry, C. (1995). Risk and saving in Northern Nigeria. *The American Economic Review, 85*(5), 1287–1300.

Van Assche, K., Beunen, R., & Duineveld, M. (2014). Formal/informal dialectics and the self-transformation of spatial planning systems: An exploration. *Administration & Society, 46*(6), 654–683.

Zeller, M. (1999, February). The role of micro-finance for income and consumption smoothing. In IADB Conference on Social Protection and Poverty. Washington DC February (Vol. 5).

6 Plight of Migrant Informal Workers in India in the Context of COVID-19 and Inadequacy of Existing Labour Legislations

Kingshuk Sarkar

6.1 Introduction and Context

The COVID-19 pandemic and subsequent lockdown exposed the vulnerability of the informal sector workers in India. They found themselves without jobs overnight. They were anyway engaged in casual and contract work and some of them were self-employed doing petty economic activities. Lockdown rendered them jobless. Usually they earn just enough to subsist and few even earn less than minimum wages. Petty economic activities are not economically remunerative and in most cases not even cover basic sustenance needs. Under such circumstances, informal workers with very little or no savings could not survive beyond few days of the lockdown (Dandekar & Ghai, 2020).

Among the informal workers, inter-state migrants were specially disadvantaged as they did not have enough money to pay rent or buy food. After a few days, they started to leave cities and in absence of public transport started their long walk back to native places, sometimes as far as 2000 km away. The entire nation witnessed these phenomena during the months of April, May, and even June. Many such workers did perish in the process too.

Relatively economically better-off section of the society could discover that these large number informal workers were subsisting right among them. The roadside vegetable sellers, domestic workers, construction workers, rickshaw-pullers are managing livelihoods right in front of their eyes and such other small economic activities being carried in full public view. Well-off sections of our society almost did not notice the existence of these informal workers till the point lockdown was announced subsequent to outbreak of COVID-19 pandemic.

Most of the labour laws do not apply to informal workers. Informal workers remain mostly undocumented. The fact that informal workers underwent relatively higher sufferings during the pandemic induced lockdown because protective labour legislations were absent (Aiyar, Kapur, Mukhopadhyay, Naik & Singh, 2020). Access to social security was inherently non-existent for almost all the informal workers particularly migrant workers. This chapter examines the legal protection or lack of it for the informal workers in India in the context of COVID-19 pandemic.

DOI: 10.4324/9781003226970-9

6.2 Informal Labour in India

The informal economy in India provides livelihood to more than 90% of the total workforce (Economic Survey, 2018–19). In terms of non-agricultural employment, share of informal employment is 83.6% in India ((ILO, 2013). Informality is found in both the traditional informal economy like establishments having less than ten workers and – increasingly – through the growth of informality in the formal sector too. There has been growing use of contract and casual labour in the formal sector over time (MoLE, 2017). Informal labour is being increasingly used as it is cheaper than regular labour. Most of the labour laws do not apply for informal labour and they are denied statutory legislative protection that is otherwise available for regular workers. That reduces the cost of hiring informal labour. For example, in 2013–14, the wage-gap between contract and regular workers in the organized manufacturing sector was 25%; this explains the dramatic rise in proportion of contract workers in the sector from 12% in 1990–91 to 33.6% in 2013–14 (; MoL&E, 2019). There is no explicit employer-employee relation in such cases and these workers particularly the migrants among them do not have access to any form of social security.

Broadly, in structural sense, there are two reasons behind this phenomenon of increasing informalization. First is the quest of employers to minimize cost in a competitive environment. When India embarked on liberalizing its economy in 1991, domestic economy experienced deregulation and they had to compete with international establishments. Production structure in majority of instances gradually got decentralized to accommodate more and more informal labour (ILO, 2013). The apparent and explicit motive is to reduce cost of production particularly through economizing on the labour cost. And informal labour is way cheaper than formal labour.

Second, over the last three decades, India's occupational distribution could not keep pace with changes in the sectoral distribution of national income. Over the years, contribution of primary sector in the national income declined steadily (presently it's share is 14.2%) but it still engages overwhelming large number of workers. Workers engaged in the primary sector did fell but not to the level it was expected. Share of workers engaged in the primary sector fell from 52.45% in 2009 to 42.39% in 2018–19. Corresponding increase in secondary sector employment was from 21.18% in 2009 to 25.58% in 2019 (Economic Survey, 2019–20). Many workers continued in the primary sector as additional hands and rest left the primary sector to look for livelihood in secondary and tertiary sectors in urban areas. Majority of such workers found ways of survival in urban areas as informal workers in the secondary sector and particularly in the tertiary sector.

These informal manufacturing and service sector workers often eke out a livelihood by engaging themselves as appendage workers of the formal sector, various extension and non-core activities, petty economic and subsistence activities on the fringe like selling vegetables at roadside, opening cycle-repairing shops, hawking at roadside and public transport, and domestic work. As per Periodic Labour Force Survey 2017–18, 52% informal workers are self-employed and survive through precarious activities. Majority of such workers are unskilled or at best low-skilled.

In this chapter, the term 'informal labour' refers to all workers who don't have written job contracts and do not have access to any form of social security. This definition has also been used to define informal/unorganized labour by the National Commission on Enterprises in the Unorganized Sectors (NCEUS, 2007). The formal sector is defined as establishments which employ 10 or more workers and terms of employment and conditions of services are guided by existing labour laws and formal arrangements. However, there are informal workers engaged in organized formal establishments in cases where these workers are engaged as contract/casual/outsourced workers without written job contracts. Such informal workers in formal establishments don't have access to any form social security unlike their regular counterparts.

The size of the formal sector is increasingly shrinking and the informal sector is expanding as formal activities are disintegrating into informal ones. The total labour force in India was 484 million in 2017–18. Out of this, hardly 34 million are employed in the organized sector and the rest 93% are employed in the un-organized sector (Economic Survey, 2018–19). The share of the unorganized sector in NDP at current prices was over 60% (Economic Survey, 2018–19). This shows the significance of the informal sector in the economy.

6.3 COVID-19 Impact

The COVID-19 pandemic and subsequent nationwide lockdown have made the situation further precarious and complex. There has been huge job loss during the months of lockdown and partial lockdown. Unemployment rate was all-time high at 8.8% in March 2020 even before the lockdown was imposed (CMIE, 2020). It is now three times that level at 27%. This is an unprecedented crisis of very high magnitude. Growth rate has fallen to almost zero for the present quarter and overall economy suffered a decline to the tune of 23.9% in the first quarter of 2020–21 (CMIE, 2020). There is uncertainty about when are these things going to be revived.

The COVID-19-induced nationwide lockdown in India pushed the labour migrants back to the villages in extreme despair, joblessness, homelessness, hunger and mass migration (Ranjan, 2020). Innumerable migrant workers walked through national highways with their kids manifesting the fault line of our society. According to a statement of Labour and Employment Minister in Parliament on 14th September 2020, COVID-19–induced lockdown led to reverse migration of 10 million workers (Sharma, 2020). Further, on 15 September 2020, the Minister stated in Parliament that there is no data available on loss of lives and jobs due to pandemic (Nath, 2020).

6.4 Informal Workers and Labour Law

Different kinds of employment are considered within informal work, including self-employment and wage employment. Self-employment includes employment in unregistered or small enterprises that includes own account workers and unpaid family workers. Wage employment is characterized by informal jobs without social protection in both informal and formal enterprises. (Chen, 2006).

One of the basic reasons why informal workers are outside the basic legislative protection is that in informal work arrangement is characterized by an ambiguous 'employer-employee' relationship. Narrowly defined employer-employee relation segregates formal and informal workers. There are layers of intermediaries between the employer and workers in the form of contractors and sub-contractors. For example, in the construction sector, workers are mostly employed through contractors. There are also a number of sub-contractors under these contractors. Even formal employers are increasingly putting out a large number of jobs through a process of sub-contracting to small firms or home-based workers. Such workers may get few labour rights from the principal employers but lack many other benefits that would accrue to a 'permanent' formal worker. Self-employed workers are primarily workers who failed to get wage employment and include own-account workers employed in their own informal enterprises that do not hire outside workers and mostly use unpaid family members as workers. India has a large share of self-employment workers. Own account workers account for a substantial share of this. About 52% of informal workers in India are self-employed (NCEUS, 2007).

Majority of labour laws do not apply to informal workers. A section of informal workers finds it difficult to get the recognition as workers like domestic workers and home-based workers. Establishment of employer-employee relation becomes basis of labour law protection in India. Almost all the labour laws have been enacted on the premise that there exists employer-employee relation. In case of self-employed informal workers such relation is non-existent or at best ambiguous as there exists layers of intermediaries. In case of informal worker in wage employment too, employer-employee relation is hazy is most cases and in occasions where it is relatively apparent, those mostly do not satisfy the threshold criteria. Most of the labour laws in India apply to establishments which employ ten or more workers. Small enterprises in the informal sector mostly employ less than ten workers.

Thus, by nature of construct, a person is recognized as employee by the contract of employment. Legal protection is available for contract employees. Extending the definition to those who are self-employed or difficult to identify the principal employer or enterprise is challenging. One of the challenges has been to extend the definition of employee to those who are not directly employed by the principal employer or user enterprise and also to extend the definition to those who appear self-employed but show characteristics of wage employment. Such self-employed persons who share 'employee-like' characteristics are sought to be brought within the ambit of legislative protection and regulation of working conditions.

In addition, the recently enacted Unorganised Workers Social Security Act, 2008 has broadened the definition of unorganized workers. The unorganized would include the self-employed so that the basic social security can be ensured. Though the Act considers informal workers in its preview it does not guarantee their position same as their formal counterparts. Most of the labour laws have minimum threshold in terms of number of employees engaged in the establishments. Workers in the informal sector mostly do not fulfil this minimum threshold criterion. Some of the important labour laws and their threshold criterion are discussed below.

Payment of Wages 1936 is an important piece legislation which is applicable to factories, mines, and plantations. These all are establishments in the organized sector. Essentially Payment of Wages Act 1936 applies to workers in formal establishments. The crux of this legislation is payment of wages within the given wage period and prevention of unauthorized deduction. This Act prohibits irregular wage payment. This issue is relevant in the prevailing COVID-19 pandemic context as wages are not paid regularly during the lockdown. There are instances of significant cut in wages without assigning any reasons. For example, in jute mills in the State of West Bengal did not pay wages during the period of lockdown. It was treated as no-work no-pay basis. Remedial measures could have been initiated under this Act but that was limited to formal workers in formal establishments only.

During the pandemic-induced lockdown, Government made an appeal to employers not to retrench workers and instructed to pay wages. The legal justification behind such appeal lies in certain provisions of industrial dispute act 1947. There are sections which provide for exigencies like pandemic when it is possible that workers are laid-off and paid wages half the normal wages. This is applicable when these establishments qualify as industry. Informal establishments do not satisfy this criterion and subsequently workers did not get this protection during the pandemic.

Factories Act 1948 lays down conditions of service and terms of employment for factory workers. But again, this is applicable in establishments which employ 20 or more workers and thus excludes the factories in the informal sector. Similar thing happens with the Contract Labour Act 1970. This piece of legislation provides certain protection to contract labour but threshold of minimum 20 workers lead to exclusion of informal workers.

Almost all the occupation-based welfare legislations like Building and Other Construction Workers Act 1996, Motor Transport Workers Act 1961, Mines Act 1952, Plantations Labour Act 1951, and Dock Workers Act 1948. have certain employee threshold attached to those. As a result, informal establishments in these occupations are outside protective welfare legislations. Almost the entire construction and transport workforce are informal but they hardly receive any social security or welfare from their employers. Construction workers spend their entire life in informality and they don't have access to institutional social security instruments like provident fund, medical facilities, and maternity benefit. During the pandemic-induced lockdown construction and transport workers lost livelihood in massive scale as these activities stopped completely (Dandekar & Ghai, 2020). As such workers did not had access to any form of legislative protection, they lost their livelihood without any compensation and suffered from lack of social security.

There is this Building and Other Construction Workers Welfare Board in every State under the Construction Workers' Welfare Act 1996. Welfare Board provides for certain social security and welfare benefits to registered construction workers. Such social security and other benefits are financed from cess collected from construction employers. To avail such benefits, construction workers must be registered beneficiaries. However, as most of the construction workers are inter-state migrant workers, they were not able to avail benefit in host states. Portability of registration and benefits are presently absent and that prevented construction workers from availing benefits from welfare boards.

Existing social security legislations apply to formal workers only. Employees' Provident fund is the primary social security instrument in India and this is governed by Employees Provident Fund Act 1952. This legislation is applicable to establishment employing 20 or more workers. This threshold of 10 workers essentially excludes workers in small enterprises (having 19 or less) from accessing institutional provident fund. Provident is kind of forced savings and there are both employees and employers' contribution at the rate of 12% to the fund and Government provides for reasonable high interest on the accumulated fund. Withdrawal from the fund is allowed in case of contingencies. During the COVID-19–induced lockdown, many employees in the organized sector who had access to institutional provident fund could survive because they could withdraw money from their provident fund account. However, informal sector workers could not avail such benefits. Even the threshold is calculated considering only regular permanent employees. An enterprise might have sizable number of workers, but the number of permanent workers is gradually declining over time as more and more contractual and casual workers are being employed. Thus, even when a large number of workers are apparently employed in an enterprise, it still might remain below the threshold level of 20 or more permanent workers and institutional provident fund would be inaccessible to many workers employed therein. In calculating the threshold of 20 workers only permanent workers are included.

Similar threshold exists in Employees State Insurance also. ESI Act 1948 is applicable to those establishments having ten or more workers. Thus, medical facility that is otherwise available to workers in the organized sector is not available to informal workers. Many informal workers fall into debt trap as they borrow to finance emergency medical expenses. Precious little savings that they could make is also exhausted in meeting medical expenditure in private medical centres.

Gratuity is also payable to workers in establishments employing ten or more workers. Thus, payment of gratuity as postulated in Payment of Gratuity Act 1972 is not applicable for the entire informal labour force.

Similar provisions exist in case of maternity benefit too. As per Maternity Benefit Act 1961, provisions of maternity benefit are applicable to workers in establishments having ten or more workers. Under this Act, in case of incidences of maternity, a women employee is entitled to 26 weeks of paid leave. Establishments having 50 or more women workers must provide creche facilities under this Act. There are several other facilities under this Act. However, all such facilities are for formal women employees. Informal women employees don't have access to maternity benefit. In other words, maternity benefit in all practical purposes is limited to miniscule of women employees in the formal sector.

In the recently formulated Social Security Code 2020 which is going to be implemented soon, all the above thresholds remain intact. Thus, exclusion of informal workers is perpetuated in the new scheme things too. This Code was passed during the pandemic itself. There are elements in the Code that try to incorporate certain social security instruments for informal workers but important universalization of social security is something that remains unfulfilled.

Two acts which provide certain legislative protection for inter-state migrant informal workers are Inter-State Migrant Workmen's Act 1979 and Minimum Wages Act 1948. However, there are severe enforcement issues with these two acts. These are discussed below.

6.5 Inter State Migrant Workers Act 1979

Migrant workers are part of the informal labour force. Last year, the entire informal migrant labour force suffered as they lost livelihood opportunities because economic activities came to a halt. At best, informal workers earn minimum wages which is just enough for subsistence. They can't save much and there is no job or social security. When lockdown was imposed last time, migrant workers lost jobs and could hardly survive beyond two weeks with their meagre saving. After a point, they could not stay any more as they were not in a position to pay house rent. Also, there was no guarantee when lockdown was going to be withdrawn. Employers mostly didn't provide any succour. Informal migrant workers didn't have options but to return back.

The issue of legal protection of inter-state migrant workers can be discussed in the present context. The most prominent legislation in this respect is the Inter-State Migrant Workers' Act 1979 (ISMW Act 1979). This act was enacted to regulate the condition of service of inter-state labourers. The act's purpose is to protect workers whose services are requisitioned outside their native states.

The interested workers are entitled to various additional allowances/provisions over and above what the general labour laws permit. These allowances are meant for suitable accommodation at the place of work and medical facilities, going back to their natives, and so on. It is visualized in the act that inter-state migrant workers are engaged only through contractors. There are recruiting agents in home state and contractors in host state. Both have to take approval in their respective states. There is an elaborate process regarding these types of documentations at both states.

The act mandates registration of all contractors who employs or employed five or more inter-state migrant workmen on any day of the preceding 12 months. All contractors registered under this act are supposed to furnish the details of workmen periodically and maintain their records. The act further mandates registration of all principal employers on whose premises inter-state workers are being employed by the contractors. Employers are to keep records of inter-state workers. This act also specifies the mechanism for distribution of wages under the supervision of representative of principal employer. This is to ensure payment of wages by stipulated amount. In this process, the principal employer is held responsible for any failure of contractor to make payment of wages and benefits.

6.6 Limitations of ISMW Act 1979

According to the 1991 census, approximately 20 million people moved to other states in search of work. According to census data from 2001, the number of inter-state migrants has doubled in a decade (from 1991 to 2001) to 40 million people. Around 80 million migrants are reported to be present at this time, with 40 million working in the construction business, 20 million as domestic workers, and 12 million working in illegal mining, also known as small-scale quarries (Dandekar & Ghai, 2020). The true number of inter-state workers is underestimated because the vast majority of such journeys are spontaneous and self-sponsored. Because the pattern of movement has altered dramatically over time, particularly after the deregulation of the economy in 1991, mapping inter-state migratory labour has become extremely complex. Inter-state migration patterns in the previous two decades have shifted due to changes in the labour market and increased informalization.

This ISMW Act of 1979 has a track record of poor implementation among states over the years. This cannot be entirely attributable to India's generally low enforcement of labour laws. There were other characteristics of this statute that made implementation even more challenging.

Section 12 of the ISMW Act of 1979 stipulates the duties of contractors. This section states that 'it shall be the duty of every contractor (a) to furnish such particulars and in such form as may be prescribed, to the specified authority in the State from which an inter-state migrant worker is recruited and in the State in which such workman is employed, within fifteen days of the date of recruitment, or, as the case may be, the date of employment, and where any change.; (b) to issue a pass book attached with a passport size photograph of the workman and stating in Hindi and English languages, and if the workman's language is not Hindi or English, also in the workman's language'.

If Section 12 had been followed in practise, we would have access to all information about inter-state migrant workers, at least in the majority of cases of wage employment. However, circumstances have changed dramatically, as have migration patterns. When the ISMW Act 1979 was implemented in the 1970s, the majority of inter-state migrations were handled by contractors. Contractors were present in both the home and destination states. The majority of migrations were escorted. However, the pattern of migration shifted later, and from the early 1990s, particularly with economic liberalization, workers have moved to neighbouring states on their own. Contractors' role has dwindled. There is no evidence of outmigration from the host countries. Migrant workers are employed in host countries in capacities other than contract labour. Even though they are hired on as contract workers, they are listed as local workers against their home addresses. The procedure stated in Section 12 of the ISMW Act of 1979 has become obsolete. The vast majority of workers travel on their own, without the assistance of contractors. Contractors exist in host countries, but they are not obligated to fulfil Sec 12 rules because migrant employees are engaged as local contract workers. In the process, migrant workers' identities are masked and disseminated in legal jargon.

The overall architecture of migration, as envisioned in the ISMW Act 1979, has undergone substantial changes over the years, and Section 12 of the ISMW Act 1979 has lost relevance in the process.

Along with it, the act's provisions for inter-state migrant workers' documentation and corresponding requirements for certain benefits fell out of use. The stipulations of the ISMW Act 1979 were extremely difficult to implement in both home and host states. As a result, inter-state migrant labourers are currently without any legal protection worth its name. This is due to both inadequate execution of existing legislation and major changes in the ways migration occurs in post-liberalized India.

The migration network operates through family members and close friends. Word of mouth is very essential. Contractors in home states, with the exception of a few well-established construction firms, play no significant role. Contractors in host countries hire these people as contract labour, but their migratory status remains ambiguous. A sizable proportion of such inter-state migrant workers are self-employed and involved in minor economic activity in cities. Employer-employee relations do not exist, and the ISMW Act of 1979 does not apply in such cases.

Migrants in the formal sector did not suffer as much because they had job security and sufficient funds to fall back on. Many of them were given the opportunity to work online, allowing them to work from home. Even if they were laid off, they were entitled to lay-off compensation under the Industrial Disputes Act of 1947. They also had access to some social security instruments like provident funds.

The point here is that a regular respectable employment will allow a person to survive a lockdown. An undocumented migrant worker cannot because he or she lacks access to appropriate working conditions and social protection. There are a substantial number of self-employed informal migrants, and there is no actual employer in circumstances where there are layers of middlemen. A nice working environment is unheard of in an informal workplace.

The sufferings of informal migrant workers during the shutdown can be related to the lack of suitable working conditions and a compensation mechanism. As a citizen of our country, you have the right to live and work wherever you want in the country.

Exigencies such as the COVID-19 epidemic and ensuing lockdown should not result in the distress conditions as witnessed during the lockdown in 2020. In terms of fundamental survival, a migrant's identity should not matter all that much. In this setting, the identity of a worker from the informal sector is critical. Migrants would not have returned if reasonable working conditions and compensation system were in place.

6.7 Minimum Wages Act 1948

The Minimum Wages Act, 1948 is one of the few labour laws that apply to the informal sector workers in India. This piece of legislation stipulates that workers are paid at least the minimum wages as fixed by the appropriate Government. In general, there are two ways of determination of wages and salaries. One way is through collective bargaining and another is through fixation of minimum wages with regard to workers engaged in different categories of employment. Usually, in the formal sector, wages and salaries are determined through collective bargaining. Collective bargaining can be bipartite as well as tripartite. If negotiation happen between employers' representatives and trade union representatives, that is known as bipartite collective bargaining. When State mediates and facilitates negotiation between employers' and trade union representatives, in that case it is called tripartite collecting bargaining. Another way of determination of wage is through fixation of minimum wages by the State. Advisory Committees are formed at both Centre and State levels. Outcome wage at the collective bargaining process is usually higher than corresponding wages determined through minimum wage fixation machinery. In majority of cases, wages that are agreed on in collective bargaining are monthly rated. In case of minimum wage fixation, wages are notified on a daily-rate basis on the pretext of working hours is limited to eight hours. Collective bargaining results in an agreement which remains valid for a definite period. When the period of existing agreement gets exhausted, a new agreement is arrived at through tripartite discussions involving all the three stakeholders.

The Minimum Wages Act of 1948, on the other hand, allows the appropriate Governments at the federal and state levels to set minimum wages for various scheduled employments within their respective domains for various time periods. The Act specifies the types of jobs for which minimum wages are required and is notified by the federal and state Governments, respectively. Only if there are more than 1,000 workers employed in a certain occupation in a given state can the state issue a minimum wage notification. Employments (also known as occupations) are added to the Schedule of Employment based on these criteria. Wages notified under the Minimum Wage Act are usually calculated on a daily basis. It's a form of subsistence income based on a family's daily calorie consumption plus a small allowance for additional requirements.

The Act requires that wages be revised every five years by the respective Governments. The basic wage and the variable dearness allowance, which is adjusted to the Consumer Price Index every six months, make up the fixed minimum wage. The minimum wage varies by state and by occupation. Within a state, there would be two types of minimum pay for a given job, as central and state minimum wages differ. Even for a specific job, there are three sorts of minimum wages: unskilled, semi-skilled, and skilled. The most basic subsistence salary is for unskilled workers, with a 10% premium for each level beyond that. The appropriate Government is entrusted with the authority to determine the hours of works for scheduled employments under the Minimum Wages Act.

6.8 Implementation of Minimum Wages Act

In India, the enforcement of labour regulations is generally lax. This is especially true in the case of the minimum wage statute. This is for a variety of reasons. When the current market wage is much lower than the stated minimum wage, enforcing the minimum wage becomes extremely difficult. This occurs when the labour supply vastly outnumbers the labour demand. Because there are so many unskilled workers out there, the market pay is under pressure. Farm's share of national income is decreasing, while manufacturing industries have been unable to absorb the surplus employees that have been liberated from agriculture. As a result, the rural labour market has a large reserve army of workers, and wages are on the decline. In such conditions, enforcing minimum wages is difficult because workers who are unable to find work at the prevailing minimum wage agree to work for less in order to earn at least something. For them, earning something is preferable to earning nothing.

In such situations, market realities take precedence over statutory limitations. Employers take advantage of the circumstance by paying workers less than the minimum wage. Because vulnerable workers do not come forward to testify, enforcement agencies have a tough time prosecuting employer. They are terrified of losing their meagre earnings. Minimum wage prosecution necessitates the submission of evidence demonstrating payment less than the minimum wage, as well as personal confirmation of the workers involved. Workers, on the other hand, are hesitant to speak up for fear of losing their employment and earnings. Employers are typically penalized for minor infractions such as failing to maintain registers, failing to submit returns and reports, and so on. As a result, in labour-surplus states, labour market imperatives make enforcing minimum wage laws extremely difficult.

It's not that minimum wages are purposefully set higher than market wages. As previously stated, the minimum wage is set at the basic subsistence level. When the labour market is skewed, market wages might fall to extremely low levels. This makes enforcing a minimum wage extremely difficult. The statutory minimum wage cannot fall to that abnormally low level because social reproduction of labour power would be adversely affected. The concept of a minimum wage is conceptually derived from the Keynesian downward rigidity of wages. Wages should not fall below that of subsistence. In most Indian states, this is in direct opposition to current labour market imperatives. Kerala is an outlier in that as wages prevailing at the market are more than double the minimum wage prescribed, owing to the state's labour scarcity (Dandekar & Khai, 2020).

In addition, there are other instances in which the Minimum Wage Act does not apply. Self-employment accounts for around half of the activity in the informal sector. The minimum wage laws will not apply in such instances. It would also be difficult to establish an employer-employee relationship in the case of certain wage jobs because there are layers of informal intermediaries in between. As a result, the applicability of the Minimum Wages Act in India is essentially confined to less than 20% of the workforce, with around 50% of the workforce engaged in self-employment and another 30% in casual employment (MoLE, 2017). In addition, newer types of work and vocations emerge over time, and there is a procedural delay in incorporating them within the act's employment schedule. According to a World of Work report published in 2013, only around 60% of wage earners in India in the mid-2000s were covered by minimum wage legislation, excluding public-sector workers.

In the evaluation studies on implementation of the Minimum Wages Act, 1948, done by the Labour Bureau under the Ministry of Labour & Employment, workers' lack of understanding of the Act was also recognized as a problem. The majority of workers in the informal sector are unaware that minimum wages that apply to them. Employers do take advantage of asymmetry in information.

6.9 Conclusions

During the pandemic-induced lockdown informal workers in India suffered a lot, particularly the migrants among those. A large number of such workers lost their livelihood and found it hard to survive. Those who were migrants faced certain additional problems as they were able to stay back at their places of work, were not in a position to access free rations Such sufferings of the informal workers got further aggravated as informal workers did not had access to protective labour legislation. Most of the social security provisions available at present are applicable to those workers in the organized sector and who have a clear employer-employee relationship. Informal workers lost livelihood and at the same time did not have access to social security instruments like provident fund. For labour laws to be inclusive, it is vital that informal workers with informal employment relationships are included. This means moving beyond the traditional conceptions of work which rely on stable employee-employer associations. A significant number of informal workers are self-employed and have no employer-employee relation. State must devise a strategy to provide legal protection and access to social security to such workers too.

Inter-State Migrant Workers did not get protection of existing protective legislation. Present act found to be inadequate to deal with present day realities. Migration architecture underwent significant changes during the last three decades. Such migrations are not contractor guided as postulated in ISMW Act 1979. Role of contractors and agents in migrations have declined and migrations are mostly distress migrations and happens on its own through closely held networks. Also inter-state migrant workers keep on moving from place to another across states in search of better livelihood opportunities. This phenomenon is described as footloose workers in literature and it is very difficult to document such migrations within the framework of ISMW Act 1979. Essentially it has become very difficult to capture the essence of contemporary migrations through the existing labour legislations and particularly through ISMW Act 1979. This particular piece of legislation needs radical overhaul to become relevant in the present context.

Overall, informal workers, particularly migrants, heavily suffered during the pandemic-induced lockdown as protective legislations were either non-existent or found ineffective. Most of the existing labour laws provided some protections to permanent workers in the organized sector. Workers in the unorganized sector lacked any meaningful legislative protection. Labour market dynamics also added to the distress. Huge excess supply of labour led to fall in market wages below that of minimum wage. Informal workers did not have the means to fall back upon during the period of crisis.

References

Aiyar, Y., Kapur, A., Mukhopadhyay, P., Naik, M., & Singh, A. (2020). Redesigning India's Social Protection Financing Architecture to meet the Challenge of COVID-19. Centre for Policy Research.

Chen (2006) Chen, M. (2006). Rethinking the Informal Economy: Linkages with the Formal Economy and the Formal Regulatory Environment. In B. Guha-Khasnobis, R. Kanbur, and E. Ostrom, eds., *Unlocking Human Potential: Concepts and Policies for Linking the Informal and Formal Sectors*. Oxford: Oxford University Press. 44–59.

CMIE (2020), Economic Outlook 2020, June, Centre for Monitoring Indian Economy Pvt. Ltd., Mumbai.

Dandekar, A., & Ghai, R. (2020). Migration and Reverse Migration in the Age of COVID-19. *Economic and Political Weekly*, 55, 28–31. Economic Survey 2018–19. Accessed on https://www.indiabudget.gov.in/budget2019-20/economicsurvey/index.php

International Labour Office (2002). Decent Work and the Informal Economy; Report of the Director- General; International Labour Conference, 90th Session; Report VI; International Labour Office, Geneva, 2002.

ILO (2013). The Informal Economy and Decent Work: A Policy Resource Guide Supporting Transitions to Formality. International Labour Office, Employment Policy Department – Geneva ILO 2013.

MoL&E. (2017). Report of the Working Group on "Labour Laws & Other Regulations" for the Twelve Five Year Plan (2012–17). Ministry of Labour and Employment.

MoL&E. (2019). Standing Committee on Labour Report. Ministry of Labour and Employment. Govt. of India.

NCEUS. (2007). Report on Conditions of Work and Promotion of Livelihoods in the Unorganised Sector. National Commission for Enterprises in the Unorganised Sector.

Nath, D. (14 September 2020). Govt. Has No Data of Migrant Workers' Death, Loss of Job. *The Hindu*. Accessed on 12 June 2021at https://www.thehindu.com/news/national/govt-has-no-data-of-migrant-workers-death-loss-of-job/article32600637.ece

Ranjan, R. (2021). Impact of COVID-19 on Migrant Labourers of India and China. *Critical Sociology*, 47(4–5), 721–726.

Sharma, Y. S. Labour Minister Gangwar Clarifies His Response on Migrant Workers in Parliament. *The Economic Times*. Accessed on 21 June 2021 at https://economictimes.indiatimes.com/news/economy/policy/labour-minister-gangwar-clarifies-his-response-on-migrant-labourers-in-parliament/articleshow/78142699.cms

7 MSMEs in India during Lock and Unlock Times

Policy Responses and Coping Strategies

Soumyadip Chattopadhyay and
Partha Pratim Sahu

7.1 The Context

COVID-19 and the subsequent lockdowns have halted almost all economic activities across the globe, including India and led to an unprecedented humanitarian crisis. India's economic outlook further appears to be bleak as the second wave of the pandemic trammelling the recovery processes which is evident from recent World Bank's estimated GDP growth forecast of 8.3% for the fiscal year starting April 2021 compared to its earlier estimate of 10.1% (The World Bank, 2021). The COVID-19 pandemic has not left any sectors of the economy. Although it started in big cities and urban areas, it has now penetrated into villages and hinterlands. The micro, small, and medium enterprises (MSME) sector – with a total of just over 63 million enterprises, contributing to over 110 million jobs and almost a third of India's GDP and about half of India's manufacturing output and exports – has been severely impacted by the COVID-19 and pandemic led lockdown (GoI, 2021b). The MSME sector is not only huge and heterogeneous, but also unevenly distributed across Indian states. States with higher share of the MSMEs have witnessed higher incidences of COVID-19 cases along with stringent lockdowns of longer duration and reverse migrations, derailing the economic activities of significant majority of the MSMEs and livelihood of the workers (RBI, 2020).

Many studies have documented severe impacts of COVID-19 on the MSMEs in terms of disruptions in supply chain, decrease in product demand, decrease in labour supply, loss of revenue, inadequate access to credit and in worst case scenario, closure of unit (Indrakumar, 2020; MSC, 2020; Ramaswamy, 2020; Sahu, 2020; ILO, 2021). Importantly, the characteristics of the enterprise and type of activities have influenced the severity of these impacts. Microenterprises and their workers, especially engaged on temporary basis, have been disproportionately hit (Bartik *et al.*, 2020; Sonobe *et al.*, 2021). Out of the total 63 million unincorporated MSMEs, 98% are micro and small enterprises and are also largely informal in terms of nature of business and relationship among the businesses and workers with a significant majority of the later without written job contract or access to social security (Pandey and Pillai, 2020).[1] Laying off

DOI: 10.4324/9781003226970-10

the workers on temporary or permanent basis, delayed or irregular wage payments and lack of access to any social safety nets have afflicted a body-blow to
their livelihood options (APU, 2021; ILO, 2021; Sonobe *et al.*, 2021). Sudden
loss of job or income has also caused mental anxiety and stress among both the
entrepreneurs and workers engaged in the MSME sector (GoI, 2021a). Few of
the highly labour-intensive sectors like gems and jewellery sector, leather sector,
man-made yarn and fibres sector along with lodging, tourism, airlines, retail
sector, steel, apparel, automotive sectors have borne the maximum impact of
COVID-19, resulting in significant job losses (GoI, 2021a).[2]

The present economic slowdown of the MSME sectors predates to *at least* two
important policy changes including the demonetization followed by introduction of Goods and Services Tax (GST) regime during 2016–17. In particular, the
competitiveness and liquidity situation of MSME sectors have worsened due to
decline in capital expansion and investment in the MSME during post demonetization phase and the unresponsive nature of GST to the unique business practices of MSMEs (Rathore and Khanna, 2021). On macroeconomic front, India's
GDP growth has been on downhill since 2017–18 with a decline in employment
and overall consumption expenditure largely in rural areas, leading to significant
demand contraction for the products of MSMEs prior to the beginning of the
deadly pandemic (Dhingra and Ghatak, 2021; ILO, 2021).[3] COVID-19 has
only made the environment more hostile for functioning of the MSMEs.

The ongoing second wave and the apprehension of third wave of the pandemic
have once again disrupted the resumption of economic activities by the MSMEs.
Problems of delayed payments, non-availability of the skilled workers and raw
materials, reverse migration and low financial resilience have been amplified and
instead of revival, the MSMEs have to struggle for their survival (GoI, 2021a).
In contrast, some studies reported better resilience of the MSMEs as reflected
through 11% decline in their businesses compared to the corresponding figure of 46% after the national lockdown on 2020, *albeit* their recovery to pre-
COVID-19 remains uncertain (*The Hindu*, 2021). Since March 24, 2020 when
nationwide lockdown was announced, we have witnessed many changes ranging
from ease in lockdown restrictions, improvements in markets, vaccination drive,
resumption in transport and logistics to return of migrant workers back to their
work destinations. A series of schemes and programmes were also announced
during the pandemic times both by state and central Governments focussing
on MSME. It is an appropriate time to revisit those policies and schemes and
analyse their effectiveness in terms of awareness and access and coping strategies
and their implications for reviving the MSMEs. The paper reviews survey-based
studies, Government reports, newspaper reports and uses available secondary
data. Following the introduction, Section 7.2 reviews all the schemes and programmes announced by the Central Government to revive the MSME sector.
Section 7.3 documents and discusses the initiatives and interventions undertaken by select state Governments. Section 7.4 analyses a series of possible and
plausible coping strategies undertaken at the enterprise level and also by the

workers. Section 7.5 presents key policy measures needed to address the challenges experienced by the MSME sector.

7.2 Policy Responses towards Restarting Businesses

Taking into account the impossible trade-off between savings lives and livelihoods, several countries have introduced various policies including stimulus packages and MSME specific policy measures (OECD, 2020).[4] To smoothen the capital flow and liquidity to the MSME sector in post-COVID-19 phase, the Central Government announced fiscal stimulus for the MSMEs as part of special economic package of ₹ 20 lakh crores in May 2020. Various schemes and packages announced by the Government of India and other agencies are compiled and presented in Table 7.1.

In addition, under the Pradhan Mantri Garib Kalyan Package (PMGKP) provision were made for free or increased ration and direct monthly cash transfer of ₹ 500 for three months to women Jan Dhan Account holders for the workers. However, these schemes have generated lukewarm response as significant percentage of enterprises did not avail the benefits either due to their ineligibility in accessing the schemes or due to insufficient demand creating enough disincentives for them (GoI, 2021a; ILO, 2021).[5] The definitional change of MSMEs based on twin criterion of investment size and turnover has coincided with COVID-19-induced virtual stagnation as well as future uncertainties of global and Indian economy. Enlargement of investment size limit, for example, from ₹ 25 lakh to ₹ one crore for micro enterprises, during this juncture of economic slowdown would likely to benefit bigger units more as they obtain the MSME status to avail benefits under Government schemes. Moreover, owing to the conditionality of enterprises already having an outstanding loan being eligible for collateral free loan at concessional rate, only 7% of total estimated MSMEs could borrow 20% of their outstanding credit in February 2020 (Ghosh, 2020). In fact, more than half of the micro enterprises reported their reliance on either their own capital or informal sources (Muralidharan *et al.*, 2021; Rathore and Khanna, 2021).[6] Limited reach of emergency assistance loans in reviving the MSMEs is evident from decline in MSMEs' share in total outstanding bank non-food credit from 5.58% in March 2019 to 4.72% in March 2020, with only marginal increase to 4.86% in June 2021 (RBI, 2021). Inadequate demand for product leading to lowering of production and thereby loss of employment and income during COVID-19 pandemic has stagnated the MSMEs, especially the micro enterprises. So, the enterprises have preferred not to borrow even the sanctioned amount. There has also been serious concern about translation of collateral free loans into non-performing assets. Table 7.2 reveals that under the pre-approved Guaranteed Emergency Credit Line Scheme, the three major public sector banks in India could disburse about 85% of the sanctioned loan. This is indicative of precautionary and prudent approach of the MSMEs in coping up with the uncertainties in economic recovery.

Table 7.1 Schemes and programmes announced by Government and other agencies during the pandemic for the MSME sector

Govt. of India/ Departments and other agencies	*Description*
1 Ministry of Finance, Ministry of MSME	- ₹ 3 lakh crores collateral free loan under ECLGS for businesses including MSMEs. - ₹ 20,000 crores Subordinate Debt for Stressed MSMEs. - ₹ 50,000 crores equity infusion through MSME Fund of Funds. - MSMEs have been redefined using twin criteria of investment in plant and machinery and annual turnover with increase in investment limit and elimination of distinction between manufacturing and service sectors. - Other measures for MSMEs include (i) e-market linkage for MSMEs, (ii) amendment to discontinue the provision of requirement of global tender in procuring goods and services worthy of less than ₹ 200 crores, (iii) provision for Employees Provident Fund (EPF) Support to business and organised workers as part of the Pradhan Mantri Garib Kalyan Package (PMGKP), (iv) reduction in Statutory Provident Fund (PF) contribution of both employer and employee from 12% to 10% for all establishments under EPFO for three months, (v) provision of tax reliefs to the MSME sector. - Introduction of CHAMPIONS, an online portal, to support the MSMEs in (a) accessing financial and no-financial inputs; (b) conceiving newer production opportunities and (c) redressing disputes.
2 Reserve Bank of India (RBI)	- Liquidity enhancement through reduction in cash-reserve ratio (CRR). - Rescheduling loan payment through moratorium for three months on payments of instalments and payments of interest on working capital facilities.
3 Small Industries Development Bank of India (SIDBI)	- SAFE (SIDBI Assistance to Facilitate Emergency response against coronavirus) Plus scheme has been introduced to supply emergency working capital against guaranteed Government purchase of products necessary for fighting the pandemic, with provision for revolving working capital term loans up to ₹. 100 lakhs. - SMILESIDBI – Make in India Soft Loan Fund for Micro Small and Medium Enterprises, to provide loan to the healthcare sector.
4 World Bank, India	- $750 Million Emergency Response Program for Micro, Small, and Medium Enterprises in India to improve the funding capacity of the NBFCs and Small Finance Banks (SFBs) and make them responsive to the urgent and disparate needs of the MSMEs.
5 Amazon India	- Reviving over 1 million entrepreneurs including artisans, weavers and women entrepreneurs through 'Stand for Handmade' scheme. - Strengthening market access and showcasing the produce of indigenous craftsmen through partnering with 22 Government Emporiums and five Government bodies.

Source: Compiled by authors.

Table 7.2 Status of credit schemes to the MSMEs by three public sector banks in India

		Sanction		Disbursement	
	Item	No of accounts	Amount (in INR Crores)	No of accounts	Amount (in INR Crores)
State Bank of India[a,d]	GECL-1	5,52,797	26,461.34	2,99,523	23,349.37
	GECL-2	362	3,650.83	240	2,251.89
	Total	5,53,159	30,112	2,99,763	25,601
Punjab National Bank[b]	GECL-1		11,272	1,78,775	10,075
	GECL-2		1,689	97	1,010
	Total		12,961	1,78,872	11,085
Bank of Baroda[c]	CGSSD	2207	24	799	12

Source: Government of India, 2021a.
a   As on 31.03.2021;
b   As on 23.03.2021;
c   As on 26.03.2021.
d   Credit is under the Working Capital Term Loan Scheme.
   GECL: Guaranteed Emergency Credit Line Scheme.
   CGSSD: Credit Guarantee Scheme for Sub-ordinate Debt.

Table 7.3 State of delayed payments to the MSMEs in India

	Number of		By close of month (In INR Crores)		
Month	Central ministries	CPSEs	Total dues	Cleared dues	Uncleared dues
May-20	25	79	2349.53	1787.89	561.64
Jun-20	25	86	2553.94	1905.11	648.83
Jul-20	30	108	4124.34	3155.16	969.18
Aug-20	26	104	3811.13	2954.48	856.65
Sep-20	25	105	4858.18	3814.44	1043.74
Oct-20	26	108	5124.13	4102.43	1021.7
Nov-20	26	110	5184.92	4279.67	905.25
Dec-20	25	82	5317.75	4364.57	953.18
Total[a]			33,323.92	26,363.75	6960.17

Source: Government of India, 2021a.
a   As on 11.01.2021.

In May 2020, as part of *Atmanirbhar Bharat Abhiyan* program, the Government promised to clear the dues of Ministries under Central Government and public sector enterprises (PSEs) to the MSMEs within a span of 45 days. Despite the announcement, securing timely payment from the Government and public sector undertakings for the products and services supplied has remained a major challenge for MSMEs. As on 11th January, 2021, the central ministries and central public sector enterprises (CPSUs) have yet to clear around 21% of total cumulative dues over May to December 2020 (Table 7.3). Importantly, the MSMEs selling their products to Government are relatively better-off as they have experienced lower cancellation of pre-booked orders (Rathore and Khanna, 2021). So, timely payment of dues could benefit them, especially the enterprises suffering from the dearth of working capital and facing difficulties in accessing loans.

Several studies also have documented that by the end of October 2020, about 70% of the enterprises had either restarted their onsite economic activities or resorted to online mode business operations (ILO, 2021). However, steep increase in the price of raw materials, especially steel, coupled with their irregular supply and, in some cases, requirement of full advance payment for procuring the raw materials has seriously hampered the prospect of restarting businesses (*The Hindu*, 2021). Absence of any concession or relaxation of power charges, even when unused, has only inflated the cost of production of the MSMEs (*The Financial Express*, 2021). In Maharashtra, as part of adherence to the standard operation procedure, MSMEs have incurred expenditure on routine RTPCR test for all workers, maintenance of hygiene in workplaces and so on. Product price, in many instances, have not matched the production cost as the enterprises are being contracted to sell their product at old rates (*The Hindu*, 2021). Even, there has been lack of clarity on the type of enterprises that can resume production and their scale of operation (Money Control, 2021). Moreover, requirements of myriad charges and fees – for example, consent fee based on the gross fixed asset values of the enterprises or double licenses (trade licenses from city Government and factory license from state Government department) have continued to financially stress the MSME manufacturing units in Tamil Nadu (*The Hindu*, 2021). Although gradual opening up of economy could improve the demand for the product, the above-mentioned factors have made the business environment for the MSMEs unfavourable in foreseeable future.

Regarding the impacts of the initiatives as listed in Table 7.1, concerns may also be raised, first, in terms of their adequacy in addressing diverse challenges that can be attributed to heterogenous character of the MSMEs and, second, in terms of availability of institutional mechanisms to implement the schemes as well as monitor their impacts. The available literature indicates bank centric nature of the schemes and absence of adequate clarity among both the implementers and intended beneficiaries (Sahu, 2020). Schemes have remained oblivious to the structural constraints of MSME financing and presupposed smooth delivery of the credit/loan facilities. Irrespective of schemes and policies, MSMEs, especially the micro enterprises, generally disfavour accessing the formal financial institutions for credit/loan support. On account of absence of any records on banking or loan transactions, such institutions apprehend about loan repayment ability of the MSMEs. Although credit is fully backed up by Government guarantee, risk-averse bankers may not consider extending loan benefits to all MSMEs as financially prudent enough (Sahu, 2020). Eligible enterprises were also unsure about repayments terms and conditions of banks after the expiry of moratorium period. Further, amid the uncertainties over economic recovery and ensuant revival of demand, no enterprise would be willing to borrow to start or continue production and businesses (Ghosh, 2020; Sahu, 2020; APU, 2021).

Like many other Government schemes and programmes, the intended beneficiaries are not aware of these schemes and those who are aware are not able to access because of complicated procedural hurdles (ILO, 2021).[7] A survey of 388 MSMEs, mainly from north and central India, reveals their low awareness of

Government relief packages, especially among the microenterprises and thus entails the risks of such packages being unresponsive to the enterprises in the greatest need for the relief (Rathore and Khanna, 2021). Another survey of 2,083 women-led MSMEs documents that higher awareness about the relief package did not translate into higher application or availing of the same and, importantly, women preferred to avail the scheme of direct cash transfer (Bargotra *et al.*, 2021). Therefore, aggressive sensitization about these programmes and schemes as well as empowerment of the small and micro entrepreneurs by capacitating them with training and skill development are urgently needed. Equally important is to understand the needs and risk-taking capacities of the enterprises while designing the relief packages.

7.3 State Level Initiatives

Several state Governments in India have also announced general and MSME specific schemes and policies to complement the initiatives mentioned in the previous section. It is important to discuss state level interventions not only to draw lessons from them and but also to explore possibilities of replicating few in different contexts.[8]

7.3.1 *Uttar Pradesh*

The Uttar Pradesh (UP) Government has restructured the loan schemes for the MSMEs and disbursed a loan of ₹2505.58 crore to more than 31,542 MSMEs in July 2021 to facilitate the setting up of new units and expansion of existing units (*The Hindustan Times*, 2021). The 'UP COVID Emergency Financial Support Scheme' has been announced to promote new enterprises with minimum investment requirement of ₹20 lakh to start manufacturing COVID-19 medical equipment. It has the provision for a subsidy of 25% or ₹ 10 crores, whichever is lower, of the total expenditure and grant of all NOCs and permits within 72 hours under the UP MSME Act (*The Indian Express*, 2021). Under the One District One Product Programme (ODOP) – designed for creating product-specific traditional industrial hubs across the districts of Uttar Pradesh, Common Facility Centres have been conceived to provide entrepreneurs the production and marketing support including availability of raw material, quality improvement, environment, and energy conservation. MSME Sathi Mobile application has been introduced to help the entrepreneurs in communicating their problems and suggestions on operations of their enterprises to the Government and to ensure speedy resolution.

7.3.2 *West Bengal*

In July 2020, The West Bengal (WB) Government announced *Banglashree* scheme to provide fiscal incentives to the manufacturing MSMEs that started their operations after 1st April 2019 in the form of (a) one time subsidization of stamp duty and registration fees; registration for patents; quality compliance and setting up of plant and machinery and (b) continuation of subsidizing interest on term loan; electricity charges and state GST. In order to generate and incentivize self-employment in manufacturing, trading and service sectors for project cost up to ₹ 2 lakhs, *Karma Sathi Prakalpa* was announced in September 2020 with the provision of one-time maximum project subsidy of ₹ 25,000 and three-year interest subsidy of 50% for borrowers repaying on a timely basis (GoWB, 2021). A single window system under *Silpa Sathi* was initiated to provide detail information of state schemes, registration, application for state incentives schemes and monitoring. MSME specific mobile grievances redressal app, *Silpa Disha*, has been launched for timely and transparent solutions of the business problems faced by the entrepreneurs. The Department of MSME and Textile acted pro-actively to organize and engage the MSMEs in producing PPE kits and other essential items (GoWB, 2021). Necessary training and technical supports were provided to standardize the production process. This highlights the potential of some particular category of the MSMEs in adapting to new business opportunities, if proper handholding is given and, thus, requires careful replication of such initiatives at a greater scale.

7.3.3 Tamil Nadu

Tamil Nadu in March 2020 announced COVID Relief and Upliftment Scheme (CORUS) to support the capital expenditure and working capital needs of MSMEs with collateral-free loans. 1064 MSMEs received immediate loan of amount ₹ 125 crores by June 2020 (GoTN, 2020). Under the state Government's flagship NEEDS (New Entrepreneurship-cum-Enterprise Development Scheme) program, manufacturers of medical equipment/drugs related to pandemic were being prioritized for special incentives including 30% capital subsidy, 6% interest subsidy on working capital borrowed from formal s sources, waiving of stamp duty; and promise of buying back at least 50% of the produce at a negotiated price. Moreover, the state Government signed the memorandum of understanding (MoU) with 17 foreign investors for ₹ 15,128 crores to relocate the manufacturing enterprises which would likely to ensure the supply chain requirements of the MSMEs (RBI, 2020).

The State Government has planned to support the MSMEs by providing capital subsidy of ₹ 280 crore during the financial year 2021–22 with 60% of it earmarked for immediate release to all eligible yet excluded enterprises; proposing for disbursement of 5% interest subsidy received under CGTMSE and Technology Upgradation Scheme disbursed to MSME units; waiving of registration fees till December; extending the deadlines for numerous taxes and fees including payment of mortgage of deposit registration fee, payment of Road Tax for autorickshaws and taxis, payment of price of Small Industries Development Corporation Limited (SIDCO) plots; relaxing the requirements of legal licenses for MSMEs from several state Government departments; and provision of free COVID-19 vaccination to one Lakh employees associated with the MSMEs in

45+ age group (*The New Indian Express*, 2021a). An expert committee has also been constituted to chart out a recovery plan for the MSMEs by examining their infrastructure, ease of doing business and labour issues (*The Hindu*, 2021).

7.3.4 Punjab

The state Government of Punjab has emphasized on improving the ease of doing (small) business through rationalization, digitalization, and decriminalization of regulatory environment. In particular, the proposed reforms aim to reduce the number of pre-commissioning licenses and NOCs required for starting a new business by at least 20% and ensure availability of support infrastructure through provision of timely and hassle-free water, electricity and sewage connections. Moreover, a monthly data driven assessment mechanism is proposed to ensure timely delivery of key licenses and permits. The number labour register to be maintained by an entrepreneur was reduced from 60 to only 14 and removal of discretionary power of inspectors also features in the reform program to facilitate growth of the MSMEs (*The Times of India*, 2021).

7.3.5 Andhra Pradesh

In May 2020, a ₹1,110 crore restart package was announced by the state Government of Andhra Pradesh to cover nearly 98,000 enterprises employing more than 10 lakh workers. Guaranteed purchase of MSME products along with the promise of clearing payments within 45 days would likely to provide immediate liquidity to the MSMEs operating mostly on cash (Sahu, 2020).

It is interesting to note that although the financial health of many state Governments is not encouraging, they have come up with a wide range of schemes and programmes to help MSME to survive, revive and expand. In select states, efforts have also been made to provide job opportunities in the MSME sector to the returnee migrants, based on a skill mapping exercise. Such skill mapping exercise, especially of returned migrants have been initiated in Bihar, Uttar Pradesh, Odisha, and Jharkhand. Attempts are also being made to accommodate these workers in various rural development schemes, that is, National Rural Livelihoods Mission (NRLM), Mahatma Gandhi National Rural Employment Guarantee Act (MGNREGA) and the MSME sector.

7.4 Coping Strategies

Although the pandemic-led lockdown has thrown many challenges for the MSME sector, it has also reiterated the importance of local economy and entrepreneurs. The micro entrepreneurs including the self-help groups (SHGs) learnt to design and adopt a variety of coping strategies in response to pandemic. Household based and women led enterprises have provided the much-needed safety net to the families directly or indirectly related to the MSME sector. A variety of coping strategies including temporary (or permanent) lay-off, flexible working hours, selling at reduced margins, operating at below capacity utilization, enhanced focus on marketing and online sales, diversified products and services, exploring new and alterative supply chains, readjusting working hours, rescheduling of bank loans, mortgage and so on may have been adopted by the individual entrepreneurs.

7.4.1 Scaling Down Businesses and Change in Employment

As part of operational coping mechanisms, the MSMEs reduced their scale of operation and, even, closed down the business, either permanently or temporarily, with such impacts being more on microenterprises than small and medium sized enterprises (ILO, 2021; MSC, 2020; Rathore and Khanna, 2021; Sonobe *et al.*, 2021). Based on CMIE-CPHS data on self-employed workers, Jha and Abraham (2021) found that comparatively higher proportion of small business owners close down their businesses and resort to daily wage or casual work including farming. Announcement of lockdowns by various state Governments following the second wave of COVID-19, would likely to perpetuate the incidence of closure or scaling down.

7.4.2 Laying Off the Workers

Temporary or permanent laying off the workers has emerged as the predominant operational coping strategy with some variations among the size class, type of business and states. As compared to the microenterprises, large numbers of small and medium sized enterprises laid off their workers and are managing with only one or two workers (ILO, 2021; Jha and Abraham 2021). Incidence of laying off the workers is more among the manufacturing enterprises compared to the service enterprises (ILO, 2021). Among the three states covered in the ILO study (2021) – Maharashtra, Tamil Nadu, and Uttar Pradesh – laying off workers appeared to be least preferred strategy, especially for the microenterprises in Tamil Nadu. These enterprises instead have attempted to utilize disparate strategies including greater marketing efforts, online sales, continuing business activities at half of their actual capacity or on alternate days and so on. Workers, especially the skilled workers, are central to economic activities of the MSMEs and given the uncertainty as well costs of reengaging people, the owners negotiated with the workers in terms of reduced wage or roster-based work schedule (NOCCi, 2020).

7.4.3 Online Sales

The use of e-commerce and online sales has provided the MSMEs much required alternative marketing space to sale their products (ILO, 2021). A survey of MSMEs engaged in service-related activities and located in metro cities reported use of video conferencing and WhatsApp to run business activities, resulting in better revenue generation with the same being especially useful for

MSMEs in retail and educational services (Ramaswamy, 2020). During lockdowns and partial restrictions on economic activities, some of the enterprises used online platforms and apps to link with both the suppliers and the customers and payments are largely made on digital mode (MSC, 2020). However, the cost of making the enterprises e-commerce friendly, lack of technical capabilities and poor access to digital mode of payment have undermined the revival potential of MSMEs depending on new business arrangements (Ramaswamy, 2020). For example, lack of access to the accounting and software system among the employees at home has severely disrupted order and supplies of small businesses across India (*The Financial Express*, 2021). Inadequate access to modern technology is more severe in rural areas where a large section of MSEs are engaged in unorganized businesses (GoI, 2021a). Enterprises engaged in services and the men headed enterprises in urban areas are found to utilize these new arrangements more effectively (MSC, 2020; ILO, 2021).

7.4.4. Diversification of Products and Services

In response to demand uncertainties, in some cases, the enterprises diversified their products and services or strategized stocking of essential goods with relatively inelastic demand (MSC, 2020; ILO, 2021). The disruption in cash-flow during lockdown worsened the liquidity situation of the MSMEs, especially the microenterprises (Rathore and Khanna, 2021). Accordingly, the MSMEs either have compromised on the variety of goods or limited the credit sales or, even, in some cases charged higher prices to smoothen the cash flow (MSC, 2020). Some of the enterprises, mainly engaged in manufacturing activities, reported selling their products at average profit margin or reduced margin to moderate revenue loss (ILO, 2021). Deferment of business expansion plan till the recovery and stabilization of market has also featured as another important coping strategy by the MSMEs in Odisha (NOCCi, 2020).

7.4.5 Bank Loan and Borrowing

Disruption in economic activities inflicted significant loss of revenue for majority of the MSMEs. As part of financial coping mechanisms, the employers resorted to freeing up their savings or business cash reserves or borrowings to support business activities, with the risk of exhaustion of such funds sooner (MSC, 2020; ILO, 2021). For borrowing, both the employers and workers depended primarily on friends, relatives and other non-institutional sources of credit (ILO, 2021). Quite a significant proportion of enterprises postponed their loan repayment to cope up with the cash shortages in business and to meet the household chores. In spite of the Emergency Credit Line Guarantee Scheme (ECLGS), institutional borrowing, in practice, has failed to attain desired momentum for adequate liquidity infusion into the MSME sector (Ghosh, 2020). Nevertheless, the ECLGS has provided some financial cushions to the COVID-19 hit small and medium businesses as, for example, the beneficiaries reported the use of ECLGS

loan for meeting the price increase of raw materials in Tamil Nadu and for paying the GST and other dues in Maharashtra (*The Financial Express*, 2021; *The
Hindu*, 2021).

Following the loss of job or income, workers engaged in these enterprises
faced serious economic hardship. Workers were forced to work for longer hours
at reduced wages or with delayed wage payments, with such problem being severe
among the women workers (GoI, 2021a; ILO, 2021). In the absence of alternative employment opportunities, worker continued to work under unfavourable
working conditions. The employers provided little support to the workers as
they themselves were hard hit by COVID-19 (ILO, 2021). Workers managed
their livelihoods initially by drawing on their own savings or borrowing/support
from the friends or relatives or non-institutional sources. The coverage of the *PM
Garib Kalyan Yojana* package is far from universal and even the cash assistances
received under this package is grossly inadequate to compensate the workers
who experienced the income shock (APU, 2021). So, as part of their coping
strategies, the workers have returned to their native places and engaged in farming or working under Mahatma Gandhi National Rural Employment Guarantee
Scheme (MGNREGS) (ILO, 2021).

7.5 Concluding Remarks

The MSMEs play a critical role in employment generation in India. The pandemic induced lockdown and subsequent disruption in demand and cash economy; supply of raw materials and labour; and lack of access to affordable credit
have shattered the business operations of many MSMEs, especially the micro enterprises. Reimagining of the existing schemes and policies are urgently needed
to address the persistent as well as systematic challenges faced by the MSMEs,
especially the microenterprises, and their quick and robust revival so that they
create employment opportunities and contribute to economic recovery.

Data on MSME units and their employment are inadequate. The Udyam registration portal contains self-certified information on average employment, nature of business, investment, and turnover provided by 3,529,084 MSMEs (as
on 30th June 2021) while Goods and Services Tax Network covers businesses
with a turnover of more than ₹ 4 million. It is important to carry out national
level survey to collect data to understand better the pain points of the MSME
sector. The Odisha Government's recent announcement of state level MSME
census will be a welcome move for improved data system (*The New Indian Express*, 2021b). New comprehensive database could cover issues such as: to what
extent the unit is impacted by lockdown; what are the different constraints and
challenges faced by the unit; did the unit get benefits from any Government
schemes; nature of access to formal institutions in credit, technology, market,
skill and training during the pandemic times and so on. Equally challenging is to
estimate the number of MSME workers impacted by the COVID-19. Initiative
like *Pravasi Aayog* in Uttar Pradesh needs to be leveraged to develop database of
the MSME workers, making needs assessment and intervention more effective.

Although there is a wide and systematic network of formal institutions to provide support to the MSME sector and there are large number of schemes and programmes, a preponderant majority of enterprises, especially located in rural areas are not aware of these institutions and schemes. Therefore, there is a need to sensitize micro and small entrepreneurs about these formal institutions and the whole of range of programmes and schemes, which are meant for them. It is also equally important to simplify regulatory compliances, paper work and formalities to encourage these enterprises to come forward on their own to avail these schemes.

During the pandemic times, implementation of programmes and schemes were also badly affected. Towards creating an enabling ecosystem, interactive IT enabled digital platforms were created by various ministries and departments to provide easy access of financial and non-financial service needs of the entrepreneurs (Sahu, 2021).[9] While these initiatives are welcome moves but it may be worth noting that more than 90% of MSME units do not have access to computer or internet and they do not have the required skill to get benefited from these digital services Therefore, in addition to, sensitizing the MSME sector about these portals and platforms, adequate funding along with training and capacity development to navigate smoothly to a digital ecosystem is required. There is urgent need for subsidised digital connections, mobile handsets and other electronic gadgets for the rural micro and small entrepreneurs, especially for women and underprivileged entrepreneurs from SC and ST communities.

Access to shared services such as Common Facility Centres, Cluster Development Programmes, Farmer Producers Organization (FPO), and Producers Companies could be beneficial for micro and small enterprises to address the twin problem of supply chain disruptions and depressed market demand. MSMEs also need support in terms of new and innovative marketing plans and easy access to e-marketplaces for reaping the benefits of new found business opportunities in post-pandemic world.

During the pandemic times, the micro and small entrepreneurs and their workers have faced various psycho social problems including anxiety, low aspiration, and mental stress. Social welfare schemes and their structure need to be strengthened through, for example, increase in budgetary support for MGNREGA and public distribution system and introduction of urban job program, for MSME workers, especially targeting those who have lost employment during the pandemic period. In essence, understanding the exact needs and problems faced by the MSME sector and how they cope up with these issues is the key to successful design and implementation of all the schemes and policies.

Notes

1 In particular, nearly 62 million microenterprises with less than 20 workers do not come under the most formal regulation (Muralidharan et al., 2021).
2 From April to November 2020, commodities of gems and jewellery, leather and leather manufacturers and man-made yarn and fibres sectors recorded negative growth of 40.85, 33.25 and 27.78%, respectively (GoI, 2021a).

3 Average per capita consumption spending in India declined by 15% year on year basis by the end of 2020 (Dhingra and Ghatak, 2021).
4 For a detailed discussion on type of measures (such as wage subsidy; self-employment; social welfare schemes; exemptions or deferments of income tax, indirect tax, local tax; debt moratorium, loan guarantees, direct loan to SMEs; innovative marketing, digitalization, training and capacity building) see OECD (2020).
5 Several studies have highlighted poor coverage and inadequacy of PMGKP in addressing the economic distress of the workers (APU, 2021).
6 As per the Economic Census 2013, more than 81% of MSMEs are self-financed while only 7% of them accessed funds from formal institutions and Government sources.
7 The ILO survey carried out in 3 states (Uttar Pradesh, Tamil Nadu, and Maharashtra) found that 60% of surveyed enterprises did not access or obtain any support. Even, among them many were unaware or unsure about getting the support (ILO, 2021).
8 Selected states in this chapter account for 44% of the MSMEs in India (GoI, 2020).
9 For instance, a series of IT enabled portals have been maintained by Ministry of MSME, such as MSME 'Sambandh' to monitor the public procurement policy; MSME 'Samadhaan' to address the grievances related to delayed payments and MSME Idea Portal to offer a bank of schemes, ideas, innovations and research.

References

Azim Premji University (APU). (2021). Reviving employment and livelihoods in India: COVID-19 and After. Confederation of Indian Industry. February, 25.
Bargotra, N., Bhatotia, K., Karthick, M.P., and Narasimhan, M. (2021). How did India's women enterprises fare during the COVID-19 lockdown? *Economic and Political Weekly*, Vol. 56, No. 19, May 8. (https://www.epw.in/engage/article/how-did-indias-women-enterprises-fare-during-covid). (Accessed on 28th July 2021).
Bartik, A. W., Bertrand. M., Cullen. Z. B., Glaeser. E. L., Luca. M., and Stanton. C.T. (2020). How are small businesses adjusting to covid-19? Early evidence from a survey. *National Bureau of Economic Research (No. w26989)*.
Dhingra. S. and Ghatak. M. (2021). How has COVID-19 affected India's economy? (https://www.economicsobservatory.com/how-has-covid-19-affected-indias-economy). (Accessed on 28th July 2021).
Ghosh, S. (2020). Examining the COVID-19 relief package for MSMEs. *Economic and Political Weekly*. Vol. LV, No. 20. May 30: 10–12.
Government of India. (2020). Annual Report 2020–21. Ministry of Micro Small and Medium Enterprises. New Delhi.
Government of India. (2021a). Impact of COVID-19 pandemic on MSME sector and mitigation strategy adopted to counter it. Parliament of India, Rajya Sabha. Report No. 308. New Delhi.
Government of India. (2021b). Contribution of MSMEs to GDP. (https://www.pib.gov.in/PressReleasePage.aspx?PRID=1744032). (Accessed on 9th August 2021).
Government of Tamil Nadu. (2020). Press Release No. 447, June 25.
Government of West Bengal. (2021). Economic Review 2020–21. Department of Planning and Statistics. Kolkata.
Indrakumar, D. (2020). COVID-19 and its impact on micro small and medium enterprises in India. *Manpower Journal*. Vol. LIV, No. 3&4. July-December: 75–88.
International Labour Organization. (2021). Situation analysis on the COVID-19 pandemic's impact on enterprises and workers in the formal and informal economy in India. New Delhi.

Jha, M. and Abraham, R. (2021). Reading between pandemics economic shockwaves among worst hit are our teachers and small business owners. (https://timesofindia.indiatimes.com/blogs/toi-edit-page/reading-between-pandemics-economic-shockwaves-among-worst-hit-are-our-teachers-and-small-business-owners/). (Accessed on 28th July 2021).

Micro Save Consulting. (2020). Impact of COVID-19 pandemic on micro, small and medium enterprises (MSMEs) India Report. June.

Money Control. (2021). MSME associations in Maharashtra oppose lockdown, seek clarity on units that can operate. (https://www.moneycontrol.com/news/trends/msme-associations-in-maharashtra-oppose-lockdown-seek-clarity-on-units-that-can-operate-6771661.html). (Accessed on 8th August 2021).

Muralidharan, T., Paul, B., and Basole, A. (2021). Creating Udyog Sahayak Enterprises Network (USENET) for employment generation and scale-up in the MSME sector. Proposal developed for the Working Group of Ministers (WGoM) on Employment and Skill Generation. Government of India. (https://cse.azimpremjiuniversity.edu.in/wp-content/uploads/2021/01/USENET_Report_Final_for_Release.pdf). (Accessed on 30th July 2021).

North Odisha Chamber of Commerce and Industry. (2020). Impact of COVID-19 on MSMEs. White Paper. (http://nocci.in/Impact%20of%20Covid%2019%20on%20MSMEs.pdf). (Accessed on 28th July 2021).

OECD. (2020). Coronavirus (COVID-19): SME policy responses. (https://read.oecd-ilibrary.org/view/?ref=119_119680-di6h3qgi4x&title=Covid-19_SME_Policy_Responses&_ga=2.100275355.443141381.1629739846-1440813790.1627568025). (Accessed on 28th July 2021).

Pandey, R. and Pillai, A. (2020). COVID-19 and MSMEs: the 'identification' problem. (https://www.ideasforindia.in/topics/macroeconomics/covid-19-and-the-msme-sector-the-identification-problem.html). (Accessed on 27th July 2021).

Ramaswamy, K.V. (2020). Impact of COVID-19: micro, small and medium enterprises (MSMEs) in India pandemic shock of COVID-19 and policy response: A bird's eye view. In C. Choongjae (ed.) *Crisis and Fragility: Economic Impact of Covid-19 and Policy Responses*, KIEP Visiting Scholars Program. pp. 159–171.

Rathore, U. and Khanna, S. (2021). Impact of COVID-19 on MSMEs evidence from a primary firm survey in India. *Economic and Political Weekly*. Vol. LVI, No. 24. June 12: 28–38.

Reserve Bank of India. (2020). COVID-19 and its spatial dimension in India. (https://rbidocs.rbi.org.in/rdocs/Publications/PDFs/03CH_271020206C458AE369944258A62779FF5A2F5362.PDF). (Accessed on 28th July 2021).

Reserve Bank of India. (2021). Press releases. (https://rbi.org.in/Scripts/BS_PressReleaseDisplay.aspx?prid=51979). (Accessed on 20th August 2021).

Sahu, P. P. (2020). COVID-19 pandemic-led lockdown and MSME sector in India: towards a revival strategy. In C. Choongjae (ed.) *Crisis and Fragility: Economic Impact of Covid-19 and Policy Responses*, KIEP Visiting Scholars Program, pp. 145–156.

Sahu, P. P. (2021). Developing sustainable rural enterprise. *Kurukshetra*, July 2021, pp. 37–42.

Sonobe, T., Takeda, A., Yoshida, S., and Truong, H.T. (2021). The impacts of the COVID-19 pandemic on micro, small and medium enterprises in Asia and their digitalisation process. *ADBI Working Paper Series*. No. 1241. March.

The Financial Express. (2021). Maharashtra how MSMEs in India's economic hub are left COVID-ravaged even as they stare at worst phase now. (https://www.financialexpress.

com/industry/sme/msme-eodb-maharashtra-how-msmes-in-indias-economic-hub-are-left-covid-ravaged-even-as-they-stare-at-worst-phase-now/2232235/). (Accessed on 2nd August 2021).

The Hindu. (2021). Enterprise Limited an MSME memoir. (https://www.thehindu.com/news/national/tamil-nadu/enterprise-limited-an-msme-memoir/article33540545.ece). (Accessed on 28th July 2021).

The Hindustan Times. (2021). UP CM disburses INR 2505 cr loan to boost MSME impacted due to COVID-19. (https://www.hindustantimes.com/cities/lucknow-news/up-cm-disburses-rs-2-505-cr-loans-to-boost-msmes-impacted-due-to-covid19-101624460325467.html). (Accessed on 16th August 2021).

The Indian Express. (2021). Uttar Pradesh Cabinet approves 25% subsidy for new units making medical equipment. (https://indianexpress.com/article/cities/lucknow/uttar-pradesh-cabinet-approves-25-subsidy-for-new-units-making-medical-equipment-7316826/). (Accessed on 16th August 2021).

The New Indian Express. (2021a). TN govt gives breather to MSME sector in state. (https://www.newindianexpress.com/states/tamil-nadu/2021/may/12/tn-govt-gives-breather-to-msme-sector-in-state-2301428.html). (Accessed on 16th August 2021).

The New Indian Express. (2021b). Odisha plans MSME census to revitalise the ailing sector (https://www.newindianexpress.com/cities/bhubaneswar/2021/jun/28/odisha-plans-msme-census-to-revitalise-the-ailing-sector-2322479.html). (Accessed on 31st July 2021).

The Times of India. (2021). Punjab reforms in MSME sector to reduce regulatory burden. (https://timesofindia.indiatimes.com/city/chandigarh/reforms-in-msme-sector-to-reduce-regulatory-burden/articleshow/82091789.cms). (Accessed on 16th August 2021).

The World Bank. (2021). Overview. (https://www.worldbank.org/en/country/india/overview). (Accessed on 9th August 2021).

8 The Impact of the COVID-19 Pandemic on Domestic Workers in India

Amrita Ghatak and Kingshuk Sarkar

8.1 Introduction

In India, domestic workers mainly come from backward and relatively marginalized communities. Domestic work is not only informal in characteristics; it is also often a precarious occupation that is undervalued, underpaid and poorly regulated with very little recognition in legislation or policy. Like other workers in the informal sector, domestic workers were also severely impacted by the national lockdown enforced in March 2020 owing to complete loss or limited options of livelihood. The pandemic has exacerbated the pre-existing issues and challenges for workers in the domestic workspace.

One of the main consequences has been the reduction of working hours or loss of job resulting from fear and restricted mobility due to confinement measures during lockdown (Ghosh, 2020). After three months of lockdown in India their job-insecurity is further intensified both in terms of availability and securing deserving wages. Most of the gated communities in cities have put unreasonable restrictions on the movement of domestic workers (Ghosh, 2020) and adopted extra-constitutional measures to prevent even willing households from engaging domestic workers going beyond the Government of India guidelines. The measures by gated communities forming middle and upper middle class of the society reflect their magnified anxieties and insecurities in allowing domestic workers into their house premises. This study relies on the local definition of 'middleness' and moralized meanings ascribed to it.

Given this scenario, this chapter looks into the impact of COVID-19 pandemic–induced lockdown on domestic workers; how middle class employers perceive domestic workers and how their perceptions influence the status of employment, wages and working conditions as well as the employer-employee relationships in times of COVID-19 pandemic in two cities namely Ahmedabad and Kolkata in order to generalize the findings in pan India context.

8.2 Impact of Lockdown

During lockdown in the first phase majority of employers instructed their domestic workers to stay home and not to report at work. They paid the salaries

DOI: 10.4324/9781003226970-11

through bank transfer and in some cases domestic workers came in person to collect salaries from the doorstep. These domestic employers (mostly belonging to the middle income segment of the population and herein henceforth refereed as middle class) did pay salaries to their domestic workers during initial period of one to two months of the lockdown last year notwithstanding the fact that domestic workers could not report at work.

When unlock process started in June, domestic workers started returning to work. But quite a few of them were not allowed to resume work as employers were apprehensive. Some of these employers kept on paying salary but the rest decided to discontinue domestic workers.

Some domestic workers who earlier commuted daily from villages to cities for work, started living in cities in low rent houses (group of workers living together and sharing the cost). Cost of commuting was too high in absence of suburban trains. Their employers also supported these workers by providing them with extra money and other help. Few employers gave additional money to their domestic workers to take care of increased travel cost and few gave money such that domestic workers can buy cycles.

Another common behaviour observed among the majority of employers is that they started employing singular domestic workers in cases where earlier they used to employ multiple domestic workers to do different types domestic work. Employers tried to minimize entry of outside persons in their homes and in the process shifted from multiple to single domestic workers. As a result, a substantial number of domestic workers lost their jobs. Also, some employers told that they curtailed working days from usual six to three days or asked domestic workers to work in alternative days.

Domestic employers too could better realize the precarious nature of domestic workers in the context of COVID-19 pandemic. A section of these employers tried to stand by their workers even in cases where households suffer loss in income because of pandemic. However, there is large number of cases where employers fired domestic workers during the initial stages of lockdown itself.

By the time, second wave hit our country and local lockdowns became the norm of the day, domestic workers again started losing jobs. Apartments or households in gated communities in cities put restrictions on entry of domestic workers. Even in cases where households were willing to let workers in, they were not allowed to do so. Also, a significant number of domestic workers lost livelihood as again public transport were off roads and they could not commute.

Employers too did not support their domestic workers this second time around. No work no pay was the predominant norm in the second wave. Also, learning from the experiences of previous lock downs, employers made alternative arrangements. A section of domestic workers already lost livelihood during lockdowns and subsequent time last year itself. Those who could preserve their jobs last year, suffered during the second wave. Lockdowns and fear of infection in successive years hit domestic workers hard who were already in a precarious condition reeling from last year's crisis.[1]

8.3 Middle Class Insecurity in India during COVID-19 Pandemic

The fear of infection has been manifested in a new form of untouchability particularly among the middle class in Indian cities (Ghatak and Sarkar, 2020b; Ghosh, 2020). In big cities such as Delhi and Mumbai, the class and trust divide has been evident among the urban middle class. For instance, most of the residential complexes either have barred the entry of domestic workers, or have imposed irrational conditions on their movement by prohibiting their access to elevator, benches, parks, etc. As Ghosh (2020) cites, a recent advertisement, now withdrawn, read "Are you allowing your maid to knead atta dough by hand", playing on fears of the maid's "dirty" or "infected" hands. Evidently, group of domestic workers in Mumbai was forced to hire a bus to Kolkata because housing colonies shut the doors on them (Ghosh, 2020).

Middle class has been an important historical and sociological category in the modern India. There is no unique consensus in defining the middle class. The middle class is defined generally in terms of both self-rated and instrumentalist approaches indicated by income or expenditure. The self-perceived status implies the self-rated feeling of middleness among people reflected also in their income and consumption levels. It is highly dependent on the socio-cultural factors that differ from one country to another. The instrumentalist approach brings attention to both absolute and relative middleness in terms of distribution of income or expenditure. While the absolute definition relies on the amount of disposable income or expenditure, the relative definition defines middle class as the share of the income or consumption relative to the rest of the population (Birdsall et al., 2000). As far as the absolute approach is concerned, the range of income/expenditure in order to define the middle class varies (Brandi and Büge, 2014). For instance, India's National Council of Applied Economics Research (NCAER) defines middle class as one with disposable income of Rs.200,000– Rs. 1,000,000. Banerjee and Duflo (2008) define middle class as one with disposable income of US$2–$10 per capita per day. Similarly, Ravallion (2009) used US$2–$13 as the threshold levels.

Despite having varied opinion with regard to definition of middle class, one common notion is that the thresholds to be used for the definition of the middle class should not include those just above the poverty line as these are the households who don't have any security. Or, in other words, these are the individuals who can fall below the poverty line in case of any negative shock and are therefore in a vulnerable position. Thus, security is one of the most important characteristics for defining a middle class (Bose and Chaudhuri, 2017).

The data in this study indicate that the employers belong to the middle class or upper middle class. Depending on our data, the middle class has been defined as one with monthly household income ranging between Rs.12,650/- and Rs. 280,000/-. It has been observed that post-globalization a process of homogenization took place with respect to preferences, attitudes and habits, implying that our sample, which is identified from metropolitan and big cities, is more or less a representative sample of the Indian middle class (Bose and Chaudhuri, 2017).

8.4 Lack of Data on Domestic Workers

Having no recognition in the occupation structure even within informal sector, there is a paucity of data on domestic workspace and workers. Official statistics reveal that there are 4.75 million domestic workers employed in India. At least 3 million of them are women. However, the more accurate number could be between 20 million to 80 million workers,[2] who are part of an informal and unregulated sector, obscured in private homes, not recognized as workers but rather as 'informal help'.

The Census 2001 data set reveals that there are around 6.7 million domestic workers in India. Another source, the National Sample Survey (NSSO, 61st round 2004–05) indicates that there are approximately 4.2 million domestic workers in India. Estimated on NSSO 68th round (2011–12), the most recent Government press release from January 2019 shows that the total number of domestic workers are 3.9 million[3] in India.

These estimates lack credibility since they conceal more than they actually reveal. These are survey data based on small sample. There are about 30 million middle-class households in India. Almost, all the middle-class households hire services of one domestic worker on an average. This vouches for at least 30 million domestic workers plus at least a few million domestic workers engaged in the rich families. Official figure of 4 million is grossly underestimated.[4]

8.5 Methodology

In order to understand the impacts of COVID-19 pandemic–induced lockdown on the domestic workers this study includes both workers and employers along with the NGOs from Ahmedabad and Kolkata. In absence of a large sample data the study follows a qualitative approach of research using the data collected through primary sources. Apart from the primary information, the study also refers to the secondary literature and data sources on the given subjects.

Interviews with employers are done online or over the phone during first phase of lockdown from March to June, 2020. Interviews with the NGOs are done using semi structured schedules over the phone and in person. Mainly qualitative approach has been followed while framing the questions in the interview schedules. The interview schedule has been used for the collection of the primary responses using a personal narrative approach focussing on various features of employment, expenditure, income, perceptions, and preferences with regard to domestic work. A total number of 131 employers are included in the study. It is observed that the employers belong to mainly middle class on the basis of their monthly income. The characteristic of middleness in terms of income and the employment status particularly among women are observed to be important factors in determining the entry of domestic help to the households or workspaces.

In line with the earlier studies (Bose and Chaudhuri, 2017; Ghatak and Sarkar, 2020a), the entire sample is based on areas in Ahmedabad and Kolkata forming a reasonably representative group of the middle class in Indian cities in terms of their responses, income and behaviour.

Interviews with domestic workers are also undertaken in the same manner over the phone, and in a few cases personal interviews. A semi-structure schedule is used to interview the workers in both Ahmedabad and Kolkata cities. A total number of 165 workers are interviewed, including 81 from Ahmedabad and 84 from Kolkata.

8.6 Characteristics of Domestic Workers in India

The "domestic work" is defined 'as the work performed in or for a household or households' and "domestic worker" means 'any person engaged in domestic work within an employment relationship'.[5] In India, domestic work is informal work which is characterized by absence of written contract, social security, conventional method of wage determination, and presence of multiple household employers, very little Government intervention and lack of decent work-environment. Domestic work itself is a distress livelihood option. It's a fall back option when no other option is available.

Since domestic works are not limited to any particular set of tasks within a household, it is not possible to define this occupation in terms of type of task. Rather, it is defined by the place of work, which is the household, a private domain. The 'private, familial domain' also implies that the state regulation is absent, thereby the standardization of wages and effective unionization are also limited. The concepts of decent work are difficult to apply in this sector owing to its wide variation in the nature and type of tasks. Thus, this sector relies on mainly the employer-employee relationships within the households.

Pragmatic intimacy or the individual negotiation within the private, personalised domain of the 'madam/sir–maid relationship' embodies not just the vulnerability of the domestic worker but also certain advantages based on 'mutual dependence and reciprocity'. This is especially so in the context of little or no social security and alternative employment options for the worker.

The overall degraded position of the domestic worker rides on the logic that she is contracting in the so-called private realm of social relations where the principles of 'civic' contract are 'fleeting' (Sen and Sengupta, 2016).[6]

8.7 Lack of Legal Protection for Domestic Workers

Although a few States have made efforts to formalize the domestic workspace by including the domestic work in the scheduled of employment and fixing minimum wages, there exists no welfare legislation for domestic workers in India. However, implementation still faces challenges, as conduct of inspection at domestic space remains ambiguous and household being the employer is yet to be legally defined. The workspace of domestic work is the household, which is explained in liberal theory as a space that should be free from state intervention making it difficult to include under the ambit of regulation. A holistic legislation, encompassing different aspects of domestic labour, needs to be enacted.

Devoid of legislative protection the domestic works operate through informal arrangements influenced by local social norms, customs, culture and practices. While the local norms and practices help in developing employer and employee relationship based on benevolence and loyalty, they also marginalize the workers. Since household unpaid tasks are mainly undertaken by women the domestic workers' tasks are often considered as the 'labour of love' and not the work that warrants regulation and full remuneration. Pragmatic intimacy forms the structure of interaction between household and domestic worker.

There are mainly two alleyways through which the process of estimation of minimum wages seems to be a complex and nuanced exercise. While one alley includes the complexity in terms of employment and types of task profiles, the other alleyway involves the cumbersome method of computation. As far as terms of employment are concerned domestic workers are hired on various terms depending on the number of hours, or type of tasks, or even the intensities of tasks. They are hired as part-time workers as well as live-in or whole time ones. The skill and time required to fulfil each task also differ from household to household. Wages are sometimes determined by the location of the employer's household. Since, domestic workers are employed by households of various socio-economic status, the perceived paying capacity of the employer itself plays crucial role in determining wages of the worker. Locality of the employer's household, is thus, a proxy indicator of the income level of the employer. Moreover, the wages are also influenced by the social characteristics such as caste, sub-caste and religion. In the absence of unions, the social capital of the domestic worker contributes to empower her and enhance her ability to bargain for higher wages. Nevertheless, payment of wages in kind in addition to cash is a common practice, making the computation of wages further cumbersome.

The method of calculating minimum wage involves fixation for time rate, which is not feasible in case of domestic works. The time rate is also a complex concept particularly because of the presence of multiple employers. Wages for specific type of work-done or the number of tasks-done may be one way of standardization, but given the variation in types of employment and nature of tasks as well as the possibility of negotiating better wages only the minimum wage floor may be standardized. For instance, no wage deduction or adjustment for food or provision of accommodation is generally observed for the live-in workers who are not entitled to avail any separate residential quarter (Sarkar, 2018).

Although legislative protection is limited, there are a number of efforts that are made in the recent past to include domestic work in the ambit of the law. For example, domestic workers have been included as a specific category of workers (with home as the workplace) in the Sexual Harassment of women at workplace (Prevention, Prohibition and Redressal) Act (2013), which provides legal standing of domestic work as an occupation at least to some extent. Unions in several States have started organizing domestic workers during recent past. For example, Parichiti in Kolkata (West Bengal) and Civic in Bengaluru (Karnataka) are engaged in organizing domestic workers in their decades during the last one decade or so. Domestic Workers Sector Skills Council has also been established under Ministry of Skills Development to enhance the skill of domestic workers and enable their career progression.

8.8 Wages, Employment and Working Conditions

The observation from Kolkata and Ahmedabad reveals that most domestic workers in our sample were paid for the month of March in 2020, since the lockdown was declared during the third week of the month. Despite repeated appeals from the Government in the media the employers in many cases stopped payment to domestic workers from April, 2020 onward. As a result, domestic workers find difficulties in receiving wages in April and thereafter. The loss of wages amounted to economic hardships that threatened their survival. Important here to highlight their other family members were also involved in the different segments of the informal sector experiencing loss of wages. Workers survived on loans and charities. While they depended largely on the informal money lenders for borrowing money to make the both ends meet, they also received relief from the civil society. But, many respondents reported that in a few months they found themselves in a debt trap by the end of September, 2020.

The employers are young adults with average level of education is PG degree and above, monthly average household income of Rs. 84,500/- in Kolkata and Rs. 100, 210/- in Ahmedabad. The average age of employers in Ahmedabad is 48 years, whereas in Kolkata it is 36 years (Table 8.1). The monthly per-capita income of employers ranges between Rs. 6,765/- and Rs. 150, 010/- with an average of Rs. 44, 225.53/-. One can expect that the attributes of employers who

Table 8.1 Employers' profile both from survey and in-depth interviews

City	Average Age	Average level of education	Monthly average income of household (in Rs.)	Percentage of responders experienced deduction in salaries due to pandemic	Average household size	Total number of respondent
Ahmedabad	48	PG and above (91.66%)	100210.53	26.32	2.94 (approx. 3)	70
Kolkata	36	PG and above (84.21%)	84500	25	4.66 (approx. 5)	61
Total	45	PG and above (87.10%)	97187.50	25.81	3.61 (approx. 4)	131

Source: Online primary survey, 2020.

belong to middle class and are young, educated adults with urban aspirations will have bearing on the employment of domestic workers by means of perceiving the risk of contagion through domestic workers, protecting their wages and working condition.

8.9 Case of Kolkata

The average income for domestic workers in February was about ₹7,000 in Kolkata. The discussions with domestic workers reveal that it dropped by 25% in March, and further by 60% in April. The participants in the discussion including both the PARICHITI volunteers and the workers over the phone reported that the wages for March were expected to be paid at a later date. However, they were uncertain about receiving the wages for April onward, ever. At least 28% workers reported no income from the month of April. Within a month period from April to May, there was a steep fall of average monthly household income by 45% from Rs. 7,000/- to Rs. 4,010/-.

With the relaxation of strict lockdown from June, the workers started resuming the work, but with great difficulties. The difficulties emerged from ambiguous guidelines regarding the lockdown issued by the Government combined with jeopardized public transport services and irrational imposition of restrictions by the residential complexes in the cities. On one hand, public transport services were dysfunctional; on the other hand the residents' welfare associations or employers prohibited the entry of domestic workers. Even when the workers in other occupations such as auto rickshaw drivers, plumbers, electricians, construction workers, etc., within the informal economy started functioning, domestic workers could not resume their works particularly because the employers were reluctant to allow them inside their homes. Employers were wary of workers owing to the possibility of workers using public transport facility and being employed by multiple households. While many workers lost their jobs permanently, others returned with lower wages or lower number of employers' households. Workers were found to be aware of the precautions to be taken with regard to COVID-19 infection.

As it was observed in an earlier study (Ghatak and Sarkar, 2019), women engaged in domestic work used to contribute to the stable source of their households' incomes and share the major parts of the regular essential expenses of the households. Their income was regular and shared at least 50% of the total household income in many cases. During the lockdown period many domestic workers are found to live on either their life-long savings, or borrowings, and relief from the civil society or personal networks. The average debt of the domestic workers' households amounts to Rs. 10,000/-. However, those who lost the job suffered from the high burden of debts. For instance, Maloti in Sonarpur area of Kolkata suffered from Rs. 70,500/- debt accrued from May, 2020 and reported on the day when we arranged for a discussion with her in the month of November in 2020. Undoubtedly, the impacts of the shocks of income loss and impending debts would be borne throughout the forthcoming months.

The interviews over the phone in Kolkata reveal that a domestic worker's household in Kolkata was able to survive on saving for 20 days on an average at the time when the lockdown started in March. Over 25% of domestic workers households had savings that provided for the daily expenses only for ten days. In addition, these households also deferred the dues toward rents and utilities for the first seven weeks of the lockdown. The pending utility bill itself amounted to be Rs. 6,500/- during those seven weeks' period.

Although relief programmes were conducted frequently a limited number of domestic workers (around 25%) received it as beneficiaries of the relief organized by the State. The gap in convergence of domestic workers as beneficiaries is observed in other relief initiative, too. For instance, there were only 27% domestic workers' households received any relief extended by either political leaders, police, or the Government, and a few (around 11%) received support from within the community. The cash transfers and food-grains support seemed to be the most urgent and critical forms of relief as the respondents reported in Kolkata.

The loss of job was such a prominent experience during the lockdown that it reported by at least 62% of the respondents in Kolkata. There are only a few (14%) domestic workers who were able to retain their jobs at pre-pandemic level. However, the loss of income was not associated with any reduction in their expenditure. For instance, at least 36% workers were staying in rental houses and faced difficulties in paying rents; 23% did not have ration cards. Hence they could not access the rations during this lockdown. It was also difficult to pay for education of the children. At least 66% domestic workers could not pay for their children's education.

Interviews also revealed that domestic workers experienced increased burden of unpaid work inside the household as most family members were in the house during the period of lockdown. However, when this increase in unpaid work was compared to household size, it was seen that this burden of unpaid work was experienced by women more in households which had fewer family members than those that had a larger group of people staying together.

Similarly, in terms of care work, the majority of respondents stated a significant increase in child care work. Again when compared to household size, it was seen that the burden of increased care work of all kinds including caring for the elderly, a sick relative or pets was experienced more by women in smaller households than those who lived in larger households.

Commuting is another important consideration for live-out domestic workers. Many daily commuters come to the city by train from villages which are comparatively close to the city. Even within the city, women travel by bus or auto rickshaws and many simply walk to work. Most domestic workers who live in Kolkata prefer to take jobs close to where they live so that they can walk to work and save money on transport. Once restrictions eased, women who walk to work found it easier to go back. Employers felt that it was safer to allow in workers who were not risking exposure to COVID-19 on buses or other modes of public transport.

It was evident from the interviews that domestic workers feel that they have to rely on their own resourcefulness to best take care of themselves and their families whether it is getting services from the state or getting their jobs back. The interviewees said that they had felt insecure during the lockdown, were worried about getting their jobs back and concerned about being paid wages for the time they couldn't work because of the lockdown. Most of the women we interviewed had suffered a loss in income and were worried about the future. There were uncertainties in the job market that affected them, as well as others in their families in different kinds of informal employment.

8.10 Case of Ahmedabad

The observation from Ahmedabad is also more or less in line with that from Kolkata. The impacts of lockdown have been manifested in various ways in the domestic workspace in Ahmedabad. In Ahmedabad, the average working wages received by domestic workers used to be higher compared to Kolkata (Ghatak and Sarkar, 2019). Once the lockdown started getting relaxed the employers started employing domestic workers again. But, our data reveal that at least 26% households in Ahmedabad and 17% households in Kolkata continue to prohibit the entry of domestic workers. Most households are found to employ part-time workers who work for less than six hours daily in one household and therefore are employed by multiple households for multiple tasks. However, a few households are also observed to employ full-time workers who work for at least six hours daily in one household and thus are employed by single household (Table 8.2).

In an earlier study it was observed that domestic workers generally work for at least 69 hours in a week, longer than the average hours of work-done in a week by workers in other occupations in the informal economy (Ghatak and Sarkar, 2020). The recent discussion with NGO/civil society organisation, namely, SAATH in December, 2020, indicates that the work-load has been further intensified due to restrictions imposed to contain the COVID-19 pandemic as the employers don't want to expose themselves to multiple workers on a daily basis. Thus, the task that earlier used to get distributed among two or three workers are now being performed by one worker. This is a more prominent feature of single employer households in which case a domestic worker is hired by one

Table 8.2 Employment of domestic workers and their wages

City	Percentage of respondents employing domestic workers at the time of survey	Percentage of full – time workers (at least 8 hours a day)	Percentage of part-time workers (less than 8 hours a day)	Average monthly wages paid to full time workers (Rs.)	Average monthly wages paid to part-time workers (Rs.)	Total number of respondents (employers)
Ahmedabad	73.68	26.09	73.91	11400	2665.79	70
Kolkata	83.33	13.33	86.66	8000	1692.31	61
Overall	77.42	19.35	64.51	9125	2270.31	131

Source: Online primary survey, 2020.

household for whole time and such workers also reside at the employers' place. Although their salaries are on the higher side compared to the prevailing wage rates for the full-time/live-in domestic workers, they are now subjected to much higher work-load compared to pre-lockdown scenarios in Ahmedabad, owing to the employer households' apathy to employ any daily commuter/part-time worker.

While the support rendered by employers towards domestic workers (Table 8.3) imply the advantages of 'pragmatic intimacy' during lockdown, the increased daily workload in the absence of other workers and presence of employers for the entire day imply the disadvantages of informal labour arrangement within the private sphere of a household. The negotiation between formal arrangements of "labour" versus notion of domestic work as an act of care and love is thus observed even in the cases wherein the workers are employed through some agencies based on written agreements.

It is important here to highlight that the employment through written agreement with the help of an agency is not a common practice in both the cities. In absence of legal recognition of domestic workers as "labour" the NGOs and trade unions such as SAATH and SEWA function successfully in this domestic workspace only by providing training to the workers and bridging the gaps between employers and employees in the domestic workspace through actions, negotiations and mobilisation of potential workers.

Table 8.3 Support provided by employers during lockdown

Cities	Provided salary (in percentage)	Provided additional support (Mask, sanitizer, soap, etc.) (in percentage)	Didn't provide any support (salary or others) (in percentage)	Total number of respondents
Ahmedabad	26.32	73.68	26.32	70
Kolkata	16.66	66.66	33.33	61
Overall	22.58	70.96	29.03	131
NGOs' opinion	The support from employers varies between 8 days in the month of March to three months until June 2020	Yes, the NGO provided one set of each item including mask and sanitizer. However, some employers provide those items later on. A few employers don't provide any such item.	Yes, there are a small number of such employers.	The NGO is aware of total 445 employers in Ahmedabad and Kolkata

Source: Online primary survey, 2020.

The observation in Ahmedabad and Kolkata shows that the support from employers although evident in many cases, they are largely inadequate particularly due to the long duration of lockdown period. As the lockdown doesn't allow domestic workers to reach their workplaces, they were essentially absent from their workplaces for months. The discussion with SAATH and SEWA reveal that many employers paid the salary to the workers despite no service received from them for one month but as the lockdown continued for over a month, employers gradually stopped paying salaries to domestic workers implying the limitations of 'pragmatic intimacy'.

The prolonged absence because of lockdown combined with the fear of contagion not only leads to deduction of wages, but also the loss of jobs of domestic workers in many instances. Although employers supported their domestic helps in terms of monetary and non-monetary benefits only for a month or two, after the month of June, all kinds of support towards domestic employees subsided and stopped.

8.11 Employers' Perceptions and Fear of Contagion

With a few exceptions the findings from Ahmedabad and Kolkata reveal that there is deterioration in terms of employment and employer-employee relationship. Domestic workers lost jobs in certain cases because of two reasons. First, restriction on movements induced by lockdown prevented domestic workers to reach employers' home in cities. Second, some employers stopped engaging domestic workers because of fear of getting infected. Evidently, 26 respondents in the survey of 131 employers from Ahmedabad and Kolkata city reported to have stopped employing domestic workers ever since the pandemic has set in. The NGOs have reported a drop of 87 percentage points in the number of employers who used to employ domestic workers via them in cities of Ahmedabad and Kolkata.

Most of the gated communities in cities have imposed unreasonable restrictions on the movement of domestic workers and adopted measures to prevent even willing households from engaging domestic workers going beyond the Govt. of India guidelines. Hence, domestic workers still struggle to retain their employment in the cities (Table 8.4). There are over 80% of the respondents who prohibit the entry of domestic workers to their household premises or residential apartment premises. There are at least 19% of the households that want to restrict domestic workers even after the lockdown is lifted.

In order to examine the extent of perception about the risk of exposure to contagion through domestic workers this study relies on the self-reported perceptions of the respondents (employers) about the possibility of contacting the contagion by allowing domestic workers inside their households. Their responses were recorded on a vignette scale of one to ten wherein one represents 'No additional exposure compared to any other daily activities' and 10 represents 'Severely high exposure compared to other daily activities'. It is observed that on an average the respondents believe that entry to domestic workers is moderately

Table 8.4 Entry restrictions imposed on domestic workers

City/group	Entry barrier imposed by the respondent at the time of survey (in percentage)	Entry barrier imposed by respondents or others during the lockdown? (in percentage)	Entry barrier imposed by the respondent or others after the lockdown started getting relaxed from and partially withdrawn from August? (in percentage)	Restriction imposed on domestic workers other than wearing masks, using sanitizers, washing hands, and maintaining physical distances at present? (in percentage)
Ahmedabad	Yes (15.78)	Yes (89.47)	Yes (52.63)	Yes (5.26)
Kolkata	Yes (3.11)	Yes (83.33)	Yes (8.33)	Yes (8.33)
Overall	Yes (9.67)	Yes (83.87)	Yes (19.35)	Yes (9.67)
NGOs opinion	Yes, still, as on the date of survey in December there are building societies that bar domestic workers commuting daily.	Yes, no residential societies allowed domestic workers commuting daily. But they allowed live-in workers based on medical report of COVID-19 infection.	Yes, there are many building societies and employers didn't allow entry of daily commuting domestic workers. But they allowed live-in workers based on medical report of COVID-19 infection.	Yes, the daily commuting workers are asked to change clothes. The live-in workers are not allowed to go out.

Source: Online primary survey, 2021. Percentages are in the parentheses.

risky in terms of contacting the contagion. While nobody believes that the entry of domestic workers can expose severely to the contagion compared to any other daily activity, around 13% of the respondents perceive that the presence of domestic worker in the household could be highly contagious (Table 8.5).

Owing to the fear of exposure it is also observed that many employers in the middle and upper middle class tend to rely on the machines and automation in getting the households' tasks done. At least 39% respondents in Ahmedabad and 21% in Kolkata have reported to prefer machines over the manual domestic help in getting the clothes washed, utensils cleaned and floor mopped.

Over 29% of the households that earlier used to employ domestic workers have now stopped it due to COVID-19 pandemic. At least 36% of the respondents have stopped appointing domestic workers in Ahmedabad even after the lockdown is relaxed whereas there are 11% households that have stopped hiring domestic workers during the same period in Kolkata. Although there are around 26% employer households in the survey experienced deduction in monthly income due to lockdown measures, it is the overall pre-existing economic status of the household that influences the decision regarding recruitment of domestic

Table 8.5 Percentage distribution of households by perceived risk of exposure to the contagion through domestic workers as reported by the employers (respondents)

Levels of perceived risk of exposure to the contagion through domestic workers	Percentage of households		
	Ahmedabad	*Kolkata*	*Overall*
Low risk (1–3)	11.43	36.07	22.58
Moderate risk (4–6)	42.86	88.52	64.51
High risk (7–9)	15.71	9.84	12.9
Total number of households	70	61	131

Source: On-line survey, 2021.

workers after lockdown is lifted. It is evident that the households that bar domestic workers are also those that fall in the lower or middle bracket of per capita income as reported in the survey.

There are two major changes observed in the employers' households – one is the reduction of their monthly income and another is the change of their workplaces from office to home – influencing their behaviour and decision regarding recruitment of domestic workers negatively.

The fear of contagion among the middle class households seems to have huge implications on the relatively poor domestic workers' households as a large number of them lost jobs or remained unemployed for a long period. Interviews with domestic workers further reveal that even after the lockdown is lifted, domestic workers are not able to get back to work immediately. The workers are able to find work only from September, but in fewer houses compared to the pre-pandemic scenarios.

As a consequence, the workers are found to be extremely worried about their children's education. The closure of schools and the initiation of online classes for children create another burden because they have to buy a smartphone and bear its recurring costs. While 75% of respondents identify children's education as a significant challenge, 45% also highlight recurring cost of mobile phones as a matter of concern. Also, due to a significant decline in their work and income, many workers had to stop private tuitions for their children.

In West Bengal, in addition to pandemic and lockdown restrictions, all of the respondents are affected by Cyclone Amphan, which devastated many parts of West Bengal in May 2020. Domestic workers overall tend to not rely on the state for welfare or health services. Both central and state Governments fall short in meeting the needs of domestic workers during the pandemic, which could potentially have long-term impact on their income, health, and well-being.

8.12 Conclusion

The COVID-19 crisis has exposed the particular vulnerability of informal domestic workers, emphasizing the urgent need to ensure they are effectively included in labour and social protection. The pandemic has magnified and intensified the pre-existing issues. Very few domestic workers have access to social security, no paid weekly leave or sick leave, no institutional access to health care, employment injury benefits or unemployment insurance. Earnings are meagre and savings are not adequate to meet any form of financial exigencies.

In the wake of pandemic and subsequent lockdowns, sizable number of domestic workers lost their livelihood. Few, who could retain work, suffered deterioration in terms of employment condition. Overall domestic workers experienced significant decline in earning capacity. Domestic workers in India lack minimum wage protection and access to social security instruments. Such vulnerabilities worsened further during pandemic-induced lockdown.

This further strengthens the need to have a comprehensive legal protection for domestic workers. Wages are low and based on informal bargaining. Domestic workers should get minimum wage protection. They should have access to institutional social security measures like pension, death benefit, medical and maternity benefit. Domestic workers should be included within the legislative protection accorded in various labour laws and association of domestic workers in the form of trade unions should be encouraged. State should find a mechanism to conduct inspection in domestic space such that relevant laws can be enforced in true spirit. Crisis emanating from COVID-19 pandemic clearly demonstrated the fact that domestic workers did not had access to almost any form of legislative protection as workers. It is high time such protections are accorded within a comprehensive inclusive framework.

Notes

1 Available on https://thediplomat.com/2020/05/covid-19-lockdown-india-needs-laws-to-protect-domestic-workers/; accessed on June 18, 2021.
2 Available on https://www.ilo.org/newdelhi/areasofwork/WCMS_141187/lang--en/index.htm, accessed on June 14, 2021.
3 Available on https://www.wiego.org/blog/coping-covid-19-sewas-domestic-workers-pandemic-and-beyond), accessed on June 14, 2021.
4 Available on https://thewire.in/labour/domestic-servants-informal-workforce; accessed on June 14, 2021.
5 Convention No. 189 of ILO; Available on https://www.wiego.org/blog/coping-covid-19-sewas-domestic-workers-pandemic-and-beyond; accessed on June 14, 2021.
6 Available on https://oxford.universitypressscholarship.com/view/10.1093/acprof:oso/9780199461165.001.0001/acprof-9780199461165; accessed on June 15, 2021.

References

Banerjee, Abhijit V. and Esther Duflo. (2008). "What is middle class about the middle classes around the world", *Journal of Economic Perspectives*, Vol. 22, No. 2, pp. 3–28.

Birdsall, Nancy, Carol Lee Graham, and S. Pettinato. (2000). "Stuck in the Tunnel: Is Globalization Muddling the Middle Class", *The Brookings Institution Center on Social and Economic Dynamics Working Paper No. 14*, Washington DC.

Bose, Ritabrata and Trisha Chaudhuri. (2017). "Understanding middle class with reference to recent trends in India Economy", *Working Paper January 2017*, IIM Bangalore.

Brandi, Clara, and Max Büge. (2014). "A Cartography of the New Middle Classes in Developing and Emerging Countries", *German Development Institute, Discussion Paper No. 35/2014*, Bonn.

Ghatak, Amrita and Kingshuk Sarkar. (2020a). "Economic status of domestic workers and the institutional support for them in India: Evidence from NSS 2014", *Working Paper No. 255*, GIDR, Ahmedabad.

Ghatak, Amrita and Kingshuk Sarkar. (2020b). "Perils of lockdown and informal sector workers: Reflections in the time of Covid-19", *Vikalp: People's Perspective for Change*, available on https://www.vikalp.ind.in/2020/04/perils-of-lockdown-and-informal-sector.html?m=0&fbclid=IwAR3S7ZmVwTGKxWYvdmu3cAZQNhU_66neCazkb-FKC5J4Cqp4LTRkLAz2sZNI, accessed on June 5, 2021.

Ghosh, Sagarika. (2020). "Covid-19 has exposed middle class paranoia and India's class faultlines", *The Times of India*, available on https://timesofindia.indiatimes.com/blogs/bloody-mary/covid-19-has-exposed-middle-class-paranoia-and-indias-class-faultlines/, accessed on July 3, 2021.

Sarkar, Kingshuk. (2018). "Complexity in the determination of minimum wages for domestic workers in India", *NLI Research Series No. 137/2019*, V Giri National Labour Institute, Noida.

Sen, Samita and Nilanjana Sengupta. (2016). "Domestic days: Women, work, and politics in contemporary Kolkata Samita Sen and Nilanjana Sengupta, Oxford Scholarship Online", p 52, available on https://oxford.universitypressscholarship.com/view/10.1093/acprof:oso/9780199461165.001.0001/acprof-9780199461165, accessed on June 8, 2021.

Part IV

Infrastructural Challenges and Human Capital

9 Infrastructure Deficits in Indian Cities amid COVID-19

Key Opportunities and Challenges for Policy and Practice

Soumyadip Chattopadhyay

9.1 Introduction

The spread and impact of COVID-19 have put the Indian cities, especially their poorer neighbourhoods, into an entire uncharted territory. The second wave has again foregrounded the consequences of not preparing in advance. Scholars have argued that social and spatial inequalities in access to urban amenities including housing significantly shape the outbreak and impact of any pandemic in developing countries (McFarlane, 2021; Biglieri et al., 2020). In conformity with the global preventive measures, India announced one of the most stringent nation-wide lockdowns on 25th March 2020, followed up with gradual relaxations, and emphasized on the importance of following COVID-19-appropriate behaviour – frequent hand washes with soap, self-isolation, and social distancing – to arrest the spread of COVID 19.

However, these preventive measures do not sufficiently address how the challenges of adherence to COVID-19-appropriate behaviour relate to and are informed by the inadequate availability of urban services in Indian cities that predate the pandemic. Infrastructure of the public health care facilities is inadequate to meet the demand of any health emergencies. Similar is the inadequacy in access to basic urban services including housing, with the situation being more dreadful in slums and peri-urban areas. Indian cities' tryst with COVID-19 is far from over and the longer-term impacts of the pandemic and the lockdown are primarily speculative. But this will certainly not be the last epidemic of a novel infectious agent, nor stopgap measures are substitutes for inclusive cities, even in the best circumstances.

While the need for 'build back better' cities is well acknowledged, less is discussed on how inequalities are produced through contemporary forms of urban policies and practices in India. This chapter engages with pandemic responses of the Indian cities against the backdrop of prevailing state of urban services and their potential to deepen current vulnerabilities. First, the chapter assesses availability of housing and related urban services which are bare essentials to ensure COVID-19-appropriate behaviour. Second, the chapter dissects the policy trends, in both infrastructure and governance, shaping contemporary outcomes of service delivery systems in Indian cities and underscores the urgent need to

DOI: 10.4324/9781003226970-13

explore the pathways for better preparing Indian cities. To address these questions, the chapter draws on available secondary data, policy reports and scholarly literatures including recent empirical studies and the expositions move between macro trends and illustrative examples.

9.2 Grounding the Infrastructure Deficits in Indian Cities

9.2.1 An Unimaginable Luxury of Handwashing

In India, infrastructural development has not been able to keep up with the increasing population growth in the cities. In case of water supply, only 70% population coverage, out of which 62% have access to treated tap water, fall far short of Government of India's service benchmark of 100% water coverage and the same is far more inadequate in smaller cities and towns (Census of India, 2011). Out of 111 cities selected for construction of Ease of Living Index in 2020, in half of the cities only around 40% of urban households enjoy access to piped water supply (GoI, 2021). Significant inter-city variations exist as population coverage with water supply connection ranged from 55% for Chennai to 96% for Kochi (IIHS, 2020). Indian cities also experience significant intra-city variations – for example 46% households living in Mumbai used 95% of the available water (IIHS, 2017).

In general, almost one-fifths of households in urban India lack access to water within their homes while 6% of them collect water from sources situated more than 200 meters away from their homes (NSSO, 2019). Average collection time is almost an hour every day (NSSO, 2019). Moreover, water is intermittently available, on average, only for 1 to 6 hours (Water Aid, 2018). It is also found that women in almost 57% of urban households shared the burden of collecting, storing, and managing water beside their regular household activities and this only increases their mental and physical stress (NSSO, 2019). Thus, irregularity and insufficiency of water supply stamp down the advantage of availability of water supply in Indian cities. This is reflected in per capita per day availability of only 69 litres of water compared to the service benchmark of 135 lpcd in Indian cities, with the corresponding figure being as low as 58 lpcd for Chennai (IIHS, 2020). Mukherjee et al. (2020) estimated that proper adherence to the frequent hand washing for at least 20 seconds would increase 20% per capita clean water consumption for each household and amplify their water shortages. In the slums, relatively higher household coverage of water supply of 74% needs to be interpreted in terms their shared access to water using community stand posts. In a recent survey of slums in Indian cities, Auerbach and Thachil (2020) found that almost 40% of the residents did not have water taps within their homes. Soap and hand sanitizers are luxury items that a significant majority of slum residents cannot afford. The inhabitants of unrecognized and informal settlements, mainly the migrants, are not covered by any municipal network of water supply, not even temporary facilities such as municipal water tankers during any crisis.

A detailed study of migrant hotspots in Ahmedabad and Surat reveals that water access is not same for everyone, rather it is influenced by social norms of gender, caste and religion and the informal relations between the migrants and their landlords or employers and the type of arrangement made by the later (Ajeevika Bureau, 2020).

Affordability is a crucial factor for accessing water from alternative sources like self-provisioning arrangements (tube wells or hand pumps) or private water vendors or buying bottled water even in normal times. 36% of the urban households utilized supplementary sources for drinking water (NSSO, 2019). For such coping strategies, poorer households spend much higher percentage of their income. Quite a significant proportion of people in Chennai and Bangalore bought water from water vendor by paying a price ten to hundreds of times that of municipality supplied water during pre-pandemic period (Post et al., 2020). Slum residents in Dharavi of Mumbai incurred monthly expenditure of $ 20.51 to access water and in many slums, the slum dwellers could only afford to buy water once a week and practice of hand washing would only reduce the amount of water available for drinking and cooking (YUVA, 2020). So, they do not have any other option but to forgo personal hygiene in their battle for daily survival. Further, almost half of the urban households had to treat drinking water received from all the sources (NSSO, 2019), and this is indicative of questionable water quality, with the problem being severe in peri urban areas and slums – for example, 90% of the water available in peri urban localities of Bengaluru was found to be unfit for human consumption (Chatterjee and Roy, 2021). Urban residents were also unaware of the quality of water from alternative sources (Post and Ray, 2020).

9.2.2 Challenges for Accessing Sanitation Facilities

In India, 91% and 96% of the urban households have access to bathroom and latrine facilities, respectively (NSSO, 2019). However, about 16% of the urban households rely on shared facilities. Also, 8% and 4% urban households lack access to bathroom and latrine facilities respectively. Such service deficits are more pronounced among nearly 40% of slum residents Indian cities (Dasgupta, 2021). A survey of Mumbai's informal settlements reported that only one tenth of the households have personal toilet facilities, while three-fourth of them depend on shared toilet facilities (The Hindustan Times, 2020). Lack of cleanliness and associated poor hygiene have further aggravated the risk of disease transmission among the slum residents. Another study of sanitation practices among the peri-urban communities of Tamil Nadu reported open defecation by almost 27% of the surveyed households during lockdown due to lack of access to sanitation (Ashraf et al., 2020).

In case of private toilets, lockdown induced limited mobility of the family members and, in some cases, diarrhoeal symptoms of COVID-19 increased the frequency of toilet use and also the need for proper maintenance and sanitization. Users of shared sanitation facilities had to wait in queues and required to follow preventive measures like wearing mask and hand washing, resulting in inconsistent toilet use and increase in open defecation (Ashraf et al., 2020). Only 85% of the urban households have access to water with availability soap or detergent in or around the latrine (NSSO, 2019). Practice of handwashing with soap since lockdown has been higher among the households having access to private latrines (Ashraf et al., 2020). Adherence to the COVID-19-appropriate norms in public toilet use is practically impossible for the women as they could access the facilities only during restricted time and their usage time including wait time was higher, enhancing the risk COVID-19 transmission (Tandel et al., 2021; Ajeevika, 2020). Government of India's sanitation guidelines have mandated proper cleaning and disinfection of toilets at least twice daily by a trained cleaner wearing personal protective equipment (PPE) and arrangement of flush toilet or latrine for COVID-19-infected people (NIUA, 2020). However, given the resource and capacity constraints at the city levels, safe and adequate access to sanitation facilities is, indeed, challenging.

9.2.3 Impossibility of COVID-19-Appropriate Behaviour Amid Inadequate Housing

In India, practice of basic preventive measures of self-isolation and social distancing is almost impossible due to lack of adequate space or congestion. A 2012 report of the Technical Group on Urban Housing Shortages indicated a national urban housing shortage of 18.78 million, a significant majority of which is due to congestion or obsolescence and is concentrated among the economically weaker section (EWS) and low-income group (LIG) (GoI, 2012). Considering congested households as those whose persons per room is two or more, or where households have no exclusive room, significant proportions of urban households in metropolitan cities (35.7%) and large cities (30.4%) were found to live in congested condition in 2011 (Kundu et al., 2016). Roy and Meera (2020) considered the housing units which are either non-pucca or obsolete[1] or congested[2] as inadequate and estimated the housing inadequacies separately for slum and non-slum areas of Indian cities. Housing appeared to be inadequate for almost 44% of slum households as they live in houses that are non-pucca and either obsolete or congested. Incidence of congestion was lower among the non-slum households with the corresponding figure of about 20% living in congested conditions. Roy and Meera (2020) also estimated that of 47.3 million or 41% of urban households in India lived in inadequate houses in 2018 and 99% of them belonged to LIGs.

Acknowledging the non-availability of any specific norms regarding over-crowding, Tiwari and Rao (2020) considered per person available area of less than 15.23 square meters as an indicator of overcrowding. The average floor area of the urban households in India is 46.1 square meters (NSSO, 2019). Given that India's urban household size is 4.66 person, per person available area of 9.90 square meters indicates overcrowding. Moreover, considering the *Pradhan Mantri Awas Yojana – Urban* (PMAY-U) scheme specified size of affordable dwelling of 30 square meter for EWS, 60 square meter for LIG,

160–200 square meter for Middle Income Group (MIG), the incidence of over-crowding is expected to be severe among the EWS and LIG households. In slum and informal settlements of metro cities, urban poor families consisting of four to five persons or more accommodated themselves in an 8 by 10 feet or a 10 by 10 feet windowless room in the peak summer and in some cases the same rooms were used as workplaces. Maintenance of physical/social distancing is, indeed, a daunting challenge with added fears of deepening of pre-existing gendered violence (Bhide, 2020).

Following the pandemic, India witnessed large exodus of migrant workers which has reemphasized the importance of augmenting rental housing for them in cities. One-third of all the urban households in India live in rented houses (NSSO, 2019). Availability of dwelling rooms per person in rented homes is only 0.46, with the corresponding figure being even lower at 0.38 in case of urban slums in India (Mukherjee et al., 2020). Access and quality of basic urban services including water supply is found to be poor among the renters as compared to the owners (Harish, 2021). About 70% of renters do not have any contractual agreements with the landlord and their average monthly rent is $ 45.22 (NSSO, 2019). When income plummeted during lockdown, informal renting with oral contracts provided some renters flexibility to negotiate the deferment of rent payment while others compromised their daily essential expenses to pay rents and retain their accommodation (Bharati and Jotwani, 2021). Migrant workers' vulnerability to the pandemic is also shaped by their disparate occupational choices and housing options – private rental accommodation, worksite accommodation, open spaces, and so on – available to them. Nevertheless, two common features characterize these options – first, size of the houses and other basic facilities including water and sanitation fall far short of basic standards of quality and adequacy and second, given the high demand for rental accommodation, such access is embedded in the informal networks between the landlords and renters in which the latter has to give up bargaining power for demanding better services to ensure a roof over their heads (Ajeevika Bureau, 2020). Arbitrariness in accessing basic facilities is also deep-rooted as renters were discriminated owing to their religious and social identity. Governments have responded to these challenges by establishing the quarantine centres, but their locations and poor availability of basic amenities have hardly provided the urban poor with any viable alternatives for self-isolations (Bhide, 2020).

Overall, the public health advisories are undoubtedly essential for containment of the pandemic, but pre-pandemic disparities across and within the Indian cities in availability of basic urban services significantly determine the ability of their citizen to adhere to them. Non-accessibility of easy water reduces per person use of water with concomitant neglect of maintenance of personal hygiene. Significant proportion of city dwellers stand in the queue for long hours to fetch water which is time bound and limited. Also, the costs of setting up the self-provisioning arrangements or buying water from water vendors are often prohibitive for cash-poor customers. In settings where lack of easy and affordable access to water as well as overcrowding are the norms, compliance to frequent handwashing with soap, self-isolation and social distancing is not an option, rather impossible to maintain. COVID-19 and lockdown induced loss of livelihoods and incomes are likely to deepen such vulnerabilities for the poor people who face difficulty in accessing basic services which, nonetheless, the wealthy urban residents can enjoy by affording the premiums for reliable water and adequate housing. Clearly, the pandemic outbreak has diverse effects on people with different living condition and responses to the COVID-19 crisis should not miss the opportunity to address pre-pandemic disparities in service availability.

9.3 Synthesizing Urban Policies: Disjuncture between Rhetoric and Practice

The key to future proof Indian cities against any pandemic outbreak lies in improving urban service delivery for all the citizens. India needs an infusion of US $1.2 trillion in urban infrastructure by 2030 to remove the current backlogs and also to match the increasing demand for infrastructural facilities (GoI, 2020). Urban governance and local capacity are just as important factors for urban service delivery as municipal financial health. So, historical genesis and evaluation of the existing financial and governance arrangements and the lessons thereof are vital for rethinking urban policies and building inclusive cities.

9.3.1 Infrastructure Investment – The Enduring Legacy of Shift from Public Investment to Private Financing

Urban development in India is a state subject. State Governments exercise their discretion over implementation of urban development plan and policies outlined by the Central Government and funds from the central/state Governments continue to be the major source of financing urban infrastructure. Following the incidence of increasingly deficient urban services including housing and deepening fiscal crisis of the Central Government, urban policies in the mid-80s experienced a remarkable shift from public investment to private financing of urban infrastructure with a substantial reduction in budgetary allocations from Governments and opening up avenues for private sector participation in urban development. During the 1990s, the International Financial Institutions (IFIs) emphasized on restructuring of municipal finance and commercialization of urban infrastructure. Central to such aspects of financial management has been the question of revenue generation through user fees, municipal bond, and other innovative instruments, cost recovery as well as making urban infrastructure attractive to the private investors. Moreover, economic liberalization in 1991 identified these financial reforms including decentralization as structural precondition to increase the efficiency of local investment. By the late 1990s, the Union Ministry of Urban Development (MoUD) made the receipt of budgetary allocation for urban development conditional on implementation of similar policy reforms. All the central urban flagship programs during 2005–14 and afterwards – namely, Jawaharlal Nehru National Urban Renewal Mission

(JNNURM), Smart Cities Mission (SCM), Atal Mission for Rejuvenation and Urban Transformation (AMRUT), *Swachh Bharat Mission* – Urban (SBM-U), and *Pradhan Mantri Awas Yojana – Urban* (PMAY-U) – uphold the narratives of 'promoting self-financed urban growth', 'sustainable infrastructure development', and 'efficiency enhancement', and emphasize on financialization of urban services through private investment, infrastructure debt funds, municipal bonds, taxes and surcharges, and full cost recovery (GoI, 2020b).

9.3.1.1 Policy Incoherence and Entrenchment of Socio-spatial Inequality

Given the incompatibility of building financially sustainable urban infrastructure and universalizing access to urban services, these programs have endangered policy incoherence having far reaching ramifications for delivery of urban services in the coming decades and, thereby, for city-preparedness during the pandemic. First, the physical progress and coverage of the programs have been unequal, creating inequality both within and across the cities. In case of JNNURM, the bigger cities in particular and cities from economically advanced states, owing to their better managerial and financial capacities accounted for major shares (Kundu, 2020). Despite the provision of at least 20% of the fund for the Basic Services for the Urban Poor (BSUP) component, several JNNURM cities actually applied for or were allocated with much less fund under the same (Banidur and Kamath, 2009). Even the allocation of fund under the SCM is exclusionary as 80% of the funds are linked to the Area Based Development projects covering up to about one-tenth of the cities, already endowed with better urban services (Taraporevala, 2018). Even for the rest of the fund available under 'pan-city' component, there is little flexibility in its spending for making capital expenditure to improve the infrastructure provision. Second, these flagship schemes have exhibited bias towards particular types of large infrastructure projects with focus either on market logic of cost recovery by equating the citizens' access to urban services with their ability to pay or creating 'world class' cities and their financial corpus (Taraporevala, 2018; Goldman, 2011). Continued emphasis on cost recovery would likely to reinforce socio-spatial inequalities by increasing the availability of basic services in city areas that are favourably assessed for financial viability which, nonetheless, paradoxically constrain urban poor's ability to access similar services. In fact, urban poor negotiate their urban service deficiencies through informal arrangements which cannot be mapped well into a predictable risk-return profile. So, the financial institutions and Governments have rarely made any attempt to incorporate them into their plans. Third, low utilization of program funds available under these flagship programs also has regressive impact on the availability of urban infrastructure.[3] Fourth, all the Government flagship programs use census data to decide on the provision of urban basic services. However, the official enumeration processes derecognize the informal settlements with sizable concentration of migrant workers who are hard hit by COVID-19. Official documents for identifying the cities' growth potentials and planning city-level infrastructure, for example Town Planning Schemes and Development Plans for Ahmedabad and Surat, have also failed to account for the dynamic migration flows of informal workforce that India generally experience (Aajeevika Bureau, 2020). City authorities are also found to be reluctant in supplying water to the inhabitants of informal settlements on public land as that might legitimize their claim on land.[4] Invisibility of the informal settlement is further entrenched first by the type of 'knowledge' possessed by the local authorities that collect data on land ownership but miss out the aspects of service availability and livelihoods and second by fragmentation of such 'knowledge' across various institutions operating in silos (Bhide, 2020). Clearly such lack of recognition and 'knowledge' deprives significant proportion of city dwellers in accessing basic services and increases their vulnerability even in normal times, let alone in post–COVID-19 phase.

9.3.1.2 Challenges of Financial Frailty

Weak financial health of the cities has limited their ability to raise requisite financial contribution to match the Central Government grant. Even, they are unable to incur necessary expenditures for operation and maintenance of all critical urban infrastructure and services.[5] The dwindling own revenue of the city Government is evident from of its contribution of only 0.43% to GDP in 2017–18.[6] Own revenue contributed not even half of the total revenue in the million plus cities in 2017–18, with the corresponding figures being far lower at 40% and 30% for cities with population 1 to 10 lakh and less than 1 lakh respectively (ICRIER, 2019). GST-led subsumption of several taxes (e.g. octroi and entry tax) is likely to further reduce municipal revenues. Property tax, the mainstay of municipal revenue, remains grossly underutilized due to inadequate assessment of properties, inefficient collection, and widespread exemptions. City Governments hardly impose user charges for providing urban services to their citizens.

Weak financial health of the cities has come in the way of harnessing the potential of innovative sources of financing including public private partnerships (PPPs) and debt financing. In general, private sectors have demonstrated little or no interest in urban social infrastructure (e.g. water supply, sanitation, solid waste management) projects primarily due to lower scope for imposition of fees and charges to cover the project costs. Limited success of municipal bond as viable financing instrument can be attributed mainly to lack of credit worthiness of the city Governments which is evident from the receipt of investible grade rating only by 163 cities out of 469 AMRUT cities (GoI, 2020a). Notably, PPP mode of delivery of urban services in many Indian cities does not necessarily improve the service availability especially for the urban poor, who are either priced out of the system due to regressive tariff hikes or lack access even after their requisite contribution due to absence of any strict service level benchmarking and monitoring of affordability and quality criteria (Sadoway et al., 2018).

The COVID-19 has further worsened the financial health of the Indian cities. Pandemic-induced tax deferrals, decrease in tax collection from advertisement tax and real estate (real estate transaction taxes, building permits and rights, etc.), and decrease in fees collection due to closure of public facilities (e.g. cultural venues, sport venues like swimming pools) are likely to dampen the revenue collection of cities. Even, disruptions in economic activities has constrained the citizens' capacity to pay taxes. Cities have experienced simultaneous increase in expenditure on account of purchase of Personal Protective Equipment (PPE), arrangement of health facilities, disinfection of public toilets and spaces and so on. Many cities, especially the smaller ones, have responded to this crisis by adjusting their expenditures on operation and maintenance and delaying or cutting the implementation and expenditures of development projects (The Hindu Business Line, 2020). Moreover, with the post–COVID-19 shrinking of the economy, private sector participation even in urban commercial infrastructure will likely to receive a jolt. In November 2020, Viability Gap Funding (VGF) scheme has been launched to make infrastructure projects in areas like waste water treatment, solid waste management and water supply financially viable as well as attractive for private capital with a budgetary support of maximum 60% of total project costs to be shared equally by the central and state Government (GoI, 2020c). Inter and intra city disparities in access to basic services is likely to deepen further as only the financially stronger cities would find investors and that too only for the commercially viable projects. More often than not, the marginalized low-income groups are likely to be the worst sufferers and become more vulnerable to any pandemic.

9.3.1.3 Incompatibility of Housing Schemes and 'Housing for All'

In case of housing, there are stark similarities among the centrally-sponsored schemes – namely, BSUP under the JNNURM, *Rajiv Awas Yojana* (RAY), and the ongoing PMAY-U – that have jeopardized the envisaged attainment of 'Housing for All' and 'Slum Free' cities, increasing the vulnerabilities of significant section of city-dwellers amid COVID-19 and beyond. First, an overwhelming emphasis on construction of new houses instead of upgrading existing housing stocks belies the empirical reality that significant proportions of urban households live in 'legally, materially or spatially insecure' and inadequate homes (Bhan, 2019). Among the four verticals under PMAY-U, the Beneficiary-led Construction (BLC) component has recorded maximum number of sanctions as it is easier for the housing institutions to deal with households with access to land. The In Situ Slum Redevelopment (ISSR) component, which was supposed to meet about 90% of the housing shortages, has performed poorly in terms of housing sanction/construction. Limiting regulations of FSI and land use and non-availability of cheap land within the cities have forced both the Government and private builders to develop low income housing in the periphery. But poor urban amenities and difficulty in accessing as well as retaining the city-based jobs and services have increased the livelihood challenges of the urban residents housed in the peripheries (Coelho et al., 2020). Second, these policies have favoured private participation in building affordable housing with Government contribution in the form of land and policy instruments like increased FSI and TDR are also used for making the projects financially viable. However, private players, being interested in extracting economic profitability of urban space, often construct high-rise building of poor quality, resembling the 'vertical slums' that are unsuitable for habitation (Dupont and Gowda, 2020). Third, all the existing schemes require the beneficiaries to have proper land ownership titles or appropriate documents and compliance with 'cut-off dates' to become eligible for housing. Moreover, instead of incorporating urban residents' housing needs and priorities, their participation is largely equated with financial contribution for the project, with the same being justified to generate a meaningful stake of slum dwellers in their housing. These conditionalities limit urban poor's access to adequate housing, subsequently resulting in 'entrenchment of slums' (Dupont and Gowda, 2020). Even, under Credit Linked Subsidy Scheme (CLSS) vertical, recent sharp rise in income limits for the EWS and LIG categories and simultaneous inclusion of the MIG categories, have further amplified the exclusionary nature of the existing housing policies.

9.3.1.4 The ARHC – Illusion of Propriety

In July 2020, the central Government has launched the Affordable Rental Housing Complexes (ARHCs) as a sub scheme under PMAY-U to respond to the housing needs of the urban poor, especially the migrants who are hard hit by COVID-19. Considering the under-construction and un-occupied houses under JNNURM and RAY, as on December 2020, a total of 2.1 lakh Government housing units are available for utilization under this scheme (GoI, 2020d). In particular, the scheme is operationalized through (a) model 1, that is, repurposing these vacant houses to rentals through PPPs or by public agencies and (b) model 2, that is, developing rental housing by public or private entities on their own available vacant land. A closure scrutiny of the policy details, however, raises serious concerns.

First, the publicly constructed houses remain vacant due to their poor location and construction quality, non-availability of basic urban services and most importantly, fear of loss of livelihood and social networks among the occupants. Repurposing such housing stock is unlikely to generate their demand. It is also hard to subscribe the promises of provision of full range of basic services for these projects by the city Governments when they have already failed to do so in other parts of the cities. Second, the scheme hopes to rope in the private investors by proposing several concessions including tax rebates, project loan at lower interest rate, additional Floor Area Ratio (FAR)/ Floor Space Index (FSI), provision of trunk infrastructure and so on. While these measures would surely balance the risk-return portfolio of the potential private investors, the extent to which the scheme is beneficial for targeted groups depends crucially on their affordability of rent charged and the protection or safety measures available to them. In practice, the rents determined by the city Governments under model 1 or concessionary by model 2 have exceeded prevailing private rental market rent, making these 'affordable' houses unaffordable for many beneficiaries (Harish, 2021). There are no explicit income criteria mentioned for scheme eligibility and essentially, the access to houses is tied to beneficiaries' ability to pay rent and, in case of employer provided housing, their continuation in the employment. Moreover, by disallowing the use of the dwelling units for commercial purposes, this scheme is likely to constrict the livelihood options for many urban migrants who use their dwelling space for carrying out home-based work. Even, during any crisis situation, the renters are devoid of any protection under the newly proposed Model Tenancy Act, 2019. COVID-19 has caused a severe decline in earnings for the majority of workers across India, especially for poorer house-holds who are coping with such economic distress by decreasing food intake and by borrowing (APU, 2021). In such situation, the conditions under the AHRC scheme stand in contrast with the way of living for many urban poor and thus, likely to offer little relief to their problem of housing inadequacy during COVID-19 and in subsequent periods (Harish, 2021).

9.3.2 Governance Reforms: Emergence of Inflexible and Exclusionary Strategies

9.3.2.1 Narrative of Partial and Fragmented Decentralization

The potential of city governance and use of local knowledge in influencing access to basic urban services and designing emergency responses during pandemic is well acknowledged. The 74th Constitutional Amendment Act (CAA) in India has provision for devolution of decentralized powers and essential functions re-lated to city planning, poverty alleviation and provision of basic services to the city Governments and citizen participation in city governance. However, urban decentralization has been partial and fragmented. In much of India, political empowerment has been derided by irregular municipal elections and limited ex-ecutive authority of elected mayors and city councillors in managing their cities even during normal times. A recent study has reported that out of 21 selected Indian cities, not a single one has complete control over essential constitutional city functions, such as water supply, sanitation or waste management – all of them are essential to manage the pandemic (PRAJA, 2020). State Governments have created parastatal agencies and Special Purpose Vehicles (SPVs) that perform some of the specified municipal functions, leading to considerable overlapping and fragmentation of decision-making structure and further complicating task of managing disease outbreaks. Institutional framework for disaster response under the Disaster Management Act, 2005 mandates district Government to coordinate and monitor the National/State Policies of relief and response. In-adequate authority of local Governments in framing local responses and wispy inter-Government coordination, in many cases, reduced the effectiveness of pan-demic responses (Dasgupta *et al.*, 2021). This calls for urgent policy attention as city Governments have effectively spearheaded rapid response actions to manage COVID-19. Some city-level strategies – albeit too few – like sanitization of 800 houses per-day and ward-wise deployment of sanitation workers by the Ranchi Municipal Corporation; formulation of a detailed standard operating procedure for cleaning of public toilets by the Chopda municipality, and daily cleaning arrangements as opposed to weekly cleaning of toilets with additional arrangements of soap and sanitizer and a box for disposing sanitary pads in Dharavi have improved the cleanliness and maintenance of sanitation facilities (NIUA, 2020).

Progress towards institutionalization of citizen participation via Ward Committees (WCs) has been equally unsatisfactory as either in many states such committees have not been constituted properly or in case of functioning WCs in other states, irregular Annual General Meetings along with politicization of member selection and deliberation process resulted in paltry peoples' participation (Chattopadhyay, 2017). Nevertheless, the WCs' participatory potential in planning local level actions is corroborated by the involvement of the WCs in four Indian cities – Agartala, Aizawl, Guwahati, and Kochi – in formulating and coordinating localized COVID-19 management that includes monitoring and enforcement of COVID-19 norms at each ward; awareness building; safeguarding institutional quarantine facilities and distribution of food and other relief supplies (PRAJA, 2021).

9.3.2.2 *Proclivity towards 'Consultancy Urbanism' and Deepening Marginalization*

Since 2000, the move towards integrating citizen participation into design and implementation of urban projects has resulted in usurpation of participatory avenues by a disparate group of actors represented by the Residents Welfare Associations (RWA)s, state level Task Forces and internationally reputed consultancy firms to infuse efficiency and accountability in the city management. Such reconfigurations of urban governance spaces in India entail three crucial implications for city's ability to deliver urban services. First, the constellation of new actors subscribes and promotes the aspirational images of a 'global' city characterized by mega projects such as new airports, super-highways, large scale housing projects, smart traffic and the like catering largely to the needs of upper- and middle-income groups. Although the proposals related to basic services like 24/7 water supply form central plank in the flagship programs, but they do not address water shortages in parts of the city (such as informal settlements) that are still disconnected from water networks and resort to informal arrangements. Second, a fetish towards imitating 'best practice' models of international investors and planners has produced identical city development plans under JN-NURM and SCM and these plans have become locally unsuitable and deepened exclusions for lower-income people (Sadoway et al., 2018). Third, urban poor depends on 'vote bank politics' to approach the local political leaders and elected representatives for 'claiming public services and safeguarding territorial claims' (Benjamin 2008). But near absence of local planners and locally elected representatives in designing the city development plans has increased the risk of making them more elitist and, thus, unresponsive to the urban poor. 'Elite capture' of urban governance has scaled a new height of exclusivity in the SCM as citizens are deliberating on everyday urban problems through 'push button democracy of blogs, online surveys, Twitter and Facebook' and 'turning the problem of unequal access to urban services as a technological concern than a structural problem of poverty and exclusion' (Basu, 2019; Dutta, 2018).

Overall, the voices and knowledge of particular group of urban stakeholders have significantly shaped the processes of urban policy-making with crucial implications for how urban inequalities in access to urban services are understood and addressed. Given the governance deficits at the city level, it is pragmatic to capitalize the forms of urban expertise provided by the newly emergent actors, but that need not be at the expense of marginalizing the elected city Governments and their representatives through which the urban poor are represented in decision-making about the city. During the lockdown period, elected councillors have responded swiftly in arranging food, medical emergencies and even makeshift shelters overnight for homeless people and also connected people with the Governmental and non-Governmental relief work at the ward level (HUL, 2020). There is much to be gained by blending 'expert' knowledge with local knowledge from the margins to bear on key urban challenges and articulate strategies towards building inclusive cities in the post-pandemic period.

9.4 Summing Up

This paper argues that the current vulnerabilities of the Indian cities to the pandemic reflect to a significant degree of social and spatial inequalities in housing and access to basic services – all of which are essential for combating the COVID-19. This is a logical result of dysfunctional urban policies, poor financial health and absence of effective governance structures in the Indian cities and an excessive bias towards privatization of urban infrastructure and decision-making processes in recent decades. Dealing with this crisis therefore offers an opportunity to rebalance the extant urban policies.

First, addressing the inequalities is essentially about improving the availability of urban services including housing and, therefore, augmenting public investment in them will be key for longer-term recovery. Governments' policy rhetoric favouring private financing of urban infrastructure needs to be supported by an independent and robust regulatory authority with the mandate of accurately assessing the costs of services, modelling cross subsidy structure and monitoring the benchmarking of service delivery to safeguard the interests of the urban poor. Second, empowerment of city Governments in terms of functions, funds and functionaries is crucial in developing and implementing locally feasible and effective strategies. Legislations on disaster management should also clearly specify the role of the city Governments. This syncs with the pandemic led reinvigoration of long-standing agendas for a 'new-municipalism' and, also, relative success of well-resourced local Governments in Kerala in managing COVID-19 (McFarlane, 2021). Special emphasis should, in general, be placed on clear cut division and synchronization of the functions that city Governments share with other state agencies and strengthening the city Governments' own revenue mobilization power to enable them in accessing innovative sources of financing.

Third, instead of cosmetic institutionalization of peoples' participation, it is imperative to mainstream and reenergize the constitutionally envisaged Ward Committees with the involvement all the citizens and community-based organizations. Also, any good policies need accurate data. Collection and management of local data on rapidly changing dynamics of the cities, especially informal service arrangements, need to be reprioritized to address the pre-COVID-19 era data gaps. Institutionalization of informal service providers engaged in basic service delivery are needed that will benefit city dwellers, especially in informal settlements. Redesigning of urban policies must start with inclusion of residents and local knowledge in ward-level planning and finally incorporating them to the city plans. Successful involvement of community organizations in Kerala *Sannadhasena* in reaching out families in quarantine with food and dry rations, involvement of community-based organizations in better managing the toilets in squatter settlements of Mumbai and effective engagement of Slum Dwellers Associations and Women Self Help Groups in providing job opportunities to the migrants in the post lockdown period under the Urban Wage Employment Initiative (UWEI) in Odisha attest the significance of community involvement in planning local-level solutions (Dasgupta et al., 2021; Biswas et al., 2020). In essence, in the post-COVID-19 era, a more human-centric urban approach could be the key to respond to 'build back better' cities that equally value all peoples' needs and ensure their representation in city governance and planning.

Notes

1 Obsolete housing are the units more than 60 years old and are between 40 and 60 years with bad condition.
2 Units lacking a separate room for a married couple are classified as congested units.
3 JNNURM and SCM recorded only 50% utilization rates while the same for water supply and sewerage projects under the AMRUT scheme were 51% and 30% respectively (IIHS, 2020).
4 For example, inhabitants of informal settlements in central government land under Brihanmumbai Municipal Corporation are required to produce a no-objection certificate from relevant authorities for accessing water. Subsequently, nearly 20 lakh people in Mumbai are denied any access to potable water (The Hindustan Times, 2020).
5 The IIHS (2020) study shows that in terms of the per capita O&M expenditure on critical urban services including water supply, six large Indian cities spent about 40%–60% less the HPEC recommended per capita expenditure norms.
6 Own revenue of the cities consists of tax revenue (property tax, advertisement tax, etc.) and non-tax revenue (user fees, parking fees, etc.).

References

Aajeevika Bureau (2020). Unlocking the urban: Reimagining migrant lives in cities post COVID – 19. www.aajeevika.org (Accessed on 20th May, 2021)
Ashraf, S., Kuang, J., Das, U., & Bichhieri, C. (2020). Sanitation practices during early phases of COVID-19 Lockdown in peri-urban communities in Tamil Nadu, India. *The American Journal of Tropical Medicine and Hygiene*, 103(5). https://doi.org/10.4269/ajtmh.20–0830.

Auerbach A.M., & Thachil, T. (2020). How does Covid-19 affect urban slums? Evidence from settlement leaders in India. *World Development.* https://doi.org/10.1016/j. worlddev.2020.105304.

APU (2021). *State of Working India 2021: One year of Covid-19,* Centre for Sustainable Employment, Azim Premji University, Bengaluru.

Banidur, V. & Kamath, L. (2009). *Reengineering urban infrastructure: how the World Bank and the Asian development bank shape urban infrastructure finance and governance in India,* Bank Information Centre South Asia, August.

Basu, I. (2019). Elite discourse coalitions and the governance of 'smart space': Politics, power and privilege in India's Smart City Mission. *Political Geography.* https://doi. org/10.1016/j.polgeo.2018.11.002.

Benjamin, S. (2008). Occupancy urbanism: Radicalizing politics and economy beyond policy and programs. *International Journal of Urban and Regional Research,* 32(3): 719–729.

Bhan, G. (2019). Notes on a southern urban practice. *Environment & Urbanization.* https://doi.org/10.1177/0956247818815792.

Bharati, M. & Jotwani, J. (2021). Roti kapda but what about makaan? May 18. https:// indiahousingreport.in/outputs/opinion/roti-kapda-but-what-about-makaan/ (Accessed on 20th July 2021)

Bhide, A. (2020). Informal settlements, the emerging response to COVID and the imperative of transforming the narrative. *Journal of Social and Economic Development.* https://doi.org/10.1007/s40847-020-00119-9.

Biglieri, S., Vidovich, D.L., & Keil, R. (2020). City as the core of contagion? Repositioning COVID-19 at the social and spatial periphery of urban society. *Cities & Health.* https://doi.org/10.1080/23748834.2020.1788320.

Biswas, R., Arya, K., & Deshpande, S. (2020). More toilet infrastructures do not nullify open defecation: A perspective from squatter settlements in megacity Mumbai. *Applied Water Science,* 10(4): 1–9. https://doi.org/10.1007/s13201-020-1169-4.

Census of India. (2011). *House Listing and Housing Census Data.* (http://www.censusindia.gov.in/2011census/hlo/HLO_Tables.html). (Accessed on 14th June, 2021).

Chatterjee, B. & Roy, A. (2021). *Creating urban water resilience in India: A water balance study of Chennai, Bengaluru, Coimbatore, and Delhi,* Observer Research Foundation, New Delhi, March.

Chattopadhyay, S. (2017). Neoliberal urban transformation in Indian cities: Paradoxes and predicaments. *Progress in Development Studies,* 17(4): 307–321.

Coelho, K., Mahadevia, D., & Williams, G. (2020). Outsiders in the periphery: Studies of peripheralisation of low-income housing in Ahmedabad and Chennai India. *International Journal of Housing Policy.* https://doi.org/10.1080/19491 247.2020.17856 60.

Dasgupta, S. (2021). Rethinking equitable access to water and sanitation. https://idronline.org/rethinking-equitable-access-to-water-and-sanitation/ (Accessed on 16th May, 2021).

Dasgupta, S. et al. (2021). ReFORM: Lessons for urban governance futures from the pandemic. *CPR Research Report.* New Delhi: Center for Policy Research.

Dupont, V. & Gowda, M.M.S. (2020). Slum-free city planning versus durable slums insights from Delhi, India. *International Journal of Urban Sustainable Development,* 12(1): 34–51, https://doi.org/10.1080/19463138.2019.1666850.

Dutta, A. (2018). The digital turn in postcolonial urbanism: smart citizenship in the making of India's 100 smart cities. *Transactions of the Institute of British Geographers.* https://doi.org/10.1111/tran.12225.

Goldman, M. (2011). Speculative urbanism and the making of the next world city. *International Journal of Urban and Regional Research*, 35(3): 555–581.

Government of India. (2021). Ease of living index 2020. March https://smartnet. niua.org/sites/default/files/resources/final_web_ease_of_living_repor t_2020_.pdf (Accessed on 14th June, 2021).

Government of India. (2020a). Standing committee on urban development 2019–2020 third report. Ministry of Housing and Urban Affairs. New Delhi. 11 September. http://164.100.47.193/lsscommittee/Urban%20Development/17_Urban_Development_3. pdf (Accessed on 20th July 2021).

Government of India. (2020b). National urban policy framework strategic intent. https:// iica.nic.in/images/Articles/NUPF_Final_Oct%202020.pdf (Accessed on 14th June, 2021).

Government of India. (2020c). Press release. 11 November. https://www.pib.gov.in/ PressReleseDetailm.aspx?PRID=1671910 (Accessed on 28th July 2021).

Government of India. (2020d). Circular No.N-11022/51/2020-HFA-V-UD/FTS-9088338. Ministry of Housing and Urban Affairs. 31 December http://arhc.mohua. gov.in/filesUpload/Circular-31122020.pdf (Accessed on 28th July, 2021).

Government of India. (2012). Report of the technical group on urban housing shortages (TG-12) (2012–17). http://nbo.nic.in/pdf/urban-housing-shortage.pdf (Accessed on 14th June, 2021).

Harish, S. (2021). Affordable rental housing complexes scheme and private rental housing in Indian cities. *Economic and Political Weekly*, LVI(16). April: 15–19.

Hyderabad Urban Lab. (2020). Urban local bodies are critical in the fight against COVID-19. https://hydlab.in/blogposts/strengthen-urban-local-bodies (Accessed on 20th July, 2021).

Indian Council for Research on International Economic Relations (2019). State of municipal finance in India. *Report Prepared for the Fifteenth Finance Commission*, New Delhi.

Indian Institute for Human Settlements (2020). *Urban infrastructure and resilience*, Background Paper for the XV Finance Commission. https://fincomindia.nic.in/ ShowContentOne.aspx?id=27&Section=1 (Accessed on 14th June, 2021).

Indian Institute for Human Settlement. (2017). Urban water supply and sanitation in India. https://iihs.co.in/knowledge-gateway/wp-content/uploads/2017/11/RF-WATSAN_reduced_sized.pdf (Accessed on 28th May 2021).

Kundu, D. (2020). Urbanisation in India: Towards a national urban policy framework and smart cities, in D. Kundu, R. Sietchiping and M. Kinyanjui (eds) *Developing national urban policies ways forward to green and smart cities*, Springer Nature, Singapore: 89–119.

Kundu, D., Sharma, P. & Banerjee, A. (2016). Housing and basic infrastructure. *Shelter*, 17(1): 82–90.

McFarlane, C. (2021). Repopulating density: COVID-19 and the politics of urban value. *Urban Studies*. https://doi.org/10.1177/00420980211014810.

Mukherjee, A., Babu, S.S., & Ghosh, S. (2020). Thinking about water and air to attain sustainable development goals during times of COVID-19 pandemic. *Journal of Earth System Science*. https://doi.org/10.1007/s12040-020-01475-0.

NIUA (2020). Response of Indian cities to COVID-19 a sanitation perspective. National Institute of Urban Affairs in collaboration with AIILSG. New Delhi.

NSSO (2019). *Drinking water, sanitation, hygiene and housing condition in India: NSS 76th Round*. New Delhi: Ministry of Statistics and Programme Implementation, Government of India.

Post, A. & Ray, I. (2020). Hybrid modes of urban water delivery in low and middle income countries. *Oxford Research Encyclopedias.* https://doi.org/10.1093/acrefore/9780199389414.013.679.

PRAJA. (2020). National consultation on urban governance key findings from 21 states. https://www.praja.org/praja_docs/praja_downloads/National%20Consultation%20On%20Urban%20Governance-%20Key%20Finding%20From%2021%20States.pdf (Accessed on 1st July, 2021).

PRAJA. (2021). Importance of local governance in crisis management. https://www.praja.org/praja_docs/praja_downloads/ENGLISH_Report%20on%20Im portance%20of%20Local%20Governance%20in%20Crisis%20Management_Praja%2 0Foundation.pdf (Accessed on 27th July, 2021).

Roy, D. & Meera, M.L. (2020). Housing for India's low-income households a demand perspective. *Working Paper 402*, ICRIER, New Delhi, December.

Sadoway, D., Gopakumar, G., Baindur, V., & Badami, M.G. (2018). JNNURM as a window on urban governance its institutional footprint, antecedents and legacy. *Economic and Political Weekly*, LIII(2): 71–81.

Tandel, V., Gandhi, S., Patranabis, S., Bettencourt, L.M.A., & Malani, A. (2021). Infrastructure, enforcement, and COVID-19 in Mumbai slums: A first look. *Journal of Regional Science*, 1–25. https://doi.org/10.1111/jors.12552.

Taraporevala, P. (2018). *Demystifying the Indian smart city an empirical reading of the smart city mission*, Working Paper, Centre for Policy Research, New Delhi.

The Hindu Business Line. (2020). COVID-19: Drop in civic revenue to affect urban projects. https://www.thehindubusinessline.com/news/national/covid-19-drop-in-civic-revenue-to-affect-urban-projects/article31897757.ece (Accessed on 21st July, 2020).

The Hindustan Times. (2020). Amid COVOD-19 pandemic water and sanitation still a luxury for many in Mumbai. https://www.hindustantimes.com/mumbai-news/amid-covid-19-pandemic-water-and-sanitation-still-a-luxury-for-many-in-mumbai-report/story-63oanSUDpJwCkqbhaLG4jN.html (Accessed on 28th July 2021).

Tiwari, P. & Rao, J. (2020). *The housing conundrum in India*, Global Research Unit Working Paper #2020-016, City University of Hong Kong.

Water Aid. (2018). State of urban water supply in India. https://www.wateraidindia.in/sites/g/files/jkxoof336/files/state-of-urban-water-supply.pdf (Accessed on 15th May 2021).

Youth for Unity and Voluntary Action. (2020). Living with multiple vulnerabilities: Impact of COVID-19 on the urban poor in the Mumbai Metropolitan Region. Final Report. Mumbai: India. https://yuvaindia.org/wp-content/uploads/2017/03/COVID19_MMRImpact_UrbanPoor-1.pdf (Accessed on 21st June 2021).

10 Non-Covid Health Care under the Era of COVID-19

A Study from Rural Bengal

Md Sahidul Islam and Hippu Salk Kristle Nathan

10.1 Introduction

Health is a fundamental aspect of human life. Health has both intrinsic and instrumental value (Ruger, 2003). Under the human development paradigm (Sen, 1999; Fukuda-Parr, 2003; Alkire & Deneulin, 2009), health can be considered not only as means of development but also as an end by itself. Appropriately so, in the ranking of countries based on human development index (HDI) published annually in the human development reports by United Nations Development Program (UNDP, 2021), attainment in health is considered as one of the three dimensions of HDI, the other two being education and income. In short, health is not only one of the critical constituent components of development but also an important enabler for individuals' ability to live a life they value (Sen, 1999; Ruger, 2003).

Also, looking from utilitarian point of view, health is instrumental in economic development. The strong correlation between health and different macroeconomic development indicators has been established beyond doubt (WHO, 2001, 2003; Strittmatter & Sunde, 2013; Bloom, Kuhn, & Prettner, 2018). Health and economic growth have a both-way causality: healthy individuals and better health care system impact positively the income at both micro (personal or household) and macro (societal or national) level; and similarly greater personal income and higher GDP help the individuals to afford better nutrition and health care and aids the society to provide better health infrastructure to its citizens (Weil, 2014).

The current situation of COVID-19 has immensely increased burdens on the entire existing health care system. This novel corona virus (SARS-COV-2) disease, first detected in Wuhan, China in December 2019 (WHO, 2020), has turned out to be one of the worst pandemics in human history (Malki et al., 2021; Xu et al., 2021). As per the latest statistics, as of June 18, 2021, COVID-19 has spread to nearly all countries of the world and there are 178 million reported COVID-19 cases and more than 3.8 million deaths worldwide (BBC, 2021; Worldometer, 2021).

The COVID-19 pandemic has divided both the health care service infrastructure and patients into two categories: Covid and non-Covid. From the point of

DOI: 10.4324/9781003226970-14

view of health care services, separate hospitals are set up or separate sections of the hospitals are dedicated for Covid management. Similarly, among the health care professionals the responsibilities got assigned to Covid-duty and non-Covid duty. Also, there is a great divide between Covid and non-Covid patients, considering fear from person-to-person spread of infection where the infected can be asymptomatic coupled with lack of foolproof treatment on the one hand and life-threatening consequence of the disease on the other (Bajwa, Gupta, Wahi, & Goraya, 2020; Lingis, 2020; Chi et al., 2021). Owing to limited health care resources and greater attention to COVID-19, the management of non-Covid patients becomes very challenging (Nundy, 2021). The influx of non-Covid patients must have lessened because of the fear of infection, and also those who turned up must have not got the adequate medical attention during the peak of the pandemic situation.

Popular media and anecdotes reported the reluctance of non-Covid patients coming to hospital and other health care institutions due to poor management and treatment given to them during this corona pandemic. The non-Covid patients particularly pregnant women and heart patients faced lots of challenges to avail health care services (Babu, 2021). More the COVID-19 cases are reported, less the non-Covid patients have been able to access health care institutions. Consequently, an inverse relation in terms of accessibility to health care service between Covid and non-Covid patients has been found in the health care literature globally (Boeken et al., 2020; Goulabchand, Claret, & Lattuca, 2020; Hebbar, Sudha, Dsouza, Chilgod, & Amin, 2020; Santi, et al., 2021). One survey report corroborated that 'high concern of COVID-19 infection has resulted in a delay in treatment of non-Covid ailments' (NATHEALTH, 2021). Further, the survey reported 57% non-Covid patients delayed or postponed treatment due to concern of COVID-19 infections.

In this study we have attempted to understand the multitude of challenges (including health and non-health) in the COVID-19 regime faced by the non-Covid patients and their coping mechanisms (including accessing newly launched Government welfare schemes on account of COVID-19). We considered the non-Covid patients particularly from the poor communities, who suffer from various socio-economic deprivations. We have surveyed 88 non-Covid patients and their attendants of Murshidabad Medical College and Hospital, West Bengal carried out in June 2020. The results show that the majority of the non-Covid patients suffered from heightened out-of-pocket expenditure (OOPE) because of COVID-19–induced lockdown and lack of availability of medical and non-medical services. This OOPE aggravated the plight of the household more intensely when income of the household suffered severely due to the lockdown. To meet OOPE, the households got drained out of their savings and assets in some cases and in certain other cases had come under the clutch of money lenders mortgaging their meagre properties. Thus, the poor households got pushed down into the spiral of poverty further.

The rest of the paper is organized as follows. The next section gives distinguished aspects of COVID-19 with respect to health care. Section 10.3 gives an overview of the study area. The following section briefs the methodology adopted for the study. Section 10.5 discusses the results. The last section gives the concluding remarks.

10.2. Distinguished Aspects of COVID-19 with Respect to Health Care

The outbreak of pandemic caused by novel corona virus has destabilized lives and systems, and increased huge burdens on every sector of society, particularly on the health care sector. There are certain distinguished aspects of COVID-19 with respect to health care. We have put forward three such aspects in the following paragraphs.

First, COVID-19 is considered as a rich person's disease affecting the poor. For instance, the virus was imported to India by the rich and affluent people those who returned from China or other initially infected countries, particularly some of the developed economies of the West. In other words, the foreign source of the contamination made this virus to be a high-class disease at the onset of the virus spreading (Bengali, Linthicum, & Kim, 2021) and most of the cases detected in cities or metro-cities over the world. Also, at the country-level, rich countries had more cases to start with because of their greater global mobility and larger share of older population compared to poor countries, and subsequently the poor countries inherited the disease from the rich (Vilasanjuan, 2021). Like other pandemics of the past, coronavirus is considered by the poor as the disease of the rich killing the poor (*The Telegraph*, 2021).

The second interesting aspect of the novel corona virus is that it is an equalizer. It does not discriminate between rich and poor. However, the health care system, likewise its response towards any other disease, makes a discrimination among rich and poor, on account of former's greater proximity and affordability to better health care system. The rich COVID-19 patients demanded a greater attention of health care service and they have been able to access so. Nevertheless, the contagiousness of COVID-19 makes the rich-biased health care system of any society, not to ignore the poor COVID-19 patients and they need to be isolated and treated; otherwise, they become the potential source for further spread of the disease, which in turn might affect the rich. Having said this, the poor have suffered disproportionately in the COVID-19 regime because of severe strain in health infrastructure; for instance, shortage of beds, oxygen, and health care professionals during the second wave of the pandemic in India (*Lancet*, 2020; BBC, 2021; DW, 2021; Nundy, 2021).

Lastly, one of the hard realities of COVID-19 is that the health professionals treating the disease are at great risk (Nguyen et al., 2020). With the existing burdens to health care, the rapid increasing infected cases of COVID-19 patients add greater challenge to the front-line health workers (Johnson & Butcher, 2020). It is the front-line health care workers including doctors were at a greater risk to be affected by COVID-19 because of their higher exposure; so were endangering their lives in the process during this crisis. As per WHO, since the pandemic started nearly 115,000 health care workers have died due to COVID-19 worldwide (*The Hindu*, 2021). In India, as per the Indian Medical Association over 500 doctors died in the first wave of COVID-19 and more than 700 doctors died in the second wave (The Wire, 2020; *Financial Express*, 2021). It is interesting to note that despite the risk of high mortality, the doctors and health workers have discharged their duty to fight the pandemic (James, 2020; Pandey & Sharma, 2020).

These above-mentioned aspects show the extreme risky and dynamic nature of COVID-19 pandemic. Quite rightly, it has pulled up vast attention of all stakeholders including Government, media, civil society, and public at large. The entire focus of the society has been geared towards revamping the health care system of the country to tackle the impending danger posed by the corona pandemic. At this juncture, a major question arises that with COVID-19 drawing all attention to it, where does it leave the non-Covid patients? This paper is an attempt to provide some of the answers to this question.

10.3. Study Area: An Overview

10.3.1 Backwardness of Murshidabad

This study is situated at the Murshidabad district of West Bengal. The district is the fourth populous district of West Bengal having a share of 7.78% of population, that is, approximately 7.1 million population with a population density of 1334 per square km (Census of India, 2011). It is the maximum Muslim populous district of India with approximately two-thirds of its population belonging to the community (Sachar Committee, 2006; Census of India, 2011).

Murshidabad is one of the most socio-economically backward districts of the state (GoI, 2009; Parvin, Hashmi, & Ali, 2019). Values of some of the socio-economic indicators of Murshidabad vis-a-vis that of West Bengal is given in Table 10.1. As per the West Bengal Human Development Report 2004, in all the three dimensions, namely, education, health, and income, Murshidabad occupies a rank between 14 and 16 among the then 18 districts of the state (GoWB, 2004; Roy & Sen, 2010). The overall HDI value for Murshidabad was 0.46, whereas the corresponding value for the state was 0.61 (GoWB, 2004). In terms of Gender Development Index, which is male-female inequality adjusted human development index, Murshidabad with a value of 0.42 occupies a rank of 15 among the districts of West Bengal, which has state average value of 0.55 (GoWB, 2004).

The Murshidabad district is one of the poverty-stricken areas in comparison with other districts of the state (Ashraf, Ahmed, & Rawal, 2017). Though Murshidabad has a share of 0.6% of India's population (Census of India, 2011), it houses approximately 2% of India's poor (Parvin, Ali, Hashmi, & Khatoon, 2020). Out of the total 26 blocks of Murshidabad, as many as 23 are underdeveloped in terms of human development index (Ashraf, Ahmed, & Rawal, 2017). The backwardness of the district is highlighted through lower agricultural output, skewed distribution of land and higher incidence of landlessness, higher dependency on agriculture and lack of industrialization, and several other socio-economic and institutional barriers (Ali, 2018). Dutta (2017) has shown through a multi-dimensional poverty index based on illiteracy rate, primary level dropout rate, non-institutional delivery, and proportion of households having lack of access to water, electricity, and latrine facility that the Murshidabad district stood at second last position among the districts of the state indicating its extreme deprivations in all dimensions.

10.3.2 Health Status and Health Care Facility in the Study Area

Murshidabad district is also deprived with respect to both health status and health care facilities. The district ranked 471 among 599 districts in India with respect to nutritional attainment (IFPRI, 2021). The major incidence of communicable diseases prevalent in this district include acute diarrheal, acute respiratory infection, pneumonia, acute poliomyelitis, tetanus neonatal, kala azar, and so on (GoWB, 2004). In terms of various health parameters, the performance of Murshidabad is below the state's average performance (see Table 10.1).

In terms of health infrastructure and health care services provided to its citizens, Murshidabad is at a lower level compared to most of districts of West Bengal (GoWB, 2011; Hati & Majumdar, 2011). In an exercise of computing health infrastructure score by Hati and Majumdar (2011), the authors have shown the scores for all the districts of West Bengal by taking six indicators such as number of medical institutions, availability of equipment and medicine in the institutions, operating facility in the hospitals/centres, referral facility, availability and functioning of critical child care unit, and availability of beds in the medical institutions, Murshidabad district scores 50.9 out of 100 which is much below the state average score of 64.5 and the district was ranked second from the bottom (Hati & Majumdar, 2011). The authors also computed a health outcome score considering five indicators: infant mortality rate, percentage of women receiving antenatal care, share of institutional delivery, percentage of babies receiving postnatal care, and morbidity. Murshidabad district scored only 54.5 out of 100 whereas state average score was 68.5 and the district ranked third from the bottom (Hati & Majumdar, 2011).

Table 10.2 shows the status of the Murshidabad district vis-à-vis West Bengal in terms of availability of hospital beds wherein the data clearly indicate the shortage in the district. Murshidabad has large majority of population, that is, more than 80% of people living in rural areas (Census of India, 2011). However, total number of rural hospitals in the district is only 17 having a total of only 580 beds (GoWB, 2018). The headcount per bed for rural areas of Murshidabad turns out to be at 4197. The stark urban-rural disparity in hospital bed availability in West Bengal and for Murshidabad district is shown in Table 10.2. For West Bengal, there are 68% people who reside in rural areas; and rural areas only have 14% of hospital beds. Similarly, though 80% people reside in rural Murshidabad,

Table 10.1 Socio-Health condition of Murshidabad vis-à-vis West Bengal

Parameters	Murshidabad	West Bengal	Source
Total Literacy (%)	66.59	76.26	Census of India (2011)
Sex Ratio (female per 1000 male)	958	940	Census of India (2011)
Human Development Index	0.46	0.61	GoWB (2004)
Gender Development Index	0.42	0.55	GoWB (2004)
Human Poverty Index	0.396	0.282	Dutta (2017)
Household having no access to safe drinking water (%)	25.28	26.64	Dutta (2017)
Household without electricity connection (%)	65.35	45.51	Dutta (2017)
Household having no latrine facilities within the premises (%)	60.47	41.15	Dutta (2017)
Infant mortality rate (IMR)	41.5	38.0	GoWB (2004)
Children having anaemia (<11.0 g/dl) (%)	46.7	54.2	IIPS (2017)
Institutional Deliveries (%)	64	75	IIPS (2017)
Last births receiving antenatal care from ANM/nurse/midwife/LHV (%)	42.6	46.5	IIPS (2017)
Stunting (among children <5 years) (%)	41.9	32.5	IIPS (2017)
Wasting (among children <5 years) (%)	17.5	20.3	IIPS (2017)
Underweight (among children <5 years)	34.6	31.5	IIPS (2017)
Primary Health Centre Infrastructure score	52.5	67.7	Hati and Majumdar (2011)
Community Health Centre Infrastructure score	51.0	63.8	Hati and Majumdar(2011)

Table 10.2 Availability of hospital beds in Murshidabad and West Bengal

Description	Rural	Urban	Total
West Bengal Population	62,183,113 (68%)	29,093,002 (32%)	91,276,115
Murshidabad Population	5,703,115 (80%)	1,400,692 (20%)	7,103,807
Beds in West Bengal[a]	18,207 (14%)	115,331 (86%)	133,538
Beds in Murshidabad[a]	1,359 (20%)	5,225 (80%)	6,584
Population served per beds in West Bengal	3,415	252	684
Population served per beds in Murshidabad	4,197	268	1,089

Source: Dept. of Health and Family Welfare, Govt. of West Bengal, 2018 and calculated by authors.
a Excluding the beds of sub-centre.
   The number in the parentheses are the shares.

the rural areas have 20% of the hospital beds, whereas 80% of the beds were provided in urban areas where 20% people live. A study on the efficiency of hospitals in West Bengal also found the severe inequality of distribution of resources including hospital beds, equipment, and manpower among the districts of the state (GoWB, 2011).

10.4 Methodology and data base

The current study required understanding of the challenges faced by non-Covid patients along with their coping mechanism to deal with economic crisis to run their family. The study intended to investigate the difficulty in accessing public health care institutions including the problem of commuting to hospital during lockdown in the awake of COVID-19. We also studied the issues related to access of Government's newly launched schemes during this pandemic period. We relied on qualitative and quantitative data both from primary and secondary sources. For primary data, self-administered questionnaire was developed which included open ended questions to capture the experiences of non-Covid patients and caretakers. The questions were categorized under five heads: social, economic, health, transportation, and accessibility to Government schemes. A pilot study with 10 respondents was made to finalize the questionnaire. We interviewed 88 respondents. The survey was carried out during 11th to 16th June 2020. This period coincided with the state's unlock 1 period of 2020 where there was a restricted opening after more than two months of complete lockdown (Mint, 2020; NDTV, 2020). The respondents were selected randomly whosoever came to outpatient department (OPD) during the study period for treatment at Murshidabad Medical College and Hospital (MMCH). Rationality behind selection of MMCH is that this is the only district hospital cum college located at the district headquarter where people from different corners of the district come for treatment. For secondary data the available research papers, articles, Government departmental reports, district gazettes reports, and macro survey data including census data available in public domain have been taken into consideration.

10.5 Findings and Discussion

10.5.1 Social Condition

Among the respondents, approximately 92% belonged to the age group of 15–59 years, rest were 60 years or above. A large majority (more than 80%) of respondents were Muslim, the others being from Hindu religion. The gender division among the respondents was: male 59% and female 41%. An interaction with the staff at the ticket counter of the OPD reveals that the hospital has usually more female footfall than male. However, the low female footfall during pandemic is indicative of the fact that female must have faced greater restrictions in mobility during lockdown. The education levels of the respondents were: illiterates (36%), primary (std. I–V) (10%), secondary (std. VI–X) (38%), higher secondary (std. XI and XII) (8%), and higher (above std. XII) (8%). Out of the total respondents, more than one-third were illiterates of which males have a larger share, that is, 72%. Among the literate females, less than one in five had education above matriculation, whereas the same share for males was approximately one in three. This is in line with the observation of greater female dropout rates after eighth standard among the Muslim population in Murshidabad district (Hoque, 2016).

10.5.2 Economic Condition

Among the male respondents there were primarily agriculture laborers (31%), daily-wage earners (29%), and self-employed (15%). There were also farmers, drivers, vendors, students, and private job holders among the respondents. Among female, more than 90% respondents were engaged in domestic chores (housewives). All the respondents held ration cards and of them 21% belonged to below poverty line (BPL). In terms of housing type, approximately three out of 10 had *pucca*-house, five out of 10 had semi-*pucca* house, and two out of 10 had *kucha* house. The average land size of homestead was 2.8 *katha* (approximately 2,000 sq. ft.) homestead land. Average annual income of respondents' households is Rs. 82,857, that is, a monthly average income of less than Rs. 7,000. The share of households among different range of annual incomes were: Rs. 0–50,000 (19%), Rs. 50,000–100,000 (56%), Rs. 100,000–200,000 (23%), and above Rs. 200,000 (2%), but none above Rs. 250,000. Because of lockdown more than 70% of the respondents had to lose their job. Only those who have owned agriculture land and self-employed particularly grocery-shop owner continued their economic activity. Forty percent of respondents have reported their expenditure to be more than their income indicating they were borrowing money to meet their daily expenses.

10.5.3 Health Condition

We have classified respondents in terms of the health condition of the concerned patients into five groups based on the number of months they were suffering from the ailments (0–3 months, 3–6 months, 6–9 months, 9–12 months, and more than 12 months). More than 60% respondents indicated that they were suffering from last three months from different types of diseases/health conditions such as cold and cough, pregnancy, surgery-infection, or ENT, gastro, or respiratory problems. Approximately one in six respondents were suffering from three to six months, and one in five were suffering from six months or more.

Table 10.3 shows the expenditure on treatment of disease and the source from which they managed expenses during the pandemic crisis. The majority of sources of expenditure was debt from relatives and friends. More than 50% of those who were suffering from three to six months managed their expenditure by borrowing from their relatives. Among those who were suffering from three to six months, more than 40% of them drained their savings to meet the health expenses.

10.5.4 Transportation System

Murshidabad district spreads over the area of 5441 square kilometres comprising 254 Gram Panchayats, 26 community development (CD) blocks, five

Table 10.3 Expenditure on diseases and sources

Suffering by Month	Respondents(%)	Average expenditure on disease in Rs.	Source of expenditure							
			Self-saving (%)	Debt from relatives and friends (%)	Selling agri.goods (%)	Selling domestic animal (%)	Gold loan (%)	Land mortgage (%)	Group loan (%)	Loan from local lender (%)
0–3	63.64	6,803	41.07	39.29	1.79	3.57	8.93	3.57	0.00	1.79
3–6	17.05	6,860	26.67	53.33	6.67	6.67	0.00	0.00	6.67	0.00
6–9	4.55	7,000	25.00	25.00	0.00	0.00	25.00	25.00	0.00	0.00
9–12	9.09	12,500	25.00	25.00	0.00	0.00	37.50	0.00	12.50	0.00
Above 12	5.68	53,000	0.00	40.00	0.00	0.00	40.00	0.00	0.00	20.00
Total	100.00	17,233	34.09	39.77	2.27	3.41	12.50	3.41	2.27	2.27

Source: Primary survey, 2020.

sub-divisions, and seven muncipalities (District Census Handbook, Murshidabad, 2011). Out of the total CD blocks, our respondents belonged to 19 blocks. Approximately 60% of the respondents belonged to Berhampore block (where the hospital is located) and two neighbouring blocks (Beldanga and Hariharpara; Table 10.4).

The mode of travel for respondents were: by e-rickshaw (39%), followed by bus (30%), own bike (11%), and hired car (7%). Most of those who came by any transport other than own transport, reported being charged with higher fare.

10.5.5 Accessibility to Government scheme

When all economic activities halted to a standstill situation, joblessness resulted in zero income during the lockdown period. In such a crisis, India being a welfare state, it was expected to provide support to people in distress through various welfare schemes. The study showed that more than 70% people had lost their jobs and rest of the respondents being self-employed, particularly those who are in agriculture and own grocery shops could continue their activities. Among the respondents, approximately 57% confirmed benefitting from PMGKY (*Pradhan Mantri Gareeb Kalyan Yojana*) which aimed to provide Rs 500 per month for three months (IBA, 2020). Only five of 88 respondents reported to be insured under *Samajik Surakha Yojana* (SSY). The SSY-2017 is a social security scheme launched by GoWB in 2017 for the workers of the unorganized sectors aimed at providing these workers with a degree of income security when faced with contingencies of old age, survivorships, incapacity, disability, bringing up children, gender disparity, curative or preventive medical care and empowerment (GoWB, 2017). Also, only 17% of the respondents were insured through Swasthyasathi Health Scheme which is provided by Government of West Bengal for basic health coverage for secondary and tertiary care up to five lakhs per annum per family (GoWB, 2016). Apart from this insurance, all respondent barring one had no other insurance (LIC, General

Table 10.4 Mode of transport to hospital

Round trip distance (Km)	Own bike	Hired Car	E-Rickshaw	Ambulance	Bus	others	All mode	Fare paid overcharged (%)	
								Yes	No
0–20	5	2	22	0	8	1	38	77.00	23.00
20–40	5	3	8	2	8	5	31		
40–60	0	0	3	0	6	4	13		
60–80	0	0	1	0	2	1	4		
80–100	0	0	0	0	1	0	1		
>100	0	0	0	0	1	0	1		
Total	**10**	**5**	**34**	**2**	**26**	**11**	**88**	**100**	

Source: Primary survey, 2020.

Insurance, etc.). A low percentage of contingency security and insurance holders among the respondents may signal their socio-economic vulnerability and precarity, particularly during this COVID-19 regime.

10.6 Impact of lockdown and coping mechanism

There is little doubt left on the impact of COVID-19–led lockdown which has hit all segments of society irrespective of caste, creed, colour, and socio-economic class. However, COVID-19–led lockdown had hit poor households more intensely than rich households because of the former's greater vulnerability. This becomes even more challenging for the poor households when any of their family members have some non-Covid aliments and they fall sick during lockdown. In the following sub-sections, we have attempted to understand our respondents' coping mechanism and management in such situations.

10.6.1 Loss of Incomes and Increase Expenses

The available secondary data on the COVID-19 highlighted how people lost their livelihoods with closed down of marketplaces (Shylendra, 2020). Our survey reveals nearly 70% respondents lost their jobs. This has led draining of their savings and increased debt in grocery shops for their daily basic needs. In addition, the households faced OOPE due to health issues. For India, OOPE is more than 60% of the total health expenditures and has been fluctuating between 60% and 75% during 2000 to 2018 (World Bank, 2018). In Indian scenario, 4.5% people got poor because of their high OOPE (Bose & Dutta, 2018). In order to meet high OOPE, poor reduce their non-food expenditures such as expenditure on fuel, education, and clothing (Panikkassery, 2020). The OOPE of treatment for non-Covid health ailments has increased further on account of lockdown. To meet the OOPE, the households had to borrow from relatives and take loan from local moneylenders at higher rate of interest mortgaging their piece of agriculture land, gold, or also, in some cases sold their assets such as domestic animals (see Table 10.3). This situation would further push people down the spiral of poverty.

10.6.2 Changing Food Consumption

It is undeniable that provision of ration grains gave a big relief to the poor households; if not full stomach but relieved them from starvation. West Bengal positioned at moderate level of food security among Indian states (Basu, 2020). Being a coastal state, non-veg items, particularly fish, are part of food consumption of households of all economic strata (Ghosh & Bose, 2018). However, we found that food consumption had reduced in terms of items and even quantity during lockdown period. The respondents recounted their experiences of coping with food scarcity. Deprivations in food consumption of female members of households has been higher than male members: one woman respondent said, 'chele-meye ke khaoanor por dekhi haadite tarkari nei, kancha lanka tipe vaat khelam' (after feeding our children, there is no curry in the pot, we had to consume rice with green chilly). Low nutrition is going to affect the health issues of the family which might further increase their OOPE and other related plights.

10.6.3 Coping Mechanism from Sickness

Respondents had to put up with their sufferings due to lack of immediate availability of money. 'No money to buy food then how we can spend on treating disease in this situation' – was a comment by a few of the respondents. The lockdown added to the misery. More than 75% of the respondents were not frequently able to access public health care due to unavailability of vehicles because of lockdown. Though NSS (2015) report signals slightly increase of access to free medicine and diagnostic test, public health facility for poor people substantially decreased and OOPE on medical care and medicine increased in West Bengal (Bose & Dutta, 2018). Our study shows that people could not afford overcharged fares to hire vehicles because of shortage of money at hand. They managed their suffering being at home; some relied on traditional home remedies to obviate their pain temporarily. Others had to resort to rural medical practitioners or quacks and nearby private medical care providers and bought services directly from them at a higher fee. This recourse to quacks sometimes worsened the ailment and increased their OOPE.

10.6.4 Women Plights

Our survey results indicated women plight got aggravated during this period. Available studies indicated both women and men lost their jobs and economic opportunities, but women are likely to be deprived more than men folk in terms of work opportunity as lockdown caused reverse migration leading to oversupply of male laborers at the native locations (De, 2020). Traditional available literature discussed about 'double-deprivation' of poor women on account of gender and poverty disadvantages (Sahay, 1998). In this study, we found women to be 'triple-deprived'. First, they belong to poor households, which have drifted to greater poverty due to the job loss of male members, and women have lost their limited job opportunity at native locations. Second, the intra-household sharing of food-grains received through PDS is not sufficient to feed all stomachs, as a result, the women of the family eat at the last and the least, indicating unequal sharing of poverty (Ray, 1998). Third, during this crisis period, a poor household is running out of resources in terms of money that is essential to meet needs like medical treatments (or even for food expenses) and men are unlikely to sell their assets (like bike or mobile); hence the women had to sell or mortgage their ornaments or any other valuables.

10.7 Concluding Remarks

COVID-19–led lockdown, on the one hand, has helped to some extent to contain the spreading of coronavirus, but on the other hand it has intensified the sufferings of a poor household particularly a household with non-Covid patients. The health care sector is stretched to attend to the COVID-19 patients. This study situated in one of the most backward regions of West Bengal has revealed different aspects of sufferings of non-Covid households amid this pandemic. The lockdown imposed multiplied adverse impacts on non-Covid households as people had to incur additional burdens over and above ill-health induced OOPE because of restrictions in public transportation system. Selling of assets and borrowing from lenders to meet these expenses have pushed the households into poverty trap. The Government schemes at this juncture came as a welcome breather, but the assistance is not adequate and also most of the people could not avail the same. The study suggested a triple deprivation of women of the poor households because of the unequal sharing of poverty on one hand and selling and mortgaging of women owned assets on the other. Since the COVID-19 situation might likely to prevail in the country in the months to come, the Government might like to provide a transport allowance for households below poverty line in case of any future lockdown situation.

This study raises the larger question of urban-rural divide, where rural remote areas suffer from inadequate availability of health care infrastructure and human resources. Availability of medical professionals including doctors at block and panchayat level and strengthening of rural hospitals with better health care facilities would be able to address most of the health care needs of rural people. This would reduce huge influx of patients travelling long distances to the main hospital at the district level and thereby not only reduce the health expenditure of people on non-medical heads, but also decrease the burden on the main hospital.

References

Ali, D.M.H. (2018). Causes and consequences of out-migration: A study in Murshidabad District, West Bengal, India. *International Journal of Development Research*, 8(01), 18189–181894. Retrieved from https://www.journalijdr.com/sites/default/files/issue-pdf/11842.pdf

Alkire, S. & Deneulin, S. (2009). *An Introduction to the Human Development and Capability Approach: Freedom and Agency.* London: Earthscan.

Ashraf, S.W.A., Ahmed, S., & Rawal, S.K. (2017). Status of human development in Murshidabad district of West Bengal. *Indian Journal of Human Development*, 7(1), 141–160. doi: 10.1177/0973703020130106

Babu, N.M. (2021). In pandemic wave, non-COVID patients too are feeling the heat, Delhi. *The Hindu.* May 12. Retrieved from https://www.thehindu.com/news/cities/Delhi/in-pandemic-wave-non-covid-patients-too-are-feeling-the-heat/article34545945.ece

Bajwa, S.J.S., Gupta, R., Wahi, A., & Goraya, S.P.S. (2020). Exploring the unknown territories in the new normal world of COVID. *Journal of Anesthesiology, Clinical Pharmacology*, 36(Suppl. 1), S77. doi: 10.4103/joacp. JOACP35020

Basu, R. (2020). The Saga of food security in West Bengal. *International Journal of Research -Granthalayah*, 8(1), 189–202. doi: 10.29121/granthaalayah.v8.i1.2020.267

BBC (British Broadcasting Corporation) (2021). Covid map: Coronavirus cases, deaths, vaccinations by country.

Bengali, S., Linthicum, K., & Kim V. (2021). How coronavirus—a rich man's disease—infected the poor. *Los Angeles Times*. May 8. Retrieved from https://www.latimes.com/world-nation/story/2020-05-08/how-the-coronavirus-began-as-a-disease-of-the-rich

Bloom, D., Kuhn, M., & Prettner, K. (2018). Health and economic growth, Discussion Paper Series, IZA Institute of Labor Economics, November. Retrieved from http://ftp.iza.org/dp11939.pdf

Boeken, T., Le Berre, A., Mebazaa, A., Boulay-Coletta, I., Hodel, J., & Zins, M. (2020). Non-COVID-19 emergencies: Where have all the patients gone? *European Radiology*, 30, 5220–5221. doi: 10.1007/s00330-020-06961-z

Bose, M. & Dutta, A. (2018). Health financing strategies to reduce out-of-pocket burden in India: A comparative study of three states. *BMC Health Services Research*, 18(1), 830. doi: 10.1186/s12913-018-3633-5

Census of India (2011). Murshidabad district: Population 2011–2021 data. Retrieved from https://www.census2011.co.in/census/district/7-murshidabad.html

Chi, X., Chen, S., Chen, Y., Chen, D., Yu, Q., Guo, T., ... Zou, L. (2021). Psychometric evaluation of the fear of COVID-19 scale among Chinese population. *International Journal of Mental Health Addiction*, Jan 11, 1–16. doi: 10.1007/s11469-020-00441-7

De, I. (2020). Pandemic likely to reverse women's empowerment gains made in rural India. *The Hindu Business Line*. June12. Retrieved from https://www.thehindubusinessline.com/opinion/pandemic-likely-to-reverse-womens-empowerment-gains-made-in-rural-india/article31811862.ece

Dutta, A. (2017). Modified poverty index of West Bengal: A human development approach. *International Journal of Multidisciplinary Research and Development*, 4(10), 43–50. Retrieved from http://www.allsubjectjournal.com/download/3532/4-10-22-589.pdf

DW (Deutsche Welle) (2021). COVID: Why is India facing an oxygen shortage? May 4.

Financial Express (2021). Over 700 doctors died of Covid-19 during second wave: Indian Medical Association, by FE Online, June 12. Retrieved from https://www.financialexpress.com/lifestyle/health/over-700-doctors-died-of-covid-19-during-second-wave-indian-medical-association/2270155/

Fukuda-Parr, S. (2003). The human development paradigm: Operationalizing Sen's ideas on capabilities. *Feminist Economics*, 9(2–3), 301–317. doi: 10.1080/1354570022000077980

Ghosh, M. & Bose, K.S. (2018). Anthropometric study of adult male brick-kiln workers of Murshidabad district, West Bengal (Doctoral dissertation, Vidyasagar University, Midnapore, West Bengal, India). Retrieved from http://inet.vidyasagar.ac.in:8080/jspui/handle/123456789/2154

GoI (Government of India) (2009). A note on the backward regions grant fund program. *Ministry of Panchayati Raj*. Retrieved from https://ininet.org/a-note-on-the-backward-regions-grant-fund-programme.html

Goulabchand, R., Claret, P.G., & Lattuca, B. (2020). What if the worst consequences of COVID-19 concerned non-COVID patients? *Journal of Infection and Public Health*, 13(9), 1237–1239. doi: 10.1016/j.jiph.2020.06.014

GoWB (Government of West Bengal) (2004). West Bengal human development report 2004. *Development and Planning Department*, GoWB.

GoWB (2011). Hospital efficiency in West Bengal: A study on secondary level hospitals. *Department of Health and Family Welfare*, GoWB.

GoWB (2016). About the scheme, Swasthyasathi. *Department of Health and Family Welfare*, GoWB.

GoWB (2017). Samajik Surakha Yojana 2017 (SSY-17). *Labor Department*, GoWB. Retrieved from https://ssy.wblabour.gov.in/Content/pdf/257.pdf

GoWB (2018). Health on the March 2016–2017 & 2017–2018 (Combined) West Bengal. *State Bureau of Health Intelligence Directorate of Health Services*, GoWB.

Hati, K.K., & Majumder, R. (2011). Health for development: A district level study in West Bengal. *Munich Personal RePEc Archive* (MPRA), Paper No. 45849. Retrieved from https://mpra.ub.uni-muenchen.de/45849/

Hebbar, P.B., Sudha, A., Dsouza, V., Chilgod, L., & Amin, A. (2020). Healthcare delivery in India amid the Covid-19 pandemic: Challenges and opportunities. *Indian Journal of Medical Ethics*, 5(03), 215–218. doi: 10.20529/IJME.2020.064

Hoque, M.Z. (2016). Muslim education in Murshidabad district of West Bengal: Problems and solutions. *International Journal of Humanities and Social Science Studies*, 2(4), 268–272. Retrieved from http://oaji.net/articles/2016/1115-1464939345.pdf

IBA (Indian Banks' Association) (2020). Pradhan Mantri Garib Kalyan package in the light of COVID-19 pandemic. Retrieved from https://www.unionbankofindia.co.in/pdf/Final-June2020-English.pdf

IFPRI (The International Food Policy Research Institute) (2021). District Nutrition Profile, Murshidabad and West Bengal, POSHAN (Partnership and Opportunities to Strengthen and Harmonize Actions for Nutrition in India).

IIPS (International Institute for Population Sciences) (2017). National Family Health Survey (NFHS-4), India, 2015–16: West Bengal.

James, N. (2020). Last line of defense: How healthcare workers soldier on in the Covid fight. *The Hindu Business Line*. May 21. Retrieved from https://www.thehindubusinessline.com/news/last-line-of-defence-how-healthcare-workers-soldier-on-in-the-covid-fight/article31638329.ece

Johnson, S.B. & Butcher, F. (2021). Doctors during the COVID-19 pandemic: What are their duties and what is owed to them? *Journal of Medical Ethics*, 47(1), 12–15. Retrieved from https://jme.bmj.com/content/47/1/12.

Lancet, T. (2020). India under COVID-19 lockdown. *The Lancet*, 395(10233), 1315. doi: 10.1016/S0140–6736(20)30938-7

Lingis, A. (2020). The new fear of one another. *Bioethical Inquiry*, 17, 471–472. doi: 10.1007/s11673-020-10035-6

Malki, Z., Atlam, E.S., Ewis, A., Dagnew, G., Ghoneim, O.A., Mohamed, A.A., ... Gad, I. (2021). The COVID-19 pandemic: Prediction study based on machine learning models. *Environmental Science and Pollution Research*, Apr 10, 1–11. doi: 10.1007/s11356-021-13824-7

Mint (2020). Covid-19: West Bengal to extend lockdown till 30 June, A. Banerjee (Ed.). June 08. Retrieved from https://www.livemint.com/news/india/covid-19-west-bengal-to-extend-lockdown-till-30-june-says-mamata-banerjee-11591617256785.html

NDTV (2020). Bengal extends lockdown till June 15 with some relaxations, all India, home. May 30. Retrieved from https://www.ndtv.com/india-news/coronavirus-lockdown-west-bengal-extends-lockdown-till-june-15-with-certain-relaxations-2237975

Nguyen, L.H., Drew, D.A., Graham, M.S., Joshi, A.D., Guo, C.G., Ma, W., ... Chan, A.T. (2020). Risk of COVID-19 among front-line health-care workers and the general community: A prospective cohort study. *The Lancet Public Health*, 5(9), e475–e483. doi: 10.1101/2020.04.29.20084111

NSS (National Sample Survey) (2015). Key indicators of social consumption in India: Health. NSS 71st Round, 2015. Report No. NSS KI (71/25.0), Ministry of Statistics & Program Implementation, Government of India.

Nundy, S. (2021). Covid-19 in India: Oxygen supplies run low; hospital fees run high. *The BMJ Opinion*. Retrieved from https://blogs.bmj.com/bmj/2021/05/07/covid-19-in-india-oxygen-supplies-run-low-hospital-fees-run-high/

Pandey, S.K. & Sharma, V. (2020). A tribute to frontline corona warriors--Doctors who sacrificed their life while saving patients during the ongoing COVID-19 pandemic. *Indian Journal of Ophthalmology*, 68(5), 939. doi: 10.4103/ijo.IJO75420

Panikkassery, A.S. (2020). Impact of out of pocket health expenditure on consumption pattern of below poverty line households in India. *Millennial Asia*, 11(1), 27–56. doi: 10.1177/0976399619900608

Parvin, F., Hashmi, S.N.I., & Ali, S.A. (2019). Appraisal of infrastructural amenities to analyze spatial backwardness of Murshidabad district using WSM and GIS-based kernel estimation. *Geo Journal*, 86(2). doi: 10.1007/s10708-019-10057-7

Parvin, F., Ali, S.A., Hashmi, S.N.I. & Khatoon, A. (2020). Accessibility and site suitability for healthcare services using GIS-based hybrid decision-making approach: A study in Murshidabad, India. *Spatial Information Research*, 29, 1–18. doi: 10.1007/s41324-020-00330-0

Ray, D. (1998). *Development Economics*. Princeton, NJ: Princeton University Press.

Roy, D., & Sen, M. (2010). Final report on poverty, hunger and public action: An empirical study of on-going decentralization initiatives in West Bengal. Loka Kalyan Parishad Government of India.

Ruger, J.P. (2003). Health and development. *The Lancet*, 362(9385), 678. doi: 10.1016/S0140–6736(03)14243-2

Sachar Committee (2006). Social, economic and educational status of the Muslim community of India. Prime Minister's High-Level Committee, Cabinet Secretariat, Government of India, New Delhi.

Sahay, S. (1998). *Women and Empowerment: Approaches and Strategies*. New Delhi: Discovery Publishing House.

Santi, L., Golineli, D., Tampieri, A., Farina, G., Greco, M., Rosa, S., ... Giostra, F. (2021). Non-COVID-19 patients in times of pandemic: Emergency department visits, hospitalizations and cause-specific mortality in Northern Italy. *Plos one*, 16(3), e0248995. doi: 10.1371/journal.pone.0248995

Sen, A. (1999). *Development as Freedom*. Oxford: Oxford University Press.

Shylendra, H.S. (2020). How is Covid-19 playing out in rural India? *The Hindu Business Line*. May 25.

Strittmatter, A. & Sunde, U. (2013). Health and economic development—evidence from the introduction of public health care. *Journal of Population Economics*, European Society for Population Economics, 26(4), 1549–1584. doi: 10.1007/s00148-012-0450–8

The Telegraph (2021). Disease of the rich, killer of the poor'-How Covid-19 brought Latin America to its knees, science & disease, news global health security.

The Wire (2020). IMA says at least 515 doctors have died of COVID-19. October 02.

UNDP (2021). Human development reports 1990–2020. Retrieved from http://hdr.undp.org/en/global-reports.

Vilasanjuan, R. (2021). A virus for the rich and for the poor? Is Global Barcelona Institute for Global Health. March 18. Retrieved from https://www.isglobal.org/en/healthisglobal/-/custom-blog-portlet/virus-rico-virus-pobre/90649/0

Weil, D. N. (2014). Health and economic growth. In P. Aghion & S. Durlauf (Eds.), *Handbook of Economic Growth* Vol (1st ed.; pp. 623–682). Amsterdam: North Holland.

WHO (World Health Organization) (2001). Macroeconomics and health: Investing in health for economic development: executive summary/report of the Commission on Macroeconomics and Health. Retrieved from https://apps.who.int/iris/handle/10665/42463

WHO (2003). Investing in health: A summary of the findings of the commission on macroeconomics and health. Retrieved from https://apps.who.int/iris/handle/10665/42463

WHO (2020). Coronavirus disease 2019 (COVID-19) Situation report–94. *WHO*. Retrieved from https://apps.who.int/iris/handle/10665/331865

World Bank (2018). Out-of-pocket expenditure (% of current health expenditure) 2018. *The World Bank*.

Worldometer (2021). Covid-19 coronavirus pandemic. Retrieved from https://www.worldometers.info/coronavirus/

Xu, Z., Ho, M., Bordoloi, D., Kudchodkar, S., Khoshnejad, M., Giron, L.B., … Muthumani, K. (2021). Techniques for developing and assessing immune responses induced by synthetic 1 DNA vaccines for emerging infectious diseases. Retrieved from https://www.researchgate.net/publication/350291166_Techniques_for_developing_and_assessing_immune_responses_induced_by_synthetic_DNA_vaccines_for_emerging_infectious_diseases

11 Impact of Pandemic on School Education in India

Generations at Risk

Saswati Paik and Roshan M Samuel

11.1 Introduction

The pandemic caused by COVID-19 has impacted human life in several ways. Additionally, it has resulted in serious threats to human development. Followed by the economic crisis, it has further triggered an anxiety for future generations. This pandemic is unique, considering the unprecedented scale of impact. The last pandemic of a similar scale was the Spanish Flu in 1918–20. Right before COVID-19, UNESCO's Global Education Monitoring Report 2020 stated that one-sixth or 260 million children (both adolescents and youth) across the world were not attending school (Sahlberg, 2020). With the pandemic, approximately 214 million children globally have missed more than three-quarters of their in-person learning due to school closure (UNICEF, 2021). This cannot be ignored as 'Preventing a learning crisis from becoming a generational catastrophe requires urgent action from all' (De Giusti, 2020, p. 3). Since March 2020, schools in India were not physically operational owing to the pandemic, some states decided to reopen schools for select classes since the beginning of 2021; however, this couldn't continue considering the advent of the second wave. In such a situation, it is important to highlight the educational crisis and related long-term challenges associated with children in India caused by the pandemic.

11.2 Literature Review

Several epidemics and pandemics have affected human civilization historically and caused not only fatality but also long-lasting social impact. Globalization ensured that the spread of COVID-19 was accelerated in a short time making matters worse. The literature reviewed for this study focus on the following: (a) the historical trajectory of pandemics, (b) the short and long-term impacts of a pandemic on society and children, (c) the specific impact of a pandemic on India's human development, specifically the youngest generation due to the closure of academic institutions, especially schools.

a   The Historical Trajectory of Pandemics and Epidemics
    A century ago, when the total world population was less than 2,000 million, an influenza virus caused the biggest pandemic in human history

DOI: 10.4324/9781003226970-15

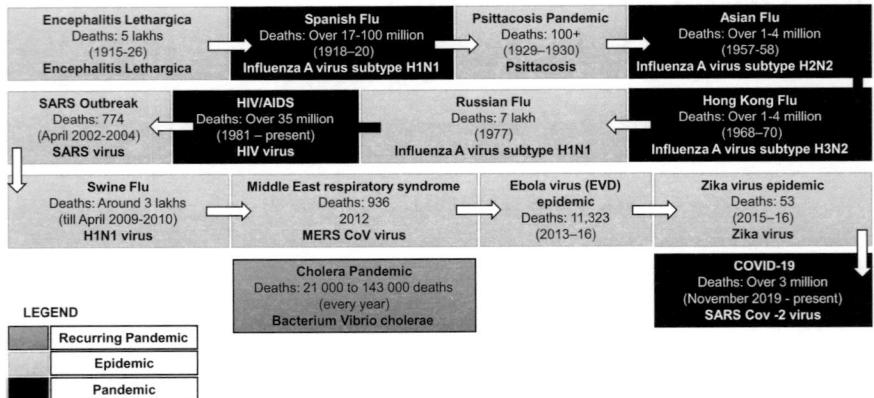

Figure 11.1 The historical trajectory of various epidemics and pandemics across the world since 1915.

which was known as the 'Spanish Flu'. The impact of this pandemic went beyond 1918–19. Taubenberger and Morens (2006) suggest that all influenza since that time (except the infections from avian viruses such as H5N1 and H7N7), have been caused by variants of the influenza virus of 1918. Figure 11.1 shows the historical trajectory of various epidemics and pandemics across the world since 1915. The pandemic and epidemic events are shown by different shades with the exception of one that stands alone since it prevails for a longer period and recurringly impacts us, the cholera pandemic.

b   Short- and long-term impacts of a pandemic on society and children

Several literatures focused on impacts of a pandemic on society. While highlighting the reason behind the continuity of the Spanish Flu to be the object of substantial interdisciplinary attention, Aassve et al. (2020) argued that during an epidemic or pandemic, only social distancing may have limited effects, but high mortality and deaths of young adults can disrupt the entire society. A pandemic is inversely linked to a nation's economic growth and therefore directly linked to the toll on children's health and nutrition. This is because children are mostly dependent on their immediate family and caregivers for their survival as well as upbringing; they are therefore the most vulnerable in a pandemic.

c   Impact of the pandemic on school closure and academic progress of children

The International Federation of Red Cross and Red Crescent Societies have classified pandemics as a natural hazard (Seddighi, 2020). Such a hazard may harm children disproportionately. Research shows that closure of schools increases the financial burden of families using daycare facilities or their reliance on vulnerable older relatives nearby. At the same time, working parents might either leave children unsupervised or give up employment to stay at home with them. School closures during the Ebola epidemic in 2014–16 'increased dropouts, child labor, violence against children, teen pregnancies, and persisting socioeconomic and gender disparities' (Armitage and Nellums, 2020).

Azevedo et al. (2000) have presented a range of estimates that came from simulations based on three scenarios: (a) Optimistic scenario where schools are closed only for three months of a school year of ten months, and the effectiveness of mitigation measures put in place by Governments like remote learning are high; (b) Intermediate scenario where schools are closed for five months, and there is a medium level of effectiveness of mitigation measures; (c) Pessimistic scenario where schools are closed for seven months with low levels of effectiveness of mitigation measures. Such a dataset might be useful for future planning for schools.

11.3 Objectives

The objectives of this research are:

i   To analyse the trends of the pandemic and their impacts on school-going children in India;
ii To analyse the existing vulnerability of school children in India, its nature, scale, and impacts on society and its enhancement due to the pandemic;
iii To propose possible solutions to address the issues associated with the vulnerability of children.

11.4 Approach of the Study

The study has three parts. Part 1 highlights the existing vulnerability of children in India with a few comparisons globally. This is discussed with secondary data

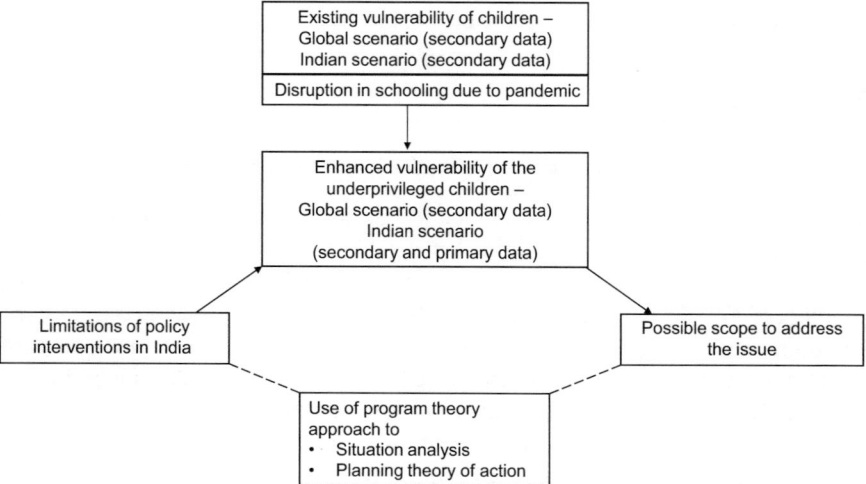

Figure 11.2 Approach of the study.

analysis. Part 2 focuses on the pandemic's impact on the academic progress of children with the help of primary data and discusses the limitations of policy interventions and possible scope for the future with a special focus on the Right to Education (RTE) Act and NEP 2020. Part 3 illustrates a probable intervention designed using the program theory approach to indicate some viable methods to overcome the upcoming crisis associated with children's lack of academic progress. The diagram below shows the approach of the study (Figure 11.2).

11.5 Methodology

This study is conducted as a qualitative, inductive research. Both secondary and primary data corroborate the research. The sources of secondary data consist of literature published by international organizations such as UN Agencies, World Bank, World Health Organization (WHO), Centre for Budget and Governance Accountability (CBGA), Child Rights and You (CRY), and national bodies in India especially the Ministry of Education, National Commission for Protection of Child Rights (NCPCR), and Ministry of Labour. A primary survey was conducted for this research to understand the perception of various stakeholders about the school closure, the participants constituted teachers, head teachers/principals, parents of school-going children, NGO workers associated with school-related works, and university/college students. In total, 152 participants from 15 states responded to the survey questionnaires. Both secondary and primary data helped to validate the arguments supporting the recommendations and suggestions which are made for the school systems, following the program theory approach. 'A program theory is an explicit theory or model of how an intervention contributes to a set of specific outcomes through a series of intermediate results' (Funnel and Rogers, 2011). The approach has been used for illustrating the theory of change and theory of action as this chapter aims to portray the issues associated with a disruption in school education during the pandemic and suggests actions to overcome some of the challenges.

11.6 Analysis

11. 6.1 Existing Vulnerability of Children in Indian Context

The World Bank's Orphans and Vulnerable Children (OVC) toolkit defines vulnerability as 'the group of children that experience negative outcomes, such as the loss of their education, morbidity, and malnutrition, at higher rates than their peers' (World Bank, 2005, p. 7). India has been identified as a country with the highest rate of malnutrition. About 37.9% of children under five years are stunted and 20.80% of children are wasted. These percentages are much higher than the Asian averages (Global Nutrition Report, 2020).

Chronic undernutrition is linked with other issues such as underdeveloped brain as well as prolonged-lasting harmful consequences like weakened mental ability and learning capacity, poor school performance, and increased risks of nutrition-related chronic diseases. This has a direct impact on adult income generation, due to reduced economic advancement, loss in productivity, poorer cognition and poorer educational outcomes. Across the globe, stunting and various forms of under-nutrition are responsible for nearly half of all child deaths (UNICEF, 2016). Stunted children are found more in rural areas than urban areas in India. It is important to note that inequality in nutrition does not simply stem from the class divide that exists in India. The largest democracy in the world, that is, India also struggles with serious cases of discrimination among the various castes and sub-castes in the society.

11.6.2 Enhanced Vulnerability of Children during Pandemic

Around 140 million of India's rural poor migrate seasonally in search of work. These migrants, who are part of India's unorganized workforce estimated at over 350 million, move back and forth undertaking a vast array of casual work in the construction, manufacturing, services, and farm sector. They remain excluded from services and rights as workers and citizens, in their rural homes and their places of work (Aajeevika Bureau, 2014). Imagine the case of a family where there is an ailing member or one who is disabled, a family drowning in debt or one with a single parent. Children from such families are more at risk of consuming drugs, indulge in child labour, or even in the flesh trade. For such children, school is undoubtedly a better and safer place for their holistic development.

Indian Government under the RTE Act granted the provision of free education for children from 6 to 14 years of age. Although commendable, several vulnerable children still slip through the cracks and end up in unorganized sectors as child labourers. There are three such groups of children – first are those left behind in the villages by parents employed elsewhere, the second group consists of those migrated with their parents and often engaged in the construction sector, brick kilns, and agricultural sectors, and the third group includes the children who themselves migrate for employment. The children of the first group are dependent on remittances sent back home, so the reduction or elimination of parent's wages due to the lockdown and limited movement during pandemics have immediate effects on food intake and health outcomes of these children (Unni, 2020). Similarly, the children of the second and third group get directly affected due to the closing down of economic activities. The children in India have been vulnerable for a plethora of reasons during the pandemic and resultant lockdown. The job losses faced by the migrant workers have aggravated the difficulty of these children.

11.6.2.1 Migrant Labourers' Children

A media report in 2020 highlighted the plight of a teenage boy from Bihar sold to a garment making factory. This boy with others of his age stayed in substandard conditions in a factory in Gujarat and toiled so that their employers would send money for their parents to survive (The New Indian Express, 2020). A study conducted in seven cities on informal worksites revealed the condition of accompanying migrant children, 30% of them never enrolled in schools, 80% did not have access to education, and 90% did not access Integrated Child Development Services (ICDS). Most of the children were found to be dwelling in hazardous and unhygienic conditions (Unni, 2020). The International Labour Organization (ILO) has predicted that with the pandemic, the world may witness a surge in child labour for the first time in 20 years, reversing years of progress in this domain (ILO, 2020).

11.6.2.2 COVID-19 Orphans and Children with Single Parents

By June 2021, the number of children who have lost their childhoods has only seen a higher peak. Post the second wave, a new category has been added to the list of the pandemic caused grief – the 'COVID-19 orphans'. Numerous children have become orphans or now have a single parent after the pandemic. Over 9,300 children have either lost their parents or were abandoned in the COVID-19 pandemic since March 2020 as informed by the National Commission for Protection of Child Rights (NCPCR) to the Supreme Court (Mathur, 2021). The NCPCR has initiated action and pilot launched mapping of children and families vulnerable to child trafficking and matching them with potential benefits under different Government schemes. The commission has recommended extensive mapping to be initiated in all the districts of all the states which are potential 'Source', 'Transit', and 'Destination' hotspots of child trafficking, as per the information available with Anti Human Trafficking Units (AHTUs) and National Crime Records Bureau (Indian Express, 2021). However, identifying such children will be very important given the vulnerability they might face in near future with the mere 27% functional AHTUs.

11.6.2.3 Increased Malnutrition

India is home to 40% of undernourished children of the world (Bharthi et al., 2017). Being in school, under the supervision of adults, engaged in play or other learning activities, being fed the mid-day meal (MDM) as provisioned for by the Government addressed many of the vulnerabilities. However, the pandemic and the resultant school closures acted like ripping the Band-Aid of a raw wound. The pandemic has increased the risk factors for child malnutrition. Due to the disruption of Anganwadi services and MDM, numerous children do not have access to regular, nutritious meals. The National Family Health Survey (NFHS) 2019–20 shows the prevalence of malnutrition among children has increased from the previous survey year, 2015–16 in a few states. India may fail to meet targets for improvement in nutrition indicators set under POSHAN Abhiyan (earlier National Nutrition Mission) for 2022, and even the targets set by WHO-UNICEF for 2030 (Ambast et al., 2021).

11.6.2.4 Vulnerability Due to Child Trafficking

Reports of child trafficking and abuse are rampant, in most cases, there is a direct causal link of the guardians lacking money to sustain their families. Traffickers use the vulnerabilities of the families to convince guardians to send their children away on the pretext of job opportunities for a paltry sum of Rs 5,000–15,000. Post the pandemic, with schools closed, reports of trafficked children have seen a steep rise. Between April and September in 2020, 1,127 children suspected to be trafficked were saved across India as per *Bachpan Bachao Andolan* (News18, 2020).

11.6.2.5 Vulnerability Caused by Disrupted Schooling

UNESCO (2021) lists out a few consequences of school closure that include interrupted learning, poor nutrition, unprepared parents, confusion and stress for teachers, gaps in child care, high economic cost, rise in dropout rates, increased exposure to violence and exploitation, and so on. Each pointing towards how the world would see a generation succumb holistically, this has far-reaching economic, psycho-social, and political consequences for a country like India. A report stated that India would have to face an economic loss of over 400 billion US dollars in the future and not to mention an entire generation skill-less and as a result jobless (The Economic Times, 2020). Here is a case about one such school dropout who was interviewed during the study (see Box 11.1).

Box 11.1 A Case Study from India

Since the lockdown of 2020, Ansh, a state Government school student, has been working at a nearby inverter mechanic's shop in Maharashtra. In some schools, online classes begun, but Ansh's family didn't find it feasible. 'I would like to study more' said the young boy who should be appearing for his 12th grade examinations if everything were normal. On asking what he aspires to become he promptly replied, 'an engineer, that's why I am working here'. Considering how the pandemic elongates it is most likely Ansh would not be able to complete his 12th grade and he would drop out resorting to this menial job of repairing inverters.

11.6.2.6 School Systems and Their Poor Preparedness Leading to Vulnerability

According to Unified District Information System for Education (U-DISE) data 2019–20, there are 1,507,708 schools in India under 17 different types of school management (Table 11.1). For the analysis, the schools are divided into six types

Table 11.1 Number of schools run by different school management

Type	School management	Number of schools	Percentage of schools to total schools	Main characteristics
A	Department of Education	785,106	Around 70.67	Largely non-residential schools
	Local Body	196,040		
	Government Aided	84,362		
	Total Type A Schools	**1,065,508**		
B	Tribal Welfare Department	46,279	Around 3.24	Mainly residential schools, serving specific children for a social purpose
	Social Welfare Department	1,717		
	Ministry of Labour	353		
	Jawahar Navodaya Vidyalaya	626		
	Total Type B Schools	**48,975**		
C	Kendriya Vidyalaya/Central Schools	1,259	Around 0.16	Mainly serving the children of specific people in Government service
	Sainik School	67		
	Railway School	85		
	Central Tibetan School	16		
	Other Govt. managed schools	939		
	Other Central Govt. Schools	83		
	Total Type C Schools	**2,449**		
D	Madrasa Recognized (by Wakf Board/Madrasa Board)	19,538	Around 1.30	Serve minority community
	Total Type D Schools	**19,538**		
E	Private Unaided (Recognized)	337,499	Around 22.38	Completely privately managed
	Total Type E Schools	**337,499**		
F	Madrasa Unrecognized	4,139	Around 2.23	Unrecognized schools
	Unrecognized	29,600		
	Total Type F Schools	**33,739**		
	Total number of schools	**1,507,708**		

Data Source: U-DISE 2019–20.

as described below. Figure 11.3 shows the distribution of students across all types of schools.

Table 11.2 shows that majority of enrolled children study in Type A and E type schools. While Type A schools are Government managed or Government aided schools, Type E schools are private unaided schools. According to a 2019 estimate of the Ministry of Statistics and Program Implementation (MoSPI), 70% of families in India pay less than Rs 1,000 per month in course fees in private unaided schools and only 15.7% of families pay more than Rs 1,500 per month as course fees in private unaided schools (Central Square Foundation, 2020). The unaided private schools pay the salary of teachers from the fees collected from the students and therefore, it can be assumed that teachers of low-fee private schools are paid very little. Given the kind of expense and skills of teachers involved, it is unlikely that such schools where per child payment is less than Rs 1,500 per month, would be able to afford online classes to children. As per

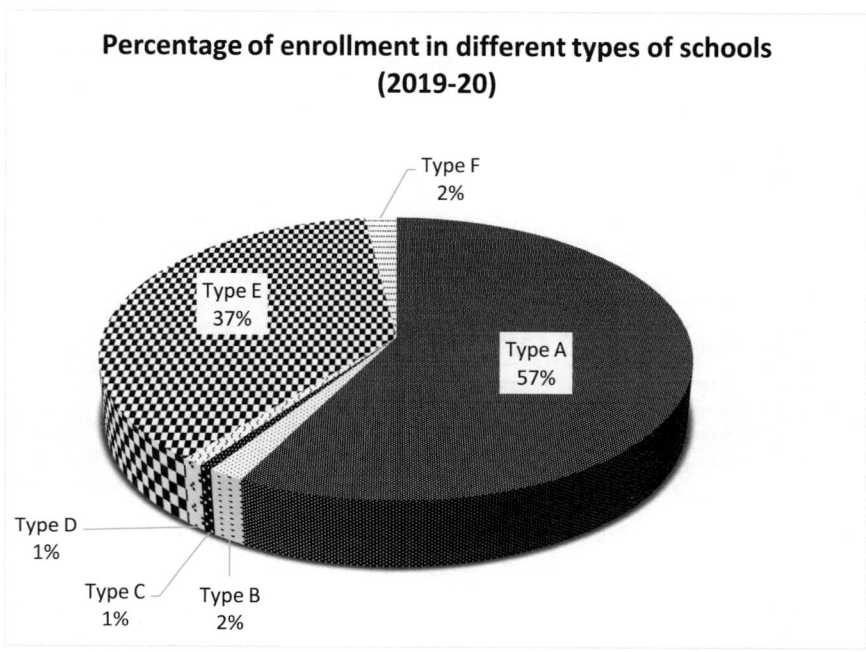

Figure 11.3 Percentage of students enrolled in different types of schools.
Data Source: U-DISE 2019–20.

Table 11.2 Probability of virtual/online learning provided to children since March 2020
as per the information received from the primary survey and media reports

Virtual/online learning – probability analysis

Type A	Type B	Type C	Type D and F	Type E
57% children	1% children	Around 1% children	Around 3%–4% children	Around 37% children
Mostly not provided regularly except for Kerala	Partially Provided to specific children	Mostly provided	Information not known	Around 15.7% of them pay more than Rs 1,500/ month as per child school fees where remote learning provision is possible

Table 11.2, if 1%–2% children from Type B and C schools and 15%–16% children studying in private unaided schools get the opportunity of online education during the pandemic years along with a few more from a few states like Kerala, the total percentage of children getting the continuity in their academics is not even 20% which is an alarming picture.

Grades of students in school/college	March 2020	March 2021	March 2022	May-June 2022	Status analysis
				3	Relatively easy to manage (Syllabus & Assessment)
			2	4	
		1	3	5	Difficult to mange (Syllabus, Advanced Conceptual Learning & Adolescence)
	Pre-school	2	4	6	
	1	3	5	7	
	2	4	6	8	
	3	5	7	9	
	4	6	8	10	
	5	7	9	11	
	6	8	10	12	
	7	9	11	Degree Year 1	Transition from school to college
	8	10	12	Degree Year 2	
	9	11	Degree Year 1	Degree Year 3	
	10	12	Degree Year 2		
	11	Degree Year 1			
	12				

Figure 11.4 Consequence of disruption of schooling for two consecutive years.

What will be the consequence of the school closure? As per the 'No Detention Policy' mentioned in RTE Act, automatic promotion of all children to the next grades is in progress without any academic engagement at least till 8th grade (Right to Education Act, 2009). Figure 11.4 shows these children's academic standing in May-June 2022 as per their age-specific grades. As most of these children are deprived of any academic engagement due to school closure in two consecutive academic sessions between March 2020 and March 2022, when they will get promoted to the next grade, many of them will have a huge learning gap. Students of a few grades might face more difficulty to manage because of the shift in terms of the expected level of learning. The students entering adolescence need a unique nurturing method. The psycho-social space of students needs to be considered as the most important factor while re-integrating them in the schooling process after the gap of two consecutive academic years.

11.7 Discussion with the Help of Program Theory

The challenges associated with these children are discussed with the help of program theory. There are four categories of children found in India now –

1 Not enrolled in the school education system due to various reasons;
2 Recently got excluded from the education system, may or may not come back;
3 Temporarily excluded and may come back after two years of disruption;
4 Continuing education with virtual learning or homeschooling facilities.

The first three categories require specific integration plans if we have to save the country from a catastrophe. The solution to most of the problems mentioned before by UNESCO is to ensure that students remain connected with online schooling. This solution has the potential to mitigate some part of the catastrophe predicted. However, merely this measure would not suffice. Adjustments need to be made at all academic and economic levels. To make the recommendations and suggestions logically aligned as per the situation, the first step of the program theory approach, that is, situation analysis has been done.

11.7.1 Situation Analysis

Situation analysis is an integral part of program theory often used to identify problems and opportunities and understand the causes and consequences of problems. A situational analysis, considering the main problem to be disrupted childhood during the pandemic reveals the reasons why this gap was created. Below provided are the causal links of the said main problem which are validated by secondary information and primary data.

The causes and consequences as displayed in the Figures 11.5 and 11.6, respectively, reveal close similarities with UNESCO's list of adverse consequences of school closure. The causes and consequences are also validated by the findings from the primary data collected from the participants through a survey across the country. Here are the main findings from the participants which validated the situation analysis done as per the secondary data:

- Most of the respondents believe that most children between 6 and 18 are vulnerable. There are short and long-term impacts on the children as perceived by most of the participants; the short-term impacts include dropout, child labour, child marriage, trafficking, and so on, whereas the long-term impact indicated by them is the lack of employability of the younger generation.
- Most schools run by the State Department of Education remained closed for a maximum time of the academic year (2020–21), a few private schools could continue online education for their students. Respondents largely believe that the major challenge schools providing no online education are facing is the lack of capacity. The causes behind such dysfunctional schools include lack of preparedness of the schools in terms of infrastructure, lack of affordability and students' feasibility of attending virtual classes, and lack of capacity of teachers to run virtual classes. The majority of them believe that schooling systems require learning resources and teacher training.

11.7.2 Focusing and Scoping and Context-Specific Theory of Action

The suggested intervention focus would be re-integration of children into school. Given the diversity existing in India, there are different models to be adapted

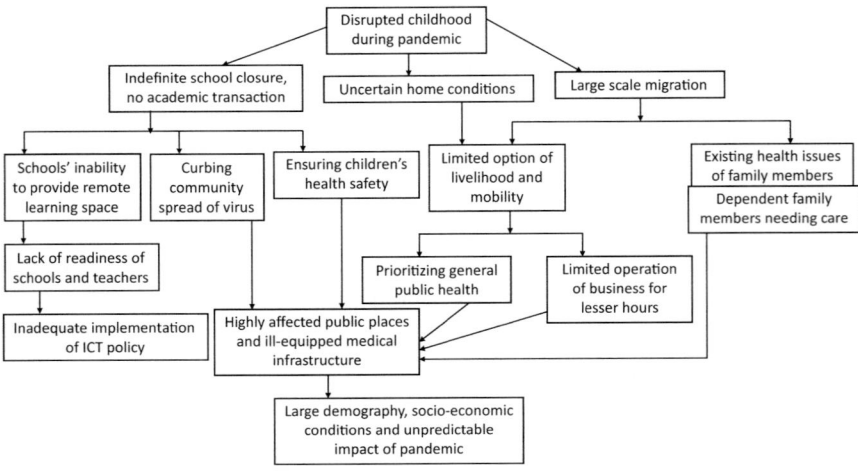

Figure 11.5 Situation Analysis showing causes of disrupted childhood and causal links of various factors.

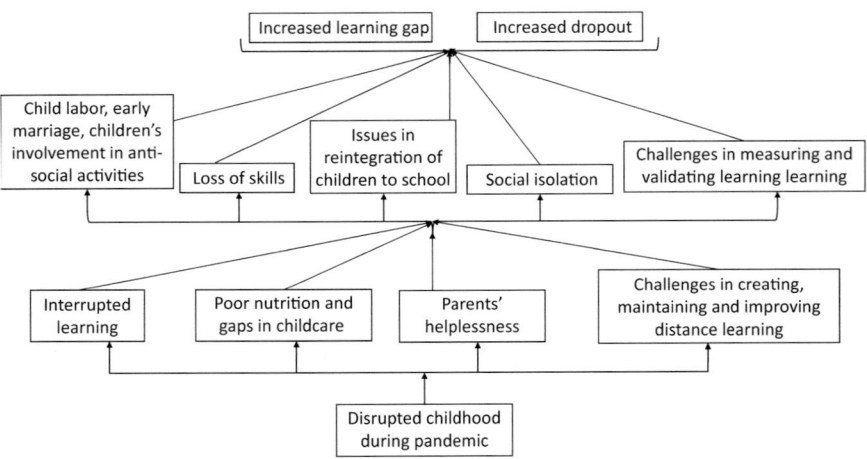

Figure 11.6 Consequences of disrupted childhood.

while re-integrating children into schools. The process might be slow; however, the focused intervention will have the scope of revamping the employability of the young generation to some extent at a much better pace.

Let us now look at two kinds of scenario for two different sets of contextual setting – (i) areas where offline and/or online learning options are possible, (ii) areas where online learning option is not possible. Based on the above contexts,

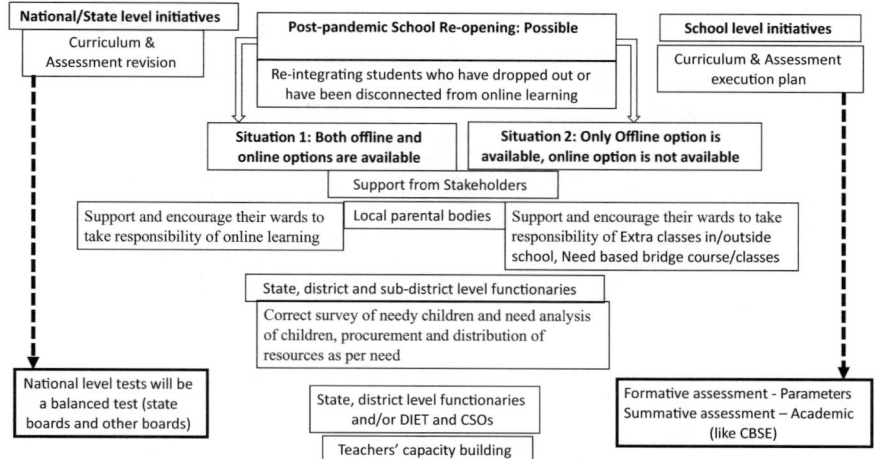

Figure 11.7 Scenarios with offline/online options.

two types of children for whom these interventions need to be planned where different stakeholders must take part as illustrated in Figure 11.7.

11.7.3 Program Theory Matrix (PTM) for Long-Term Sustainability

Based on the policy recommendations and promises made so far for education in India, a tentative plan of action is being suggested here for re-integration of disconnected/dropout children and bridging the digital divide. Table 11.3 illustrates a PTM in brief for long-term sustainable solution for building resilience in schools for any future emergency leading to long-term school closure. Here success criteria indicate how success of such an intervention may look like and success factors are the possible factors affecting the intervention.

The scenarios provided and the PTM designed is for a long-term outcome. For immediate and intermediate goals, the intervening team must target to achieve integration in small numbers. For instance, as an immediate measure targeting 35% of students to be ready for online schooling would be a reasonable target to achieve. To aid the maximum coverage of private and Government schools being online ready, school managements should actively enable their school management committees (SMCs), parent-teacher associations (PTAs), and alumni to contribute towards the resource crunch they face. Considerations are imperative for education decision-makers at national, local and school levels. The report of UNICEF titled as 'Building Resilient Education Systems beyond the COVID-19 Pandemic' also talks about short-term, medium-term, and long-term priorities similar to the strategy suggested here (UNICEF, 2020).

Table 11.3 Program Theory Matrix for long-term sustainable solution

Program Objectives

- Re-Integration of disconnected/dropout children and bridging the digital divide
- Improvement in proportion of schools, students and teachers with capacity for remote learning

Success criteria	Success factors	Resources	Activities	Outputs
Maximum children re-integrated to online schooling	Program factors 1 Willingness of state Government bodies	1 Smartphones/ Smart-tablets	1 Survey of device and connectivity needs of students per school management	1 An online school time-table made by each school management
Most Teachers are Confident about conducting Online Classes	2 Co-operation of central regulatory and funding bodies	2 Internet connection hardware	2 Procurement of devices, distribution and installation of required hardware and software	2 A uniform expectation list for students by the school
Maximum Schools started online classes	3 Agency of local governing bodies	3 Required licensed software	3 Basic operability training	3 A guideline for quality maintenance
Most parents support their ward in their online schooling experience	4 Resilient and resourceful school management	4 Training modules	4 Resilience building and motivational training	4 A uniform expectation list for parents by each school.
Maximum experts feel that tapered curriculum is necessary and sufficient	5 Accountable human resource	5 Qualified human resource	5 Career counselling	5 National standardized curriculum
Most experts feel that assessment criteria is necessary and sufficient	6 Rational participatory domicile bodies	6 Digital content (for students and teachers)	6 Parent-teacher and student counselling	6 State standardized curriculum
	7 Social justice	7 Secure physical infrastructure	7 Consensual discussion and finalization of revised curriculum, pedagogic practices, revised assessment criteria, proctored online assessment and grading guidelines (national and state), bridge course structure (state-wise)	7 National standardized vocational curriculum
	Non-program factors 1 Raging pandemic	8 NGO support	8 Qualified human resource to deliberate on user cases of assessment	8 State standardized vocational curriculum
	2 Natural and man-made disaster	9 Monetary resource		9 Pedagogic practice handbooks for states
		10 Laptops/desktops		10 National and state outline for assessment and grading
		11 Web-cameras		11 Tools for proctored online assessment
		12 2:1 Channel speakers		
		13 Microphones		

11.8 Rays of Hope

While most of the state Government-run schools remain closed due to the pandemic except for one state, that is, Kerala, few schools across the country have continued efforts to provide a virtual learning opportunity to their students, here three examples are provided based on the information obtained during the primary survey. None of these models is to be adopted as it is; however, this is evidence of possible approaches.

Example 1 Mechanism for Change – The KV Model

In the academic year 2020–21, *Kendriya Vidyalayas* successfully conducted online examinations and ensured continuity of learning (digitalLEARNING Network, 2021). The central Government school executed this feat by pooling resources through their vast alumni network. The alumni was informed of the vast digital divide within the demographics of the school and understanding the problem the members contributed towards the procurement of devices and crowdfunded the resources that would aid in schooling to be online. According to primary data, alumni members actively formed a platform where the requirements of their schools were displayed and members contributed towards the procurement of required resources.

Example 2 Social Welfare Department Schools

Andhra Pradesh Social Welfare Residential Institutions Society (APSWRIS) was established to run residential schools and colleges for Scheduled Castes under Social Welfare Department. The APSWREIS, in an understanding with the public broadcaster Doordarshan's Saptagiri TV channel, started broadcasting teachers' videos, explaining the lessons, for two hours daily from April 8, 2020, for SSC students (Verma, 2020; Subramanian, 2021). A few students studying in the schools run by APSWREIS got the opportunity of online classes throughout the school closure as they were selected by the school for intensive learning to prepare for the national and state engineering and medical tests.

Example 3 Private School

When the first lockdown was being imposed, a private school in Maharashtra was at the end of finishing its syllabus for the 10th standard. However, it was required as per their policy to conduct assessments before the batch appeared for their board exams. To accommodate this feat online, the teachers were asked to form WhatsApp broadcast groups for the classes since the application was very popular. Learning materials and mock question papers were circulated to the group and students were asked to answer them in their notebooks and submit them at the school physically. When this method could not be applied, due to strict lockdown students were instructed to study by themselves and contact their teachers to clarify doubts and answer sheets were submitted as a digital copy across WhatsApp. To streamline the process, private resources were hired to set up an online architecture on the Google platform. Live classes and a repository of learning resources were some of the features of this method. Parents who could not afford another device were helped by the resourceful ones in tandem with local mobile phone vendors who sold refurbished models for a lesser cost.

Like the Social Welfare Department run schools, if state Government-run schools and private schools were to conduct internal examinations to determine aptitude towards various career opportunities and offer selected students extra services beyond schooling, it would motivate students lacking interest, to be more focused. This would serve the purpose of garnering larger support for schooling both online and offline.

11.9 Policy Integration – Recommendations and Suggestions

A policy brief prepared by the CBGA and CRY has mentioned that the shutting down of schools and the decision of shifting traditional classrooms to digital platforms have increased learning inequality among children, numerous children are pushed out of school due to the digital divide. It states some of the issues associated with school closures that need immediate attention and suggests some short-term policy measures (Kundu and Sonawane, 2020). Following are some suggestions to be considered for the policy integration.

11.9.1 Revising RTE Provision of Admission to an Age-Appropriate Class

The RTE 2009 norm of age-appropriate admission must be relooked at. The norms must be deliberated on such that students who have dropped out during the pandemic are provided the opportunity to finish their education from the point they dropped out or by having a refresher course till their age-appropriate class which could be subject to assessment.

11.9.2 Choice-Based Credit System

In NEP 2020, promises have been made towards the reintegration of drop-out children. The third section of the policy document talks about 'Curtailing Dropout Rates and Ensuring Universal Access to Education at All Levels'. It emphasizes on 'holistic education' by providing opportunities through vocational skills. Once the schools will start functioning, there might be temporarily dropped out children who must be reintegrated in schools. During the pandemic days, the skills acquired by the children for the sake of livelihood as seen in the case study of Ansh in section 11.6, could be considered as 'skills acquired' for their reintegration and they must be encouraged further to take up skill-building courses in the form of 'vocational education' as promised in NEP 2020 in section 16.6. A choice-based credit system can provide more flexibility to the children especially of high schools for both skill-based and knowledge-based courses for reassuring better employability in the future. The state Government must incentivize vocational training institutes in the admission of students who during their years away from school acquired skill training. This should be in tandem with central and state institutes of vocational training. Both state and central Government should generate opportunities in this field aligning relevant projects (but not limited to) and incentivizing the employability chances of concerned students.

11.9.3 *Importance of Plan of Action and Systems Approach*

It would be beneficial if the policy guidelines provided in NEP 2020 were to be converted into a Plan of Action and executed as per the context-specific requirements of the schools. The intervention proposed in section 11.7 can be best executed if school complexes are set up as promised in NEP 2020. Through a survey, the number of school-going children must be identified in an area. Further, to maximize accessibility school premises should be selected strategically. The Government must seek the help of NGOs and corporates in training personnel at school to ensure the sustainability of the procedures.

11.9.4 *Monitoring to Increase Effectiveness*

The new normal mode of school education may continue with digital teaching learning platform for a while and it is difficult to predict now if a blended learning space is going to be the future trend. Considering the challenges faced during the pandemic, a major lesson to be learnt which is an effective system should be present to keep the schooling process operational. Proper resourcing, guiding and monitoring teaching processes, providing appropriate skills to teachers, teacher educators led by peers and experts may slowly improve the process. In future for any similar crisis leading to massive school closure, at least majority of the children can be served in a better manner, and many of them can be saved from unpredictable vulnerability.

11.10 Conclusion

The closure of schools considering the pandemic is justified. However, as learning organizations, schools must demonstrate the capacity to adapt to external changes. The abrupt stop in guided teaching-learning processes validates the poor preparedness towards remote learning. Considering the vast young demography in the country, it is necessary to dedicate enough attention to issues of continuing education. Therefore, a nationwide resilience approach is the need of the hour to save generations from a long-term catastrophe.

References

Aajeevika Bureau (2014) Retrieved from http://www.aajeevika.org/labour-and-migration.php

Aassve, A., Alfani, G., Gandolfi, F., and Le Moglie, M. (2020). *Epidemics and trust: The case of the Spanish flu.* IGIER, Università Bocconi.

Ambast, S., Kundu, P., and Sonawane, S. (2021). *Impact of COVID-19 on child nutrition in India: What are the budgetary implications?* New Delhi: CBGA and CRY.

Armitage, R., and Nellums, L. B. (2020). Considering inequalities in the school closure response to COVID-19. *The Lancet Global Health*, 8(5), e644.

Azevedo, J.P., Hasan, A., Goldemberg, D., Aroob Iqbal, S., and Geven, K. (2020). Simulating the potential impacts of COVID-19 school closures on schooling and learning outcomes a set of global estimates. The World Bank.

Bharthi, K., Ghritlahre, M., Das, S., and Bose, K. (2017). Nutritional status among children and adolescents aged 6–18 years of Kolam tribe of Andhra Pradesh, India. *Anthropological Review*, 80(2), 153.

Central Square Foundation (2020). *State of the Sector Report: Private Schools in India.* New Delhi. Retrieved from www.centralsquarefoundation.org

Child labor in Delhi's home-based garment industry: Adolescence lost in struggle to survive (September 24, 2020). The New Indian Express.

Covid-19 pandemic has created a second crisis in India — The rise of child trafficking (October 25, 2020). News18.

De Giusti, A. (2020). Policy brief: Education during COVID-19 and beyond. *Revista Iberoamericana de Tecnología En Educación y Educación En Tecnología*, 26, e12.

digitalLEARNING Network. (2021). KVS allows teachers to conduct online classes from home. Retrieved from http://digitallearning.eletsonline.com/2021/04/kvs-allows-teachers-to-conduct-online-classes-from-home/

Funnell, S.C., and Rogers, P.J. (2011). *Purposeful program theory: Effective use of theories of change and logic models.* San Francisco: Jossey-Bass.

Global Nutrition Report. (2020). *Action on equity to end malnutrition.* Bristol: Development Initiatives. Retrieved from globalnutritionreport.org/reports/2020-global-nutrition-report/

ILO. (2020). COVID-19 may push millions more children into child labour – ILO and UNICEF. Retrieved from http://www.ilo.org/global/about-the-ilo/newsroom/news/WCMS_747583/lang--en/index.htm

Johnson, N., and Mueller, J. (2002). Updating the accounts: Global mortality of the 1918–1920 'Spanish' influenza pandemic. *Bulletin of the History of Medicine*, 76, 105–115.

Kendriya Vidyalaya Sangathan, Government of India. (n.d.). Retrieved from kvsangathan.nic.in/.

Kundu, P., and Sonawane, S. (2020). *Impact of COVID-19 on School Education in India: What Are the Budgetary Implications?* New Delhi: CBGA and CRY.

Mathur, A. (2021). Over 9,300 children lost parents or were abandoned in pandemic, NCPCR informs Supreme Court. *India Today*. Retrieved from www.indiatoday.in.

Ministry of Education, Government of India (2021). Report on U-DISE + 2019–20. Retrieved from udiseplus.gov.in/#/Publication

Office of the Secretary, APSWREIS (2021). General Note on APSWREIS. Retrieved from www.apswreis.in/.

Over 9,000 children affected by pandemic: NCPCR submits data from states to SC (June 02, 2021). Indian Express.

Right to Education Act (2009). The right of children to free and compulsory education act. Retrieved from http://mhrd.gov.in/sites/upload_files/mhrd/files/upload_document/rte.pdf

Sahlberg, P. (2020). Does the pandemic help us make education more equitable? *Educational Research for Policy and Practice, 20*, 1–8.

Seddighi (2020). Vulnerability for response. Disaster medicine and public health preparedness. Retrieved from http://www.ncbi.nlm.nih.gov/pmc/articles/PMC7492580/.

Subramanian, S. (2021). The lost year in education. Retrieved from www.macleans.ca/

Taubenberger, J., and Morens, D. (2006). 1918 influenza: The mother of all pandemics. *Emerging Infectious Diseases, 12*(1), 15–22.

The Telegraph (2021). Teachers' online misery revealed. June 03. Retrieved from www.telegraphindia.com

UNICEF (2016). Stop stunting. www.unicef.org/india/what-we-do/stop-stunting

UNICEF (2020). *Building resilient education systems beyond the COVID-19 pandemic: Considerations for education decision-makers at national, local and school levels.* Switzerland: Geneva.

UNICEF (2021). COVID-19: Schools for more than 168 million children globally have been completely closed for almost a full year, says UNICEF. Retrieved from http://www.unicef.org/press-releases/schools-more-168-million-children-globally-have-been-completely-closed

UNESCO (2021). Adverse consequences of school closures. Retrieved from en.unesco.org/covid19/educationresponse/consequences

Unni, J.C. (2020). Social effects of Covid-19 pandemic on children in India. *Indian Journal of Practical Pediatrics, 22*, 102–104.

Verma, P.S. (June 21, 2020). Class in the room. *The Hindu.*

World Bank. (2020). The COVID-19 pandemic: Shocks to education and policy responses. Retrieved from https://www.worldbank.org/en/topic/education/publication/the-covid19-pandemic-shocks-to-education-and-policy-responses

12 Conspicuous Philanthropy or CSR in Times of the COVID-19 Pandemic

Sudhir Kumar Sinha

12.1 Introduction

Corporate social responsibility (CSR), in normal times, pursues a business to owe its obligation towards society, first as a result of the impact of its decisions and activities under the rational orientation of corporate responsibility. Second, to make it equal and inclusive under the moral orientation of responsibility, CSR seeks firms to share the wealth with the society in which it operates. The former argument for CSR is related to what the business does to a society through its specific operations, which is why it becomes reasonably a mandatory obligation on firms to mitigate those impacts and externalities. The latter, however, is what society rightfully expects and subsequently demands from businesses as being good corporate citizens to secure better living standards and quality of life for the communities. Matten and Crane (2005) have extensively discussed the business-society relationship under a concept of corporate citizenship (CC), which describes a company's responsibilities toward society. 'social responsibility refers to the decisions of businessmen and actions taken for purposes at least partially beyond the company's direct economic or technical interest' (Davis, 1960). However, whatever the case may be, CSR, in general, has been equated mostly with philanthropy, used interchangeably for each other. On the other hand, companies have always argued that they voluntarily contribute to society by supporting foundations and NGOs in normal times and also in times of crisis caused by disasters or pandemics. While this is true that companies participate in disaster/pandemic relief, such participation is often found ad-hoc and inadequate, done in a piecemeal manner at the kindness or discretion of a company. Therefore, this chapter critically reviews the reasons and substance of CSR under the premise of business-society relationships. It argues why 'CSR as Unusual' is rationally needed in times of crisis than remaining a sentimental one-off conspicuous philanthropic response to a tragedy.

In specific response to the global fight against the spread and effects of the novel coronavirus, companies globally have joined hands with Governments and civil society organizations. Many companies in India have undertaken several CSR activities for pandemic relief (Hurun India, 2020; CRISIL, 2020). However, the most visible CSR activity in response to the pandemic crisis is firms'

DOI: 10.4324/9781003226970-16

donations to the PM CARES Fund, which the Government of India created to tackle the immediate challenges. But the relief work needed quantum resources. So, the Government, to meet demands for those additional resources, expected companies to make donations. The chapter, therefore, debates why such donations to dedicated funds, although critical, are an outcome of regressive thinking.

Reports of various researches (The World Bank, 2020; Oxfam, 2020) confirm that the pandemic has caused a rise in social problems such as poverty, unemployment, and hunger. With the effects of coronavirus, the enormity of these problems has grown bigger. Therefore, CSR programs are expected to integrate the new humanitarian challenges, which have been multiplied due to the COVID-19 effects. The new normal is different and will be so during and after the pandemic. Hence, society will expect firms to be more proactive and innovative in times of crisis. However, since the immediate priorities before the country were to prevent the spread of the virus, the preferences were given to improve the health care infrastructure, equip them with required amenities, vaccination, and so on. But the bigger challenge for a company now and in the future is to strike a balance between continuing CSR commitments and responding to new (additional) social obligations created by the pandemic. So, what should companies do in such situations vis-à-vis their CSR policies intended for normal times? Does/will CSR policy acknowledge pandemics and disasters as an inclusive social concern to be included in CSR policies? Hence, this chapter analyses whether companies also consider increased problems along with urgently required health care services, and accordingly, whether they make extraordinary commitments in times of crisis.

Further, CSR in India is made mandatory by an Act, which underwent several amendments during the pandemic. As a result, companies diverted a part of their CSR funds to the PM CARES Fund to meet the new demands. Hence this chapter critically reviews how these amendments influence firms' decisions on CSR and whether these decisions can have a far-reaching effect on the CSR commitments in the future. Finally, it debates whether CSR responses to the pandemic in the absence of a dedicated policy are knee-jerk reactions and, therefore, it is conspicuous CSR/philanthropy.

Arguably, the situation is complex, demanding more intense CSR applications instead of applying standard approaches to the aggregated humanitarian problems. Therefore, with its scope limited to the role of companies in times of the COVID-19 crisis in India vis-à-vis the CSR Act, companies' CSR policies, and their continued social obligations, the chapter takes a critical review of company's philanthropic responses during the COVID-19 pandemic through a qualitative study. The research analyzes the secondary data on the CSR and disaster expenditure of 27 companies. The study selected a mix of public sector enterprises, Indian private limited companies, and multi-national companies (Tables A12.1 and A12.2). Data for the study is traced from the Ministry of Corporate Affairs (MCA) website and its national CSR portal. Also, it considered the various kinds of literature, including the annual reports and CSR policies of companies, international agencies, scholarly articles, media reports, and so on. The research is referred to as 'study' throughout this chapter.

12.2 CSR and Philanthropy: Are They the Same or Different?

Often corporate social responsibility is mentioned in reference to the philanthropic initiatives of a company. However, most arguments ascribe to academicians and experts seeking CSR to encompass economic, legal, ethical, and social dimensions under moral and rational orientations. The fundamentals of engaging in CSR in the new millennium are targeted as 'doing good to do well'. While doing good is interpreted in the broader perspective and articulated as ethical responsibility (Hategan et al., 2018), the meaning and scope of CSR are narrowed down to corporate philanthropy. According to researchers, philanthropy is largely carried out for two reasons – public benefit and personal benefit (Vesterlund, 2006). Public benefit is the outcome of the selfless services or actions that individuals, philanthropists, firms, and NGOs undertake to benefit others by creating public good, such as educational institutions, hospitals, health care services, water and sanitation, and livelihood and employment opportunities for the underserved communities. On the other hand, the private benefit of philanthropy is about feeling good, a sense of attainment, recognition in society, reputation enhancement, political mileage, and so on (Cantergil et al., 2013). As practiced earlier in the pre-industrialization and early industrialization phases, philanthropy included activities and measured success on how much public benefit it had created. For example, industrialists such as Andrew Carnegie, Henry Ford, and John D Rockefeller from the United States; John Cadbury from the UK; and JN Tata from India, to name a few, carried out meaningful philanthropic activities for the public benefit. Those philanthropies resulted in setting up many institutions that contribute to society even after 100 plus years.

On the contrary, we have more profitable enterprises and wealthier entrepreneurs today than a century before. Modern-day philanthropy, promoted as CSR, is primarily done for private benefits. Philanthropic giving is mainly driven by compliance, reputation, competition, self-satisfaction, and tradition. Therefore, it is clear from the discussions that although there is a substantial difference between the two terms philanthropy and CSR, they are often used interchangeably, mainly for securing private benefit.

12.3 Why CSR Is Needed in Times of Crisis Caused by Disasters/Pandemics

The rise in social and environmental problems due to the constant increase in disaster events is becoming a compelling social reason for businesses to integrate disasters/pandemics into CSR. According to the CRED, EM-DAT, and UN-DRR Report (2020) frequencies of disasters and pandemics have increased in the last 20 years. India is the third most-affected country after China and the United States. India has suffered a wide-ranging variety of over 300 disasters between 2000 and 2019. And now, the COVID-19 pandemic has put the world in an unprecedented crisis, which has shaken up every segment of societies – developed and developing nations, Governments and businesses, rich and poor, science and religion, and so on. This is the biggest disaster after the 1918 pandemic, which seeks everyone, who has the capability, to do something in this time of humanitarian crisis. Therefore, enterprises as corporate citizens will be expected to show compassion and discharge social responsibilities in such times of crisis. However, apart from this compassionate reason, some rational arguments determine the need for 'CSR as Unusual' in times of crisis. 'CSR as Unusual' seeks a firm to adopt a unique strategy beyond simple philanthropy or charity for relief and give long-term commitments to participate and remain invested in the reconstruction of societies. CSR-as-usual or charity in normal times will not be enough to deal with new challenges due to the impacts of the pandemic's scale and intensity. Therefore, the following three reasons are argued that determine the need for CSR in the pandemic crisis.

Reason 1: Human development problems are compounded and deepened further. It is crucial to discuss CSR in the changing context of human development due to coronavirus effects. The impacts of the pandemic on key human development areas such as poverty, hunger, illiteracy, unemployment, and inequality are estimated to be at an all-time high. For example, poverty has risen. According to the biennial Poverty and Shared Prosperity Report, the reversal of poverty is expecting to have approx. 88–115 million more people slipped into extreme poverty in 2020 (The World Bank Report, 2020; p.27). The Pew Research Centre Report (Kochhar, 2021) says, "the number of poor people (with incomes of less than \$2 a day) in India can increase by 75 million due to the pandemic effects." Similarly, unemployment has increased due to forced lockdowns and travel restrictions. Approximately half of the world's 3.3 billion global workers became vulnerable; they are at high risk of losing their livelihoods (WHO, 2020). In India, approximately 40 million internal migrant workers returned in large waves to their homes, losing their livelihoods (The Hindu, 2020), quoted the World Bank. Education got severely hit. The pandemic affected nearly 1.5 billion students in 191 countries (UN News, 2020). Almost half the world's students got impacted by part or full school closures (UNESCO, 2021a). More than 11 million girls are estimated not to go back to school after the COVID-19 crisis (UNESCO, 2021b). The study report, The Inequality Virus (Berkhout et al., 2021) says that the coronavirus crisis will deepen 'inequality' globally. The compounded and exacerbated social problems will therefore seek companies to intensify their role in society by going beyond usual philanthropy.

Reason 2: Supplementary resources for the relief and reconstruction are another big challenge, which will seek firms to do maximum. Although Governments worldwide take several measures to reach normalcy, the task is challenging because the losses are huge, and the resources required for relief, reconstruction, and recovery are enormous. It will require the accumulation of substantial supplementary resources or, say, deficit financing. For example, a report by The Harvard Gazette (Powell, 2020) suggests that the United States' aggregate losses due to the pandemic by 2021 will cost approx. $16 trillion. Many developing countries are facing difficulties in mobilizing adequate stimulus packages for their economies and societies to mitigate challenges arising from the COVID-19 crisis (UNCTAD, 2020). Although there is no such estimation done for India, it is clear that the country would also require additional financial resources to meet the losses and recovery costs.

Reason No 3: Wealth must be shared proportionately. When the world is facing a crisis, businesses (in general) have registered growth during the pandemic. The Billionaires Report 2020 (UBS, 2020) says that the total billionaire wealth globally surpassed the previous best of $8.9 trillion in 2017 and reached a record peak of $10.2 trillion in July 2020. According to Bloomberg Quint's report (Kapoor, 2020), billionaires' wealth during the COVID-19 lockdown in 2020 has gone up by over a third – 35% to $423 billion. The net worth of India's richest man (Forbes, 2020), Mukesh Ambani, rose 73% over the past year to nearly $89 billion (INR 6.52 lakh crore). Gautam Adani's, the second richest person on the list, too, rose at $25.2 billion. Vaccine maker Cyrus Poonawalla entered the top 10 at rank six as all eyes remained on the antidote. At the same time, Biocon's Kiran Mazumdar Shaw became the highest wealth gainer in percentage terms, and all the pharmaceutical billionaires on the list saw their wealth rise. Posits that the world's ten wealthiest businessmen's combined wealth increased by half a trillion dollars during the pandemic. And this wealth is more than adequate to support a COVID-19 vaccine for everybody and to guarantee that no one is pushed into poverty by the pandemic. In India, the top 10% earned 56% of the country's total revenue in 2019; the bottom 10% earned only 3.5% (Chaudhuri & Ghosh, 2021).

The data mentioned in reasons 1 and 2 present the magnitude of problems, which have risen due to the pandemic. Analysis of the said data suggests that communities have become more impoverished and vulnerable than before. Therefore, it will make them expect more from Governments. However, Governments face a shortage of additional resources to meet the losses and recovery costs, as discussed in reason 2. On the other hand, firms are reported to have made good profits. Therefore, companies with swelled affluence (as informed in reason 3) will be expected to share wealth for the humanitarian cause and creating public good. Increased societal problems, deficit financing, and the rising affluence of business strengthen the arguments of business-society interdependence under corporate citizenship. Firms can and must help the Government and society deal with increased societal problems in times of crisis. It seeks companies to take moral responsibility towards minimizing inequality, poverty, hunger, illiteracy, and unemployment. 'A great many large companies talk about having a social purpose and set of values, or about how much they care for their employees and other stakeholders. Now is the time for them to make good on that commitments. (Kramer, 2020)'. Although discussions establish CSR's definitive role in disasters/pandemics, it is crucial to examine the role of public policy measures in advancing the CSR agenda and how they influence CSR.

12.4 CSR and Disaster: Influences of Public Policy Measures

India declared the coronavirus epidemic a notified pandemic. Therefore, to combat Coronavirus challenges, it enforced the Epidemic Disease Act, 1897 and the Disaster Management Act, 2005 (Rajya Sabha TV, 2020). To administer all advisories of the Union Health Ministry and State Governments on the COVID-19 crisis, the Government of India enforced the Epidemic Diseases Act 1897. In addition, the Union Ministry of Home Affairs (MHA) imposed the implementation of lockdowns and pandemic-related guidelines by imposing the Disaster Management Act 2005. Also, some State Governments enforced their state's rules, such as Himachal Pradesh Epidemic Disease (COVID-19) Regulations, 2020; Delhi Epidemic Diseases COVID-19 Regulations, 2020; and Maharashtra COVID-19 Regulations, 2020. While the two central Acts and State regulations ensured the implementation of measures such as lockdowns, COVID-appropriate behaviour, and managing the demand and supply of essential services, the Act relating to CSR (Section 135 of the Companies Act 2013) was amended several times to increase the participation of corporations in the pandemic relief operations. These amendments allow companies to undertake various activities such as supplying PPE kits, setting up makeshift hospitals, providing medical oxygen concentrators, ventilators, other medical equipment, and so on. All such activities relating to COVID-19 health care promotion are qualified CSR activities under item nos. (i) and (xii) of Schedule VII of the Companies Act, 2013 (Ministry of Corporate Affairs, 2020a). The amendment also permitted one-time ex gratia payments to workers (temporary/casual/daily) as eligible CSR. Additionally, the expenditure on vaccines, medicines, medical instruments for COVID-19 is allowed under CSR for a limited period of three financial years from 2020 to 2023.

Furthermore, as a policy measure, on March 28, 2020, the Government of India set up a charitable trust, 'Prime Minister's Citizen Assistance and Relief in Emergency Situations Fund' (PM India, 2020). It is a national fund created to deal with any national tragedy or emergency and provide relief to the affected communities. In a move to mobilise additional financial resources required for pandemic-related activities, the Government of India encouraged companies to make donations to the PM CARES Fund. In addition, by a notification issued on March 28, 2020, the MCA clarified that all contributions to the PM CARES Fund would qualify under CSR (Ministry of Corporate Affairs, 2020b).

Under public policy measures, the creation of the PM CARES Fund and subsequent amendments made in CSR Rules influenced and impacted CSR. The analysis draws two conclusions. First, there is a shortage of funds to manage the scale and volume of the crisis. Therefore, by setting up a central fund, the Government subtly planned to meet the deficit financing from corporates, mainly through CSR. This conclusion gets substantiated by the Government's followed-up actions, which subsequently brought in several amendments in CSR rules that facilitated firms to make donations. And, this is the second conclusion. While the public policies, from this argument, may be held accountable for limiting CSR's role in making donations to the Government funds, the internal CSR policies of companies are likewise, rather more, responsible for having an indifferent approach to disasters. The study's findings suggest that companies are inconsistent in their responses to disasters. It is because disasters have not been made integral to the internal CSR policy.

12.5 Why Should Firms Include Disasters in CSR Policy – Is It a Gap?

As discussed earlier, since frequencies of disasters and pandemics have been on the constant increase, why don't corporations then acknowledge disasters as one of the leading humanitarian causes under CSR? If firms make contributions for disaster relief, then why isn't disaster philanthropy integral to CSR policy commitment? Why is disaster philanthropy perceived as knee-jerk reactions in times of crisis? The qualitative study of CSR policies of 27 firms in India helped to analyse these questions.

The study views that because espousing a CSR policy in India is made compulsory in the Act, all eligible companies now have a CSR policy. However, disaster/pandemic management does not find a grounded space in CSR policy. In contrast, the relief, rehabilitation, and reconstruction activities in response to disasters are inserted as item no XII in schedule VII of the companies Act (The Gazette of India, 2019). But only a few companies under the study have mentioned the term 'Disaster Response' in one of their internal documents, such as expenditure reports, CSR policy, or action plans. Although the mention of disaster in such records may arguably support the point of having a policy on disaster, the same is opposed because companies are not found to have made planned budget allocations for disaster management. Some companies have reported the expenditure on disaster management, but no evidence confirms those expenditures as part of the committed budget. Therefore, the expenditure on disasters under CSR is found ad hoc and knee-jerk (Table A12.2). However, some may argue that planned budget commitment for unknown events (disasters) is not advisable because companies must mandatorily spend CSR funds within that year. If there is no disaster during the year, the company will fall short of spending the fund. Therefore, the firm will fail to comply. But this is a weak argument as companies can establish a special fund and create a corpus, which is allowed in the Act. In fact, such an approach will help companies prevent them from diverting CSR funds to disaster response by affecting the ongoing commitments. Also, in the absence of a policy on disasters, it is unclear how companies allocate and donate funds to multiple disaster events if they happen during the same year. For example, companies extended their contributions to the pandemic relief in 2020. However, there was no evidence of companies extending support for the relief and reconstruction work in Odisha and West Bengal, which suffered losses due to the Amphan disaster in the same year.

The study reveals that businesses are indifferent and inconsistent in responding to disasters because (a) disasters are not yet recognized as one of the severe humanitarian causes, (b) disasters are unplanned activities as they are not made part of the annual action plans, (c) annual budget to disaster management is not allocated, and (d) decisions to make donations are not aligned with a dedicated policy on disasters/pandemics. Therefore, having no policy on disasters is a big gap. However, although disaster response lacks consistency and policy support, it is also a fact that firms contribute to relief operations as unplanned CSR activities when disaster/pandemic hits societies.

12.6 CSR and COVID-19: How Have Businesses Responded to the Crisis?

209 global billionaires contributed $7.2 billion between March and June 2020. India also could quickly mobilize a significant donation of $541 million. "That's the most in the world after the United States and China. Regarding companies' contributions in India, Mukesh Ambani's Reliance Industries Limited contributed INR 556 Cr towards PM Cares Fund and the Chief Minister's Fund for COVID-19 related activities from its CSR funds (Reliance Industries Limited, 2020). The next wealthiest man in India is Gautam Adani, whose group pledged INR 114 Cr to central and state Governments' funds (Adani Group, 2021). Tata Sons, known for philanthropies, pledged INR 1000 Cr, while the Tata Trusts has separately contributed INR 500 crore to protect and empower all affected communities. Also, Azim Premji, through his enterprise and foundation, has donated a total of INR 1125 crores (Singh, 2020). Almost all public sector enterprises (PSEs) made contributions to the COVID-19 pandemic relief. For example, State-run Coal India Ltd contributed INR 221 Cr to the Prime Minister's CARES Fund. SBI Foundation, CSR arm of State Bank of India (SBI), pledged INR 30 Cr to implement various COVID-19 relief measures across the country. Power Finance Corporation contributed INR 200 Cr under CSR to PM CARES Fund. MNCs such as Coca-Cola India committed initial support of INR 100+ crores for improving the health care system. Bosch Group in India donated INR 5 Cr to PM CARES Fund and pledged an additional INR 45 Cr for various community welfare initiatives. The list of corporate donors to the pandemic relief is exhaustive.

Nonetheless, Table A12.3 gives more information about some of the leading corporate/entrepreneur donors. From this, it is evident that firms across have responded to the need of the hour. For example, India Inc. spent INR 7,537 Cr as CSR obligations in the first two months of the pandemic outbreak in 2020, of which INR 4,316 Cr of donations went to the PM CARES Fund .

12.7 CSR, COVID-19, and PM CARES Fund: What Is the Concern?

The study confirms that most companies have either made donations to the PM CARES Fund or announced their commitments as per their financial capacity. However, no official data is available in the public domain regarding how much funds have been collected under the PM CARES Fund and disbursed. Therefore, for developing an understanding of the utilization of CSR funds that were mainly donated (rather diverted) to the PM CARES Fund, an analysis of some media reports from reputed media houses for this chapter was done. The analysis of data indicates that PM CARES Fund is utilized typically for meeting the challenges of COVID-19 in health care. For example, funds have been used for the purchase of ventilators, installation of dedicated pressure swing adsorption medical oxygen generation (PSAMOG) plants, the first phase of vaccination drive to inoculate frontline health care workers, and establishment of makeshift COVID-19 hospitals in many cities, mainly during the second wave. Some funds were also utilized for the management of migrant workers' relief during the lockdowns. One may argue that funds donated by companies under CSR to the PM CARES Fund are, after all, best utilized. Then why is there a public cry for companies contributing to the national fund? The argument here is not about giving funding support to the national fund. Instead, some initiatives like this help Governments arrange additional resources to meet the resource deficiency in times of crisis. However, no one would ask if companies give additional capital (over and above CSR Funds) to the PM CARES Fund. Data analysis reveals that companies have diverted a significant part of their CSR budget to the PM CARES Fund without increasing the CSR budget. Contributing to PM CARES Fund is absolutely not a concern. Companies must do it. However, it must not be done at the expense of continuing CSR, which is already committed. It is, of course, a concern. In another finding, the study views that the emphasis is given on spending in times of crisis as a short-term strategy by overlooking potentially detrimental consequences.

12.8 Not All CSR Spending in Times of Crisis Is Genuine Compassion: It's Illusory

In CSR discourse, too much importance has been given to financial numbers and figures – budget and expenditure. However, while *spending* is a critical element, it cannot be a substitute for compassion. In fact, at times, it is deceiving; CSR spending is strategically used to mask *irresponsible* business conduct. For example, NIKE Inc was reported having made a $250,000 donation to United Way Worldwide's India COVID-19 Relief Fund and Save the Children's India COVID-19 Crisis Relief Fund (Nike News, 2020). Similarly, Levi Strauss & Co. donated US$ 3 million (Bergh, 2020) for the pandemic control. Likewise, H&M USA provided over US$ 2 million of products for communities impacted by COVID-19 (Cision, 2020). On the other hand, according to a report, 9,843 garment workers and their families faced wage theft at eight factories supplying 16 fashion brands, including Nike, Levi's, and H&M. These companies together recorded profits of at least US$10 billion in the second half of 2020 alone. Therefore, CSR spending on community affairs or pandemic relief measures cannot be justified as social responsibility when companies in the value chain of their business are involved in irresponsible business practices, such as underpayment of wages and discrimination of workers.

Furthermore, CSR spending in disasters/pandemics is *deceptive* and used to build entrepreneurs' image and/or brand reputation. It is hard to make clear distinctions between personal charities by entrepreneurs and CSR of enterprises. Often, philanthropic contributions made by firms under CSR are channelled through family-controlled Foundations and presented as the generosity of entrepreneurs. Although it is a common practice worldwide, it is widespread in India. For instance, Reliance Industries (an enterprise) contributed ₹510 Cr to the PM CARES and State Funds for pandemic management in F.Y. 2019–20. According to the EdelGive Hurun India Philanthropy List, Mukesh Ambani emerged as the third-largest philanthropist after Azim Premji (Wipro) and Shiv Nadar (HCL) by donating INR 458 Cr. Mukesh Ambani received admiration from all corners for this charity. It is, however, unclear whether he donated from his (personal) wealth or it was part of his company's CSR fund. Who makes donations – enterprise or entrepreneur? It is blurred in most cases. It appears as if entrepreneurs are cleverly hitting two birds with one stone.

Similarly, making donations to PM CARES Fund or other Government funds may look like a company's prudent CSR commitment. This is because it helps the Government meet the funding deficit and so much more in times of crisis. However, CSR is not just *Chequebook Philanthropy* (Foundation Source Philanthropic Services Inc, 2007). It is not merely signing off a cheque of donations and giving it away to Government funds or NGOs and running away from its responsibility towards society. On the contrary, responsibility becomes much bigger and engaging in times of pandemics. Hence, companies need to commit to better coordinated and involved community initiatives. For instance, Ambuja Cements and ACC collectively contributed INR 3.3 crores to NGOs to support daily-wage and migrant workers, slum-dwellers, and homeless who got stranded across the country due to the lockdown (The Hindu Business Line, 2020).

Corporate philanthropic spending, done in whatever manner during the pandemic, is undoubtedly a sympathetic act. It receives people's recognition and admiration. However, some questions need to be countered in the larger context of seeking explanations whether corporate spending is/was ever an act of genuine compassion? Is spending the proper manifestation of CSR? Did/does CSR do enough to meet the needs during the crisis? Did/do companies contribute to the pandemic control and relief measures without affecting their ongoing CSR commitments? Did/do companies increase CSR spending to overcome the crisis of the present and future?

12.9 CSR in Times of the Pandemic Crisis: Consequences and Concerns

The study makes some direct revelations, which are critical. However, they present macro perspectives to corporate managements, CSR practitioners, policymakers, and researchers who may further debate the following findings for micro-level actions.

- Companies did not exceed their committed CSR budget while they contributed to the pandemic relief. Therefore, even if some companies, such as Reliance Industries, ended up spending more by 2%–4% (2019–20), no evidence suggests that overspending was done due to the contributions made for the pandemic-related activities. Nor did any report indicate that companies made announcements for increased CSR budgets (2020–21 and 21–22) beyond 2% of the prescribed limit of the mandatory commitment under the law.
- Since companies did not increase the CSR budget, an obvious conclusion was drawn. It confirmed that businesses manoeuvred the overall CSR budget to contribute to the pandemic relief. They diverted funds for the pandemic relief from the CSR budget to the dedicated funds like PM CARES Fund and other funds, including their own foundations.
- Diversion of funds for the COVID relief impacted the ongoing CSR commitments. This is a major finding which has been observed by other researchers too. For example, Maya Vengurlekar, COO of the CRISIL Foundation (CRISIL, 2020), said, "India Inc has already allocated over 80% of the annual CSR budget to address the pandemic. This could impact spending on other areas in 2021.". Further, FSG research (Rathi, et al., 2020) also claims that COVID-19 will lead to a drastic reduction in NGOs' funding in 2020 and 2021. As a result, CSR funding would see a significant decline, which FSG estimated to be about 30%–60%.
- The study fears that corporate donations to Government funds will impact CSR's voluntariness and independent nature. If such a trend of philanthropic giving continues, firms will fail and forget to proactively and voluntarily discharge social responsibility. In that case, this model of philanthropy and regular interferences from the Government may bring CSR under regulatory frameworks and end up with the Governmentalization of CSR. It is against the philosophy of CSR. It is the biggest worry.
- One-time donations to Government funds and doing away with primary responsibilities under CSR will have far-reaching implications. This mode of CSR implementation for a company is relatively easier than doing it by itself. This mode avoids operational complexities for companies. It also helps them save some costs. Paying one-time contributions to the approved Government funds under the Act in India helps companies meet compliance in the most legitimate way with greater visibility. Therefore, it is feared that it will hurt the philosophy of CSR that seeks direct involvement of companies in society.

– The analysis further suggests that such repeated transactions of transferring CSR funds to Government funds will strengthen the arguments for levying social cess or tax by scrapping CSR (Jain, 2019).

Findings suggest that corporate compassion is selective and limited to charitable/philanthropic giving. Therefore, CSR is restricted to spending only. However, as discussed earlier, CSR is a comprehensive responsibility and goes *beyond charity*. It pursues a company to be the best corporate citizen and use all its other resources to bring disruptive innovations in CSR. Such innovations do not restrict companies to meet compliances or doing minimum under the legal obligations as box-ticking social responsibility (Frith, 2015). Instead, companies will be appreciated for broadening the boundaries of compassion to all those directly/indirectly associated with companies who need help in such times of crisis. For example, Tata Steel, apart from its unwavering commitments to community activities, pledged to pay the monthly salary (for the remaining service period up to the age of retirement) to the families of those employees who died due to the coronavirus infection. The company will also provide medical benefits and residential facilities along with the salary. Although, as per the Act, the cost of social security for the pandemic affected employees will not qualify as CSR, nothing can be a greater or better demonstration of social responsibility than this.

12.10 Conclusions

Although CSR has emerged as a fundamental tenet for business-society relationships under the concept of corporate citizenship, overall understanding and practices in India limit the meaning of responsibility to philanthropy, which, too, is not strategic. At times, philanthropic actions are strategically engineered to downplay other critical dimensions of CSR – moral and rational. The rational obligations seek firms to increase investments in societies during the pandemic because their profits are multiplied during this period, as discussed early in this chapter. In the same breath, the moral dimension of CSR pursues businesses to own more responsibilities in times of crisis to address increased social problems such as poverty, hunger, education, and inequality. However, throughout the chapter, the analyses show that firms in India largely lack commitments on both fronts. CSR interventions of companies in response to the pandemic are found superficial and shallow, mainly cash donations made to Government funds, own foundations, or NGOs. The tick-the-box approach to meet compliance encourages the practices of chequebook philanthropy under CSR at the expense of its unique characteristics – voluntary and self-governing. The frequent amendments in CSR Act and its rules during the pandemic to meet the resource deficits are unwanted and unnecessary Governmental interferences. Hence, as a result, CSR, in a way, is on the verge of being indirectly regulated. In addition, as a policy measure, the Government constituted the PM CARES Fund to mobilize funds for the disaster/pandemic response. Although such policy measures are legitimate and needed to mobilize additional resources to meet the deficit, the analysis suggests that it has caused indirect harm to CSR, the ethos of which is feared to be hugely compromised. Companies' CSR policies are also found inconsistent in response to disasters/pandemics. Although a few companies only have included disaster response in their CSR policies, commitments to disasters go without budget allocation. Therefore, in the absence of budget commitment, disasters often get knee-jerk responses from companies.

Moreover, the ad hocism and spend-centric approaches to pandemic relief and reconstruction are typical corporate activities, mostly done for the image make-over of the entrepreneur and/or the brand. The bigger the CSR spending is, the larger the image has become an established norm now. Therefore, firms put preconditions for CSR spending, which often follows barter rules to bargain for private benefit. Thus, CSR is (mis) used as a business strategy that firms adopt to self-benefit during the pandemic. While *giving* as the letter is legitimized, the true spirit of CSR, that is, *sharing* (of wealth), is dying. And when the soul of CSR is compromised for private benefits, it is called Conspicuous CSR.

References

Adani Group. (2021). Battling COVID with Goodness. May 20. Retrieved from: https://www.adani.com/covid19updates

Bergh, C. (2020). LS&Co. Commits $3 Million to COVID-19 Response. April 2. Retrieved from: https://www.levistrauss.com/2020/04/02/lsco-commits-3-million-to-covid-19-response/

Berkhout, E, Galasso, N, Lawson, M, Andrés, P, Taneja, A, & Alejo, D (2021). The inequality virus. *Oxfam*. January 25. Retrieved from: https://www.oxfam.org/en/research/inequality-virus

Business and Human Rights Resource Centre. (2021). Wage Theft and Pandemic Profits: The Right to a Living Wage for Garment Workers. March 11. Retrieved from: https://www.business-humanrights.org/en/from-us/briefings/wage-theft-and-pandemic-profits-the-right-to-a-living-wage-for-garment-workers/

Cantergil, M., Chanana, D., & Kattumuri, R. (2013). *Revealing Indian Philanthropy*. Retrieved from: https://www.ubs.com/content/dam/ubs/global/wealth_management/philanthropy_valuesbased_investments/indian-philanthrophy.pdf

Caroll, A. (1999). Corporate Social Responsibility: Evolution of a Definitional Construct, *Business & Society*, 38, 268–295. doi.org/10.1177/000765039903800303.

Chaudhuri, D. & Ghosh, P. (2021). Why Inequality Is India's Worst Enemy. Down to Earth. March 5. Retrieved from: https://www.downtoearth.org.in/blog/economy/why-inequality-is-india-s-worst-enemy-75778

Cision. (2020). *H&M USA Provides Over Two Million Dollars Of Product For Communities Impacted By COVID-19*. April 15. Retrieved from: https://www.prnewswire.com/news-releases/hm-usa-provides-over-two-million-dollars-of-product-for-communities-impacted-by-covid-19-301040569.html

CRED, EM-DAT, and UNDRR Report. (2020). *Human Cost of Disasters: An Overview of the Last 20 Years*. Retrieved from: http://www.indiaenvironmentportal.org.in/files/file/Human%20Cost%20of%20Disasters%202000-2019.pdf

CRISIL. (2020). *Doing Good in Bad Times.* June 9. Retrieved from: https://www.crisil. com/en/home/our-analysis/reports/2020/06/doing-good-in-bad-times.html

Davis, K. (1960). Can Business Afford to Ignore Social Responsibilities? *California Management Review, 2,* 70–76. doi: 10.2307/41166246.

Forbes. (2020). India's 100 Richest People. *Forbes.* Retrieved from: https://www.forbes. com/india-billionaires/list/

Foundation Source Philanthropic Services Inc. (2007). Strategic Philanthropy: Five approaches for making a difference. Retrieved from: https://arthaimpact.com/wp-content/uploads/2019/09/d57a775e-fcf0-4408-b2c4-b51ade54e569_10.pdf

Frith, B. (2015). CSR Is Not a 'Box Ticking Exercise'. HR Magazine. November 3. Retrieved from: https://www.hrmagazine.co.uk/content/news/csr-is-not-a-box-ticking-exercise

Hategan, C., Sirghi, B., Curea-Pitorac, R. & Hategan, V. (2018). Doing Well or Doing Good: The Relationship between Corporate Social Responsibility and Profit in Romanian Companies. *Sustainability, 10*(4), 1041. doi: 10.3390/su10041041

Hurun India. (2020). *EdelGive Hurun India Philanthropy List 2020.* Retrieved from: https://www.hurunindia.net/edelgive-hurun-india-philanthropy-l

Jain, S. (2019). Best to Abolish CSR, Just Add It to the Overall Tax. Financial Express. August 2. Retrieved from: https://www.financialexpress.com/opinion/ best-to-abolish-csr-just-add-it-to-the-overall-tax/1662291/

Kapoor, M. (2020). Indian Billionaires' Wealth Rose By A Third in Just Four Months. Bloomberg Quint. October 15. Retrieved from https://www.bloombergquint.com/ business/indias-billionaires-earned-a-third-of-their-wealth-in-just-one-year

Kochhar, R. (2021). In the pandemic, India's middle class shrinks and poverty spreads while China sees smaller changes. *Pew Research Centre Report.* , March 18. Retrieved from: https://www.pewresearch.org/fact-tank/2021/03/18/in-the-pandemic-indias-middle-class-shrinks-and-poverty-spreads-while-china-sees-smaller-changes/

Kramer, M. (2020). Coronavirus Is Putting Corporate Social Responsibility to the Test. *Harvard Business Review.* April 1. Retrieved from: https://hbr.org/2020/04/ coronavirus-is-putting-corporate-social-responsibility-to-the-test

Matten, D., & Crane, A. (2005). Corporate Citizenship: Toward an Extended Theoretical Conceptualization. *The Academy of Management Review, 30,* 166–179, doi: 10.2307/20159101

Ministry of Corporate Affairs. (2020a). Clarification on contribution to PM CARES Fund as eligible CSR activity under item no. (viii) of the Schedule VII of Companies Act, 2013. eF. No. CSR-05/1/2020-CSR-MCA. March 28. Retrieved from: https:// www.mca.gov.in/Ministry/pdf/Circular_29032020.pdf

Ministry of Corporate Affairs. (2020b). Clarification on spending of CSR funds for 'creating health infrastructure for COVID care', 'establishment of medical oxygen generation and storage plants' etc. E-file no. CSR-01/5/2021-CSR-MCA. May 5. Retrieved from: https://www.mca.gov.in/Ministry/pdf/GeneralCircularNo9_05052021.pdf

Nike News. (2020). COVID-19 Community Response. April 3. Retrieved from: https:// news.nike.com/news/nike-covid-19-community-response

Ministry of Corporate Affairs. (2021). National CSR Portal. Retrieved from: https:// www.csr.gov.in/

PM India. (2020). About PM CARES Fund. Retrieved from: https://www.pmindia.gov. in/en/about-pm-cares-fund/

Powell, A. (2020). What might COVID cost the US? Try $ 16 trillion. *The Harvard Gazette*. November 10. Retrieved from: https://news.harvard.edu/gazette/story/2020/11/what-might-covid-cost-the-u-s-experts-eye-16-trillion/

Rajya Sabha TV. (2020). Epidemic Act and Disaster Management Act enforced to combat COVID-19. March 31. Retrieved from: https://rstv.nic.in/epidemic-act-disaster-management-act-enforced-combat-covid-19.html

Rathi, S., Karamchandani, A., & Thuard, J. (2020). The Impact of COVID-19 on CSR Funding for Indian NGOs. *FSG*. April 28. Retrieved from: https://www.fsg.org/blog/impact-covid-19-csr-funding-indian-ngos

Reliance Industries Limited. (2020). Annual Report 2019–20. Retrieved from: https://www.ril.com/getattachment/299caec5-2e8a-43b7-8f70-d633a150d07e/AnnualReport_2019-20.aspx

Singh, N. (2020). Azim Premji Becomes World's 3rd Biggest Donor To COVID-19 Relief Efforts. *The Logical Indian*. May 13. Retrieved from: https://thelogicalindian.com/story-feed/get-inspired/azim-premji-covid-19-relief-efforts-21060

The Gazette of India (2019). Ministry of Corporate Affairs Notification. May 30. Retrieved from: https://egazette.nic.in/WriteReadData/2019/204898.pdf

The Hindu. (2020). Lockdown in India has impacted 40 million internal migrants: World Bank. April 23. Retrieved from: UBS Billiohttps://www.thehindu.com/news/international/lockdown-in-india-has-impacted-40-million-internal-migrants-world-bank/article31411618.ece

The Hindu Business Line. (2020). Ambuja Cement, ACC Give INR 3.3 cr to NGOs Working on Covid Relief. Retrieved from: https://www.thehindubusinessline.com/companies/ambuja-cement-acc-give-33-cr-to-ngos-working-on-covid-relief/article31441870.ece

The World Bank (2020). Poverty and Shared Prosperity Report: Reversals of fortunes. The World Bank Group. doi: 10.1596/978-1-4648-1602-4

UBS Billionaires Report (2020). Riding the Storm. Retrieved from: https://www.ubs.com/global/en/global-family-office/reports/billionaires-insights-2020.html

UN News (2020). Startling disparities in digital learning emerge as COVID-19 spreads: UN education agency. *UN News*. Retrieved from: https://news.un.org/en/story/2020/04/1062232?fbclid=IwAR3NmmEKq3finyVJ8Ld3GCCQYXmuqDk5rmCX0VbzstIWmXUEYkH8TzMCw0Q

UNCTAD (2020). Response and Recovery: Mobilising financial resources for development in the time of Covid-19. UNCTAD. Retrieved from: https://unctad.org/project/response-and-recovery-mobilising-financial-resources-development-time-covid-19

UNESCO (2021a). One year into COVID, UNESCO convenes global meeting of education ministers to ensure learning continuity. March. Retrieved from: https://en.unesco.org/news/one-year-covid-unesco-convenes-global-meeting-education-ministers-ensure-learning-continuity

UNESCO (2021b). Over 11 million girls may not go back to school after the COVID-19 crisis. Retrieved from UNESCO: https://en.unesco.org/covid19/educationresponse/girlseducation

Vesterlund, L. (2006). Why do People give. The Nonprofit Sector: A Research Handbook. *Researchgate*. Retrieved from: https://www.researchgate.net/publication/248439486_Why_Do_People_Give/citation/download

WHO (2020). Impact of COVID-19 on people's livelihood, their health, and our food systems_ Joint statement by ILO, FAO, FAD and WHO. Retrieved from: https://www.who.int/news/item/13-10-2020-impact-of-covid-19-on-people's-livelihoods-their-health-and-our-food-systems

Appendix

Table A12.1 CSR expenditure (INR in crores)

Sr. No.	Company	Expenditure in 2019–20
1	Reliance Industries Ltd	908.71
2	Tata Consultancy Services Ltd	602
3	ONGC Ltd	582.35
4	HDFC Bank Ltd	535.31
5	Indian Oil Corporation Ltd	518.49
6	Infosys Ltd	359.94
7	Bharat Petroleum Corporation Ltd	346.21
8	Power Grid Corporation of India Ltd	346.21
9	ITC Ltd	342.24
10	NTPC Ltd	304.92
11	Hindustan Zinc Ltd	266.93
12	ICICI Bank	134.35
13	NMDC Ltd	199.99
14	Tata Steel Ltd	183.8
15	Hindustan Petroleum Corporation Ltd	182.24
16	Wipro Ltd	181.8
17	HCL Technologies Ltd	176.29
18	Coal India Ltd	172.31
19	Maruti Suzuki India Ltd	169.38
20	Mahanadi Coalfields Ltd	165.5
21	Coca-Cola India Ltd	17.43
22	Nestle India Ltd	0
23	Nike India Pvt Ltd	0
24	IBM India Pvt Ltd	4.36
25	Microsoft Corporation India Pvt Ltd	13.94
26	Samsung India Pvt Ltd	81.66
27	Honda Motorcycle and Scooter India Ltd	54.59

Source: Ministry of Corporate Affairs (2021).

Table A12.2 Comparative statement of expenditure on disaster philanthropy under CSR(INR in crores)

Sr. No.	Company	2014–15	2015–16	2016–17	2017–18	2018–19	2019–20
1	Reliance Industries Ltd	0.79	9.45	10.56	1.09	26.08	518.83
2	TCS	18.55	71.3	86	131	296	176
3	Infosys	0	121	5.02	0	7.05	50
4	Wipro	0	3.8	0	0	0	0
5	ONGC	0	0	0	0	0	0
6	HDFC	0	0	0	0	0	0
7	ITC	0	0	0	0	0	33.14
8	Tata Steel	0	0	0	0	0	0
9	NMDC	0	0	0	0	0	0
10	Mahanadi Coalfields	0	0	0	0	0	72.7
11	Coca Cola India Ltd	0	0	0	0	0	0
12	Nestle India Ltd	0	0	0	0.25	0	0
13	Nike India Pvt Ltd	0	0	0	0	0	0
14	Microsoft Corporation India Pvt Ltd	0.06	0.04	0	0	0.13	1.49
15	Powergrid	0	0	0	0	1.47	0
16	Honda	0.2	0	0	0	1	0
17	ICICI	3.78	3.87	0	0	10	26
18	Samsung	3	0.7	0	0	0.4	0

Source: Ministry of Corporate Affairs (2021)

Table A12.3 List of corporate donors to pandemic relief

Date of Announcement	Company	Commitments (INR Crore)	Key Personalities
28-Mar-20	Tata Sons	1,510	Ratan Tata
01-Apr-20	Wipro	1,125	Azim Premji
01-Apr-20	Reliance Industries	510	Mukesh Ambani
30-Mar-20	Paytm	505	Vijay Shekhar Sharma
04-Apr-20	Aditya Birla	500	Kumar Mangalam Birla
02-Apr-20	Vedanta Resources	201	Anil Agarwal
04-Apr-20	Avenue Supermarts	155	Radhakishan Damani
30-Mar-20	Larsen & Toubro	150	AM Naik
26-Mar-20	Bajaj	110	Rahul Bajaj
01-Apr-20	ArcelorMittal	100	LN Mittal
29-Mar-20	Adani	100	Gautam Adani
29-Mar-20	JSW	100	Sajjan Jindal
31-Mar-20	Bharti Airtel	100	Sunil Mittal
30-Mar-20	Torrent Pharmaceuticals	100	Sudhir Mehta and Samir Mehta
25-Mar-20	Hero Cycles	100	Pankaj Munjal
30-Mar-20	Hero Motocorp	100	Pawan Kant Munjal
04-Apr-20	United Phosphorus	75	Rajju Shroff
29-Mar-20	Kotak Mahindra Bank	60	Uday Kotak
30-Mar-20	Mankind Pharma	56	Ramesh Juneja and Rajeev Juneja
27-Mar-20	Godrej	50	Adi Godrej
30-Mar-20	CESC	50	Sanjiv Goenka
08-Apr-20	Eisher Motors	50	Vikram Lal

Source: Hurun India (2020)

Index

Note: **Bold** page numbers refer to tables; *italic* page numbers refer to figures and page numbers followed by "n" denote endnotes.